An Introduction to Medical Decision-Making

Jonathan S. Vordermark II

An Introduction to Medical Decision-Making

Practical Insights and Approaches

Jonathan S. Vordermark II
Ranchos de Taos
NM
USA

ISBN 978-3-030-23146-0   ISBN 978-3-030-23147-7 (eBook)
https://doi.org/10.1007/978-3-030-23147-7

© Springer Nature Switzerland AG 2019
This work is subject to copyright. All rights are reserved by the Publisher, whether the whole or part of the material is concerned, specifically the rights of translation, reprinting, reuse of illustrations, recitation, broadcasting, reproduction on microfilms or in any other physical way, and transmission or information storage and retrieval, electronic adaptation, computer software, or by similar or dissimilar methodology now known or hereafter developed.
The use of general descriptive names, registered names, trademarks, service marks, etc. in this publication does not imply, even in the absence of a specific statement, that such names are exempt from the relevant protective laws and regulations and therefore free for general use.
The publisher, the authors, and the editors are safe to assume that the advice and information in this book are believed to be true and accurate at the date of publication. Neither the publisher nor the authors or the editors give a warranty, expressed or implied, with respect to the material contained herein or for any errors or omissions that may have been made. The publisher remains neutral with regard to jurisdictional claims in published maps and institutional affiliations.

This Springer imprint is published by the registered company Springer Nature Switzerland AG
The registered company address is: Gewerbestrasse 11, 6330 Cham, Switzerland

Preface

This book is about how physicians make decisions. It examines the approaches available for decision-making and problem-solving and the rationale for choosing one approach over another. Physicians must become good thinkers and problem-solvers, and medical educators are obligated to develop these skills in those they mentor. Decision-making and problem-solving are subjects that have occupied researchers from many disparate fields, but the insights from this work have not penetrated the world of clinical medical practice in any practical or easily accessible form. To explain the principles behind a particular decision-making process or to discuss decision-making in a meaningful fashion, we need a common language that describes those processes. Unfortunately, these skills are not taught in any codified or deliberate manner—decision-making is a skill learned by clinical experience, formal and informal discussion of patient management and outcomes, and by imitation of one's mentors. Physicians have become experts at analyzing the how and why of medical practice, but they do not have an epistemological approach to explain how they arrived at a decision or a common language to describe how a particular decision was made or a problem solved. These shortcomings make it difficult to discuss the process of decision-making in a meaningful way, creating an environment which, for students and residents, is unnecessarily confusing or obscure and ultimately inefficient and inexact. The exponential growth of medical and scientific knowledge has profoundly changed how medicine is taught and care delivered, but having knowledge and being able to apply technology do not necessarily lead to better decision-making. It is necessary to examine the processes we use to make decisions at a deeper, more fundamental level.

This book is not about how to make a decision—it does not provide formulas, algorithms, or checklists. It is about the processes we use. Much of medical practice and teaching is about obtaining good outcomes—what must be done to achieve the desired result. We are a pragmatic and practical lot—not philosophers. It is difficult to step out of that mindset and spend time considering the theories and processes behind making decisions, but, if we are to become better decision-makers and if we are to do a good job of teaching decision-making and problem-solving, we must first understand the principles and processes behind the act of, and the art of, making decisions.

This book has been written from the vantage of someone who spent a career on the front lines, practicing medicine and training medical students and residents. I am not someone who has studied these problems at a distance or from a theoretical orientation. Researchers in fields as disparate as education, the cognitive and behavioral sciences, and philosophy bring valuable expertise to bear on the subject of decision-making, but I have no such claims—I was a clinician. Researchers in the fields of cognition and decision-making would, by virtue of their training and orientation, have a more detached or scholarly approach than me and might find fault in the conclusions or the theories I present. I accept such criticism and hope that what I present sparks a debate that will improve how we educate physicians and how physicians can better understand the process of clinical decision-making.

More importantly, this book explores how medical educators can teach students and junior physicians to be good decision-makers. I hope this book will be of benefit to anyone who is responsible for providing health care, but the book is primarily intended for those who teach medical students and physicians in training. There are no practical resources available to teach medical decision-making and no resources that outline the elements of this process for the student or post-graduate trainee. I hope that clinicians will find this book a stimulating and a useful resource for understanding and improving their decision-making skills, but, especially, I hope this book will be useful for those engaged in the monumental role of teaching students and residents to think like doctors.

I present not only ideas that are my own but also the observations and teachings of others. I take no credit for the work that my predecessors have already published. I have presented several concepts in graphic or schematic form that can, hopefully, be easily taught and can be used to stimulate further discussion and introspection.

I have used the terms physician and surgeon interchangeably. The fundamental concepts for problem-solving and decision-making are independent of specialty or approach. There is no area of medicine where decision-making skills are not the foundation of good clinical practice. I have emphasized the terms that are new or not commonly used by placing them in bold letters.

Physicians are, of necessity, lifelong learners and must continually challenge themselves to refine and improve their thinking and decision-making skills. I hope the concepts presented here will stimulate the reader to study the original sources, as this book can only touch the surface of this critical and fascinating topic.

Ranchos de Taos, NM, USA   Jonathan S. Vordermark II

Introduction

I have spent a lifetime thinking about how decisions are made. Growing up in a military environment, and having served in the military myself, brought me face-to-face with the issues of leadership and decision-making from earliest memory. A concept that occupied my thinking from the beginning of my clinical training was—how do doctors think and how do they go about deciding what needs to be done for a particular situation? Medical decision-making seemed a mystery. Facts and knowledge were obviously not enough—physicians must have relied on other skills to care for patients successfully.

My first clinical rotation was obstetrics and gynecology. I had no particular interest in this field but chose to start there with the naïve belief that it would be a good introduction to taking care of patients without having to worry about dealing with those who are really sick. After all, aren't pregnancy and delivery natural? Was I ever wrong! I immediately encountered situations where patients were sick, really sick, and for whom monumental, life-impacting decisions were required, often in situations of extreme urgency.

A task assigned to medical students on their clinical rotations was to examine a particular patient; review their records, laboratory, and imaging studies; and present that information in a conference setting. I was asked to present such a case to the chairman of the department, other faculty, residents, and students in a high-risk obstetrics conference. High-risk patients were those with complicated medical problems or pregnancies that warranted intense monitoring and consideration as to the optimal management of the mother and fetus. These patients presented us with very difficult decisions. The patient I was asked to present was a young African-American woman with her first pregnancy who had diabetes, obesity, and premature uterine contractions. Each of these problems individually posed a risk to the mother and fetus, and the combination of her problems presented a very high-risk situation.

To maintain the pregnancy presented risk to the mother and to deliver the fetus early might expose the infant to the many complications of extreme prematurity—problems we could not manage in the 1970s as well as obstetricians and neonatologists do today. As part of a university medical center involved in cutting-edge research, the department was using the relatively new technique of amniocentesis to obtain measurements of the levels of hormones secreted by the fetus and to measure the pulmonary development—a critical parameter in determining whether the fetus could be safely delivered early, but a technique still very new at that time.

This mother was doing well from a medical standpoint, and her fetus appeared to be growing and thriving. The problem was that serial hormone level values that had been measured were erratic and showed no definite evidence that the baby's lungs were mature enough to risk early delivery.

I presented this story to include the extensive laboratory testing that had been performed to the entire department and breathed a sigh of relief that I had managed to give a creditable account of the problem. Not bad for a medical student just beginning his third year, I thought. I took my seat and the staff conducted an extensive discussion of the scientific knowledge we had at that time, and each presented their individual experience and input.

To my horror, the chairman asked me to stand and provide my recommendation as to the best way to manage this unfortunate mother and baby. I was, in no way, prepared to do that. My knowledge of obstetrics could have been inscribed on the head of a pin, yet the chairman, a renowned and highly respected expert in this field, chose to ask me for my opinion. I had never made any medical decisions. I had never been asked to synthesize a complex problem and provide recommendations as to what should be done. I did not have a grasp of what the options might be, much less the best option. I had learned about the hormone called surfactant and its role in pulmonary development in the lectures I received during the first 2 years of medical school. I knew that diabetes was bad and that diabetes got worse in pregnancy. Beyond that, I was lost. All I knew was that, at some time, this baby needed to be delivered. The chairman wanted an answer, and I wanted to be anywhere else on Earth than in that conference room. I thought a moment and replied, "I would do nothing at this time."

I was not out of the woods. The chairman smiled, nodded his head wisely (medical school professors do this), and then asked me to justify my answer. I explained that both mother and baby were doing well, and all we had to consider were laboratory results which, at best, were equivocal. There was no scientific basis for my answer, and certainly, I had no experience to fall back on, but I did think my assessment was a logical way of analyzing the problem. Without knowing it, I was relying on common sense; what we will see later in this book could be defined as heuristics and judgment.

At such times, the student or resident braces for the inevitable onslaught of criticism or ridicule as the senior faculty pounces on the hapless trainee before enlightening all present with their knowledge and wisdom. Instead, the chairman smiled again and announced, "And that is what we shall do." He then went on to add his thoughts about the patient's management. I was too shaken to remember a word he said. I had made a decision, one the chairman thought right, but had little understanding of how I had analyzed the information and formulated an answer. I had not been given any lecture about that part of medicine. Thus, I began a long search to answer the question—how do physicians make decisions?

This book is the result of my efforts to answer that question; it is the result of years of experience and thinking about decision-making in medicine—how we teach others to become good decision-makers. It is a distillation of many concepts and approaches from a variety of sources and some concepts that are my own. I have tried to present this information in a logical and organized fashion that will allow the reader to follow my thoughts, integrate at least some of my observations into their decision-making, and be able to help students and post-graduate trainees at all levels become better decision-makers.

Physicians are generally good decision-makers, so why is it necessary to think about how we make decisions? Training and experience acquired over years of practice have made physicians adept at analyzing situations and reacting effectively. The skill is almost intuitive. Most physicians do not give a second thought to their ability to make time-sensitive decisions in stressful situations with limited data. This book was not written with the intent of proposing a better model but to explain the process of decision-making with the goal of suggesting ways in which we can teach this skill more effectively and more logically to students and residents. Being able to analyze the processes involved in medical decision-making will result in improved patient care and help us distinguish poor outcomes due to faulty decision-making from poor outcomes due to systems or communication failures or the vagaries of disease and human biology.

Physicians must work to improve their decision-making skills from the first day of medical school to the day they retire. Every patient or colleague you encounter in the course of your practice depends on your decision-making skills. Physicians make dozens of decisions every day. Some decisions are trivial and even reflexive, requiring little thought or deliberation. Some decisions, however, require considerable knowledge, gathering of data, consultation with others, and consideration of the emotional, social, and personal aspects of the patient's life and family. Some decisions can be made with a high degree of confidence and others with uncertainty or trepidation (Beresford 1991). We make decisions with confidence but rarely give thought to the processes we use to get there.

If we are to improve our decision-making skills or teach the process to others, it is necessary to be able to analyze a decision in a formal and reproducible way. Decision-making is not an arbitrary process—it can be formally studied (Birkmeyer et al. 2004). It can be broken down into its components, and a decision can be analyzed for validity or appropriateness at each step in this process. Medical decisions are cyclic or iterative—we do not make a decision and then walk away. The decision regarding the diagnosis or treatment plan is only the beginning of the process we call patient care.

This book attempts to address all of these issues, and it is my hope that everyone who reads this book will commit to become a better maker of decisions and teacher of decision-making and will be rewarded with an improvement in patient care and a positive impact from their efforts on behalf of their patients, colleagues, co-workers, staff, and institutions.

I spent most of my career training students and residents as a medical school faculty member and as a residency program director. For years, I thought my role was to teach medicine, specifically urology and more specifically pediatric urology. Teaching is an art that one develops slowly and only after much reflection and practice. It was several years before I was comfortable with my teaching skills and confident that my students and residents were receiving high-quality instruction and mentoring. Teaching medicine is not just lecturing to a room of students who learn passively or providing facts so that students can pass an examination, obtain a certification, or complete a course. After much frustration (and, I am sure, frustration on the part of my students and residents), it became apparent that my role was something more. Teaching medicine was providing students with the knowledge, skills, and judgment to identify and solve problems. As a teacher of surgery, my role was not just telling residents where to cut and how deep to cut but, more importantly, when and why to cut.

As an experienced surgeon, problem-solving was, for most situations, almost intuitive but not so obvious to the learners around me. They first had to learn to gather and access the required information critically and effectively and, then, develop an appropriate plan for the patient's problem. These are not skills learned in the classroom. The process is long, arduous, and occasionally overwhelming. It is not just an issue of learning more or being able to do well on exams. Medical students and young physicians are highly educated, bright people who got to where they are after years of hard work and struggle, and we take it for granted that these young physicians have mastered the skill of thinking and decision-making. That assumption is not necessarily correct. The process of making good decisions is vastly more difficult than it appears. Teaching students and young physicians to think lucidly and decisively, recognize untoward events or errors promptly, and solve problems accurately is perhaps the educator's greatest challenge.

Medical students start with an undergraduate education that includes exposure to the biological sciences and hopefully some training in critical thinking. Most students have spent their lives in passive learning environments and have minimal experience making real-world decisions with real consequences. Scary. They are good students but not necessarily good decision-makers. The challenge of getting students to "think like a physician" is not unique to medicine or medical training. It is a hurdle for all professions to include engineering, architecture, law, the sciences, and the arts. The learning curve is not just the accumulation of information or knowledge but a process that requires the ability to grasp the fundamental nature of that field and also to be able to use those concepts in the context of communicating with others within the discipline. A period of immersion similar to being thrown into a swimming pool and told to swim is necessary. In my experience, and in the experience of my peers, the consensus was that it takes at least 2 years before the average resident is able to approach problems within their discipline in a logical, organized fashion.

Physicians are not born thinking like physicians. After 1–2 years of on-the-job clinical experience, the proverbial light bulbs start turning on as residents become comfortable in their role. Was it having danced the dance enough to be able to move across the floor without thinking about where your feet were? Was it having an adequate fund of knowledge to finally speak and understand the new language they were mastering? They were no longer the tourists who had to refer to their English/Spanish dictionary to order a simple meal but could ask and give directions to the closest restaurant with ease. After 3 or 4 years, they could approach all but the most sophisticated and complex problems in a logical, organized fashion and develop efficient solutions. This process is fascinating, yet perplexing. Medical educators do a good job, and students and residents are highly motivated, so there must be more going on than the dissemination of knowledge. I have concluded that one major problem in teaching students and residents to be good decision-makers is the fact that we do not present this art in a formal way, using universally understood terminology and approaches. Decision-making is well recognized as a formal discipline in the cognitive and behavioral sciences, but for some reason, not medicine, even though several authors have published insightful work on how doctors think (Bosk 2003; Montgomery 2006; Groopman 2008; Shiralkar 2011).

The concept that decision-making can be approached as a discipline is recent. Multiple disciplines, such as economics, psychology, sociology, anthropology, management, and neurobiology, to name but a few, have looked at the process of decision-making in an effort to determine how decisions are made. As these disciplines are not closely related, it takes some effort to discover where this information can be found. Decision-making, at least practical decision-making in the medical sciences, has not been widely explored in the medical literature, although some nursing and medical journals have published studies about the process in select groups such as students, residents, intensive care units, and emergency departments. Unfortunately, much of what has been written about decision-making in medicine is not practical or immediately useful for the busy clinician or trainee.

Not all decisions are made using the same processes or pathways. How then does one begin a study of decision-making? First, one must consider the fundamental and somewhat existential topics of what thinking and knowledge really are. How do we analyze information and how do we reason? What are the fundamental tasks and requirements in making a decision, and, finally, what considerations are necessary to provide the most appropriate and compassionate care in a given situation? Diseases do not present in a vacuum, so decision-making must always be tailored to the situation.

Not everyone makes decisions the same way, and most decisions in medicine are not made using the formal rules of logic or the scientific method. We develop several different decision-making skills and use them selectively depending on the situation. What are these decision-making pathways, and which is the most appropriate in a given situation? We also have a personal decision-making style. We prefer to work in environments where our decision-making skills will best serve the work we are tasked with and the type of decisions we feel most comfortable making. Not everyone approaches making decisions in the same way, and most decisions can be approached from several different directions. We are more comfortable with or feel that one approach is more natural for us than another. One's individual decision-making styles and preferences should be an important part of the decision to pursue one specialty over another, yet we never focus on the unique decision-making styles of each student. The choice of a specialty is very personal, but given the number of students and physicians who change their career path in the course of their training, it is obvious that we do not always make the right choice the first time around. The attrition rate for those entering a post-graduate training has been reported to range from 6 per cent to 23 per cent in published studies, rates that are intolerably high (Andriole et al. 2008; Longo et al. 2009). Being more aware of how an individual prefers to manage problems and make decisions may allow the student to make a more informed decision as to which medical career or specialty they are best suited for and reduce residency attrition rates.

If we are to improve our decision-making skills or teach the various processes that can be used to arrive at a decision to others, it is necessary to be able to analyze a decision in a formal and reproducible way. Decision-making is not an arbitrary or impenetrable process—it can be formally studied. It can be broken down into major components, and a decision can be analyzed for validity or appropriateness at each step in this process.

Decision-making is a learned skill, a skill that demands constant attention throughout one's career. We become better decision-makers with practice and experience, but our skills can be even more finely honed if we pay deliberate and conscious attention to how we go about the business of making decisions on behalf of those who put their trust in our care.

Decision-making requires acquisition and manipulation of information. We assume that medical students and post-graduate trainees have acquired the skills necessary to learn, process, assimilate, recall, and apply information efficiently and accurately. This assumption may not be valid if the student is not taught how to most effectively master a large volume of technical information, sifting through data to determine what variables are crucial in the decision-making process. Even the best student can improve his or her learning skills, and even the most proficient clinician can improve their capability for retaining, refining, and prioritizing their knowledge (Ericsson et al. 2007; Schmidt et al. 1990).

We all make bad decisions. Bad decisions result from a variety of causes to include faulty information gathering or management. Bad decisions can result from not taking our emotions and prejudices into account, as well as relying on outdated or inaccurate beliefs. No one endeavors consciously to make a poor decision, but it is possible to identify and be aware of the stumbling blocks we encounter in the course of our interactions with patients and colleagues. Responsible decision-making requires an almost Zen-like approach—we rarely make a decision that does not involve those we will need to interact with in the future. Our decisions therefore have a ripple effect on those we work with, those who may refer patients to us, and, of course, those patients we treat, their families, and their communities.

Is it possible to teach the skill of decision-making more effectively and efficiently? An investigation of what other professions do would suggest the answer is a resounding "yes." Consider military, fire and police departments, SWAT, and rapid response teams, to name a few—all conduct pre- and post-operation briefings to review how well their decisions worked. Jet pilots and disaster relief teams do so as well. Their continued success, safety, and expertise depend on the critical analysis of their decision-making processes. Military officers, as well as strategic and operational planners, and many other professionals spend their careers learning to make decisions. The decision-making process is recognized as a skill just as important and teachable as the technical aspects of their craft. Medical problems, especially complex, multifaceted problems, that involve multiple teams or areas of expertise also demand good planning and decision-making skills. We do have venues for evaluating our results and examining our outcomes and failures, but we fall short of other professions when evaluating whether good or appropriate medical care was provided. Were our plans adequate, and did we consider the appropriate variables? Did we need to rehearse? Were support teams adequately trained, staffed, and communicated with? Is there a role for including video recording or monitoring of procedures to improve our processes? Did we obtain the right data? Too little data? Too much data? Airliners carry flight recorder data boxes. Is such technology of help in teaching or assessing outcomes, or would we become more interested in the technology than the process and the human element that such data could capture? Are we focusing too much on outcomes and not enough on planning and processes? Do we have a formal approach to making decisions, and, as a result, do we have a formal way of analyzing those decisions? Many have noted the benefit of this type of analysis, and to that end, we have created committees and processes to evaluate the quality of care provided or situations where the processes in place could be improved. These efforts are important and worthwhile (Reeves and Bednar 1994).

We all would admit that we can do a better job of making decisions for our patients. It is my hope that looking at the process of making a clinical decision from several points of view and describing what the steps we unconsciously take in this process will allow us to teach better decision-making, spur an interest into the formal research of clinical decision-making, and improve our own individual decision-making.

Ranchos de Taos, NM, USA   Jonathan S. Vordermark II

Contents

1 **Thinking About Thinking** 1
   1.1   Thinking and Our Paleolithic Ancestors 1
   1.2   Why Is Solitaire Popular? 3
   1.3   Thinking and Emotions 4
   1.4   Bias and Prejudice 8
   1.5   Thinking and Bias 10
   1.6   Thinking Fast and Slow 15
   1.7   Recognition and Elimination 16
   1.8   Logic 17

2 **Ways of Thinking** 19
   2.1   Words, Words, Words. 19
   2.2   Empiricism. 20
   2.3   Reasoning. 20
   2.4   Deductive, Inductive, and Abductive Thinking 20
   2.5   Prescriptive, Descriptive, and Normative Thinking 24
   2.6   Optimizing and Satisficing. 25
   2.7   Bounded and Unbounded Thinking 26
   2.8   Concepts of Knowledge. 29
   2.9   Simple, Complex, and Complicated 31
   2.10 Of Chaos, Butterflies, and Black Swans 32

3 **Problem-Solving and Decision-Making** 37
   3.1   Problem-Solving and Decision-Making Are Not the Same. 37
   3.2   Learning Problem-Solving and Decision-Making: What Medical Education Is Really About 39
   3.3   Summary 41

4 **The Decision-Making Cycle** 43
   4.1   The Decision-Making Cycle 45
   4.2   GPS-RADAR. 47

5	**The Elements of Medical Decision-Making**		51
	5.1	The Patient Comes First	51
	5.2	Virtue and Ethics: The Good Doctor	53
	5.3	Ethics	55
	5.4	Quality	55
	5.5	Clinical Presence	57
	5.6	Communication	58
	5.7	Teamwork and Leadership	59
	5.8	Developing Management Plans	59
	5.9	Technical Skills	60
	5.10	Organizational and Operational Awareness	60
6	**Information: Gathering, Storing, and Retrieval**		63
	6.1	Narrative Thinking	63
	6.2	Observation	65
	6.3	Centripetal and Centrifugal Thinking	67
	6.4	The Learning Cycle	71
7	**Mind-Mapping**		75
	7.1	Mind Mapping: An Overview	75
	7.2	How to Mind-Map	78
	7.3	Clinical Application	82
8	**The Processes of Decision-Making and Problem-Solving**		87
	8.1	The Elements of Problem-Solving	87
	8.2	Identifying the Problem	88
	8.3	Out with the Old and in with the New	91
	8.4	Risk and Uncertainty	92
	8.5	Multitasking: The Shadow Side of Decision-Making	93
	8.6	The Kaleidoscope Model	93
9	**Towards a Unified Approach**		97
	9.1	Approaches to Decision-Making	97
	9.2	Decision-Making Strategies: A Conceptual Model	98
	9.3	The Decision Threshold	100
	9.4	Decision Support Systems and Search Orders	101
		9.4.1 The Search Rule	102
		9.4.2 Tally Systems	103
		9.4.3 Strategy Selection and Learning (SSL)	104
		9.4.4 Search Restrictions	106
	9.5	The Hierarchy of Information	109
	9.6	The PICO Format	111
	9.7	The Decision-Making Continuum	111
		9.7.1 Decision-Making by Recognition	112
		9.7.2 Decision-Making by Elimination	113
		9.7.3 Transitional Approaches	114

	9.8	Selecting a Strategy	115

- 9.8.1 Formulaic Versus Cognitive Approaches 115
- 9.8.2 Cognitive and Heuristic Approaches 118

10 Decision-Making by Recognition 121
- 10.1 Maxims and Rules of Thumb 121
- 10.2 Mnemonics 123
- 10.3 Chunking 123
- 10.4 Pattern Recognition 125
- 10.5 Heuristics 127
  - 10.5.1 How Do Heuristics Work? 128
- 10.6 Approaches to Using Heuristics 132
  - 10.6.1 How We Make Choices 132
  - 10.6.2 Fast and Frugal 133
  - 10.6.3 Examining Fewer Cases 134
  - 10.6.4 Limiting Consideration or Retrieval of Variables 134
  - 10.6.5 Simplifying the Weighting of Variables or Cues 134
  - 10.6.6 Examining Fewer Alternatives 134
  - 10.6.7 Less Is More 134
  - 10.6.8 Ignoring Part of the Information 135
  - 10.6.9 Recognition Memory 135
  - 10.6.10 Take-the-First 135
  - 10.6.11 Heuristics Can Be Taught 135
- 10.7 Intuition 136
  - 10.7.1 The Shadow Side of Intuition 139
- 10.8 Flow 139
- 10.9 Deliberate Practice 141

11 Transitional Models 145
- 11.1 Checklists 145
- 11.2 Standard Operating Procedures 146
- 11.3 Algorithms 146
  - 11.3.1 Computer Enhancement of Algorithms 148
  - 11.3.2 The Shadow Side of Algorithms 148
- 11.4 Decision Trees 148
- 11.5 Decision Support Systems 149

12 Decision-Making by Elimination 151
- 12.1 Statistics and Mathematical Models 151
- 12.2 Statistics and Mathematical Models: The Shadow Side 153
  - 12.2.1 Statistics and the Individual Patient 153
  - 12.2.2 Computational Intractability 154
  - 12.2.3 Ethical Considerations 155
- 12.3 Evidence-Based Approaches 155
  - 12.3.1 What EBM Is Not 156
  - 12.3.2 The Shadow Side of EBM 157

	12.4	The Differential Diagnosis..................................	159
		12.4.1 The Differential Diagnosis and the Beginner	161
		12.4.2 The Intermediate Learner............................	162
		12.4.3 The Master...	162
13	**Managing Errors**..		165
	13.1	Errors: An Overview	165
	13.2	Technical Errors...	167
	13.3	Normative Errors	167
	13.4	Bias and Cognitive Errors	168
	13.5	Judgment Errors...	169
	13.6	Errors in Preparation	169
	13.7	Dealing with Errors	170
		13.7.1 Are Conferences an Effective Way of Looking at Errors?.	170
14	**Decision-Making Styles and Specialty Choice**		173
	14.1	The Quadrants of Care.....................................	173
		14.1.1 Specific Characteristics of Problems by Quadrant.......	176
	14.2	The Quadrants of Care and Choice of Specialty	177
	14.3	Does the Expert Make Better Decisions?	178
	14.4	Beyond Clinical Practice	180
15	**Conclusions**		183
	15.1	Sitting by the Fire...	183
	15.2	Decision-Making in the Future	184

Disclaimer.. 187

Bibliography 189

Index 195

Chapter 1
Thinking About Thinking

> *Different situations require different cognitive strategies. How we decide should depend on what we are deciding.*
> (Lehrer 2009, page. 166)

Summary

Thinking, problem-solving, and decision-making are skills we often take for granted but are at the core of providing good medical practice. Medical schools and postgraduate training programs do not include any formal instruction of the principles and mechanics of clinical decision-making. They assume that the medical student or resident will develop good thinking and decision-making skills almost by osmosis in the course of their training. We would like to think physicians and other care providers are somehow "scientific" or "logical" when making decisions. This viewpoint is flawed and inaccurate. Our thought processes may be, based on outdated or erroneous knowledge, illogical or influenced by our memories, emotions, and biases—errors we may be totally unaware of. We are not always the best judge of our knowledge or capabilities, factors important to making the best decision or obtaining the best result for the patient. We make decisions using many different approaches, approaches usually chosen subconsciously, and our decisions are often influenced by time constraints, the urgency of the situation, or the presence of flawed or inadequate information. As a result, the approach chosen to solve a problem may be inappropriate for the problem at hand. Good decision-making requires an understanding of the principles and approaches available for making a decision. Decision-making is a discipline that can be studied and learned.

1.1 Thinking and Our Paleolithic Ancestors

Our brains have evolved to help us to reason and solve problems, traits that distinguish humans from all other species. Sociologists or biologists may argue that many animals, especially mammals and nonhuman primates, do exhibit behaviors that show they can think and solve a problem, but the ability humans have to analyze and process information is so unique and so refined as to be a trait truly peculiar to our species. Like so many of the activities we perform routinely, we rarely think about the phenomenon of thinking in an objective or analytical way.

Consider a gazelle peacefully munching on grass in the African savanna 50,000 years ago. He hears a rustle in the grass and spots a lion poised to pounce. The gazelle does not require a sophisticated prefrontal cortex to respond to this threat—it relies on subcortical, autonomic reflexes to bolt, run, maneuver, or do what is necessary to escape winding up as the lion's breakfast. If you succeed in escaping, you catch your breath and resume munching grass. A gazelle has limited, if any, ability to reflect on this incident, analyze what just happened, and then plan a better avoidance or escape strategy. The gazelles may replay the same event tomorrow without having learned from today's encounter.

Now, consider the plight of a primitive man walking on the same savanna at the same time, who encounters the same, now very hungry, lion. You have no hooves, horns, speed, or strength like the gazelle, but you manage to outwit the lion by scaling a skinny tree the lion cannot climb. Despite his weaknesses, our Paleolithic friend had immense advantage over the gazelle—he could analyze the event, perhaps talk about it with the members of his tribe, and then develop strategies to avoid the lion or respond better in the future. It may take effort, experimentation, and time to develop the best response to the next predator he encounters, but he could learn how to better avoid a dangerous situation (Ross 2006). We do not often have to worry about escaping from a hungry lion today, but the metaphorical predators that stalk us, consciously or unconsciously, are still there and must be remembered and accounted for.

How we process, store, and retrieve information is a complex phenomenon and not isolated to one part of our brain. Unravelling the mysteries behind how the brain functions has been pursued by cognitive scientists from many disciplines, and we have a long way to go to understand the inner workings of our thinking, reasoning, and approaches to analyzing the world around us. For the purposes of making decisions, it is not necessary for us to have an extensive understanding of neuroanatomy or neurophysiology, but we can describe the fundamental ways in which we go about that process. Thinking is not only a very individualized process, but we use different approaches for different problems just like our Paleolithic ancestor who used one process when deciding how to escape from the lion and a totally different process when evaluating his actions and deciding how to react when faced with a new and different situation.

Physicians, in spite of their education and training, are not some subspecies or rarefied form of the human race. We solve problems just like every other human being. Our thought processes are no different than lawyers, engineers, or any other professional trained in a narrow discipline. We all must develop the skill of thinking and problem-solving within our individual domains. The budding engineer must learn to think like an engineer, and the medical student must learn to think like a physician.

We like to think our cerebral cortex governs and controls our analytical, rational, and creative efforts, but we are never free from our emotions, our prejudices, and our human penchant for taking shortcuts or disregarding data that is uncomfortable. Thinking and decision-making involve many parts of our brain to include our limbic system, hippocampus, thalamus, amygdala, and brain stem. We do not make any decisions, formulate any memory, or process any sensory input without filtering it through the more primitive layers of our brains. We are not, as Descartes or Plato would have us believe, entirely rational creatures. We are emotional creatures and also rely heavily on our less sophisticated parts of our brains. Eliminating emotions or denying that decisions are influenced by our emotions might give us a sense that man is more sophisticated than other animals, but this view it is not only incorrect from a neuro-biological perspective. Our subcortical brain centers allow us to make decisions more quickly, organize and store information more effectively, and react more quickly in stressful situations (Lehrer 2009; LeDoux 1996). The clinician must remain ever vigilant and remember that while we like to think of ourselves as rational and analytical, we are also susceptible to the more primitive elements of our thinking that lie just below the surface. We cannot forget that our intellectual capabilities are the product of thousands of years of evolution and experience without the benefit of the knowledge of science and technology we take for granted today.

1.2 Why Is Solitaire Popular?

Many play the game solitaire on their computer when they have a few minutes of down time. That is interesting, given that it is not a challenging game. What is the attraction? Aside from the fact that it is a relatively mindless way to spend a few minutes and aside from the fact that it is harmless in terms of risk (no one I know of bets on the outcome of a game of solitaire) and as the game is, well, a solitary pursuit, it is still remarkable that the game is so popular. I wonder if the popularity has something to do with the phenomenon of seven plus or minus two, a concept developed from research on our short-term memory (Miller 1956). His work showed that people can recall a string of five to nine numbers or words without any special training. Very few do well with a string of nine numbers, the ideal number being seven. That research may explain why we can remember phone numbers but not necessarily the area code. We probably remember the area code by knowing where the person lives as a separate bit or chunk of information, rather than being a part of the seven digits of the phone number. Miller's research is a key to understanding the limitations of human short-term memory, a limit important for us to be aware of as we consider how we process information.

The game of solitaire starts with seven stacks of cards, and the challenge is to remember the color and face value of each card. It is not nearly as challenging as trying to count cards when playing bridge or poker, but the format of the game does conform to the seven plus or minus two rule. If the rules of the game were changed so that the game started with five stacks of cards, it would be boring. If it started with nine stacks of cards, there would be more variables to deal with than the human brain is primed to deal with, and the game would be frustrating for all but a polymath. There is something comfortable and appealing about dealing with only seven stacks of cards and something very boring about the game of tic-tac-toe.

In similar fashion, we do our best decision-making when the number of variables we consider in a decision is limited. Automobile manufacturers and realtors understand this phenomenon. If we shop for a new car and are able to limit the number of requirements in terms of cost, color, size, and options, we can easily compare one model to another. Likewise, when shopping for a new home, our decisions are much more rational when we limit the number of essential variables to lot size, number of bedrooms, and access to shopping and good schools. The prospective buyer is now able to comparison shop in a meaningful fashion.

When we venture beyond a reasonable number of established variables, rational comparison becomes impossible, and we start looking at features such as a sunroof, racing stripes, or granite countertops. Such variables may not have been critical when we began our search, and such variables have nothing to do with making a sensible decision.

Our thinking is also limited by our short-term memory. As Miller showed, our prefrontal cortex can deal with seven items simultaneously. We can reliably recall a new telephone number but have difficulty to remember the new number and a new area code. Our brains are not computers that can handle a large volume of data at the same time, and when required to process larger amounts of data, we resort to well-described techniques that will be discussed in detail later. It has been demonstrated in various fields that the quality of decisions is degraded when too much data is incorporated into the process. The key is deciding which variables are pivotal and critical. Experience matters. Experts are better at recognizing what variables are most critical.

Physicians can be overwhelmed with data. The number of values measured by serum chemistry panels, the rapid availability of very sophisticated laboratory tests, and the ability of imaging studies to provide greater detail provide more information than anyone can readily process. It takes experience to ignore what may appear as significant findings on computerized axial tomography (CAT scan) or magnetic resonance imaging (MRI) and still be able to recognize when a subtle or even overlooked abnormality is really important. Not all abnormal values or abnormal findings are relevant to good decision-making (Saposnik et al. 2016; Bilalic and McLeod 2014).

1.3 Thinking and Emotions

Our emotions often override our logic. Our emotional brains are responsible in forming many of our ethical and moral decisions. Solving mathematical formulas, or a problem in physics, may seem remote from our emotions, but our attitudes towards mathematics and the elation we get from finding the correct solution to a problem do involve our emotional brain and reinforce our ability to deal with mathematics as a discipline. How many potentially good mathematicians are thwarted by

1.3 Thinking and Emotions

their belief that they are not good at math or that the problem does not make sense. Our emotional brain is just as important to achieving success in mathematics as our prefrontal cortex.

Our prefrontal cortex may filter the information used in making decisions, but decisions almost always include input from our deep brain where our emotional centers reside. It is well known that the decisions of political analysts and stockbrokers, groups that may purport to take a highly analytical approach to their decisions, and yet are often as not wrong, still are highly emotionally driven in their approaches to decision-making. Such decisions include much data that is subject to interpretation, difficult to quantify or qualify, and dependent on variables that cannot be controlled or even considered. Medical problems are often fraught with the problems of too much or too little data, "soft" data, misleading data, or unknowns. And, yes, physicians also make decisions that rely heavily on input from their emotional centers. If we receive information that is contrary to our beliefs or prejudices, we are likely to dismiss that information, no matter how creditable. We can be like lawyers who are able to make eloquent and superficially rational arguments to defend the most despicable and guilty of clients. What about the physicians who have invested in a radiation therapy facility or outpatient surgical center? Even the staunchest advocate of surgical intervention might find himself concluding that the patient is not a good surgical candidate or will argue to convince the patient and his family that "in this particular case" radiation therapy would be best. Such decisions are probably a product of our emotional or subconscious thinking, and not from our prefrontal cortex, no matter how logical and well thought out they may seem and should raise the concern that we may be making decisions not in the best interest of our patients. Some decisions, especially in situations that are unique or anomalous, should not be made quickly—there are too many variables to consider. The outcomes of those variables need to be assessed and compared, and that process cannot be made on the spur of the moment. There is a fine balance between being rash and being overwhelmed by options and data to the point of becoming unable to act. The best decision may require relegating the issue to our subconscious brain for reflection.

I remember being stymied by what I found after starting a complex reconstructive procedure in a child who had undergone several unsuccessful procedures. The situation was not what I had anticipated, and the extensive intra-abdominal scarring would not permit proceeding with my original plan. After a couple hours of work to unravel this child's anatomy, I realized that I needed a new plan. I was working with a rather impetuous and impulsive pediatric surgeon who was shocked when I admitted that the best thing to do was to take a break and have a quick lunch so that I could think about the best way to proceed. The concept of stopping to reflect on surgical options instead of laboring on was not in that surgeon's repertoire. I took a break and had lunch. After a few minutes of quiet reflection, I felt comfortable proceeding with a new plan. I advised the parents of the change in plan and, refreshed, proceeded with an uneventful and ultimately successful solution for the problem. The pediatric surgeon has, to my knowledge, never learned that lesson.

My practice was replete with complex problems without an obvious solution. Frequently there was an obvious textbook or most commonly recommended solution, but what does one do when your experience and instinct questions if the "obvious" solution is really the best for this patient or this family. In those instances, I would inform the family of the problem and ask for time to reflect. I never had a family that preferred an immediate answer or thought that a request to think first before committing to therapy was a weakness. I am sure that some families preferred a more assertive and stalwart approach. I am sure some of those families sought a second opinion or went elsewhere for care. It is best, I believe, to not let that reaction bother me—one's concern should be what is the best interest of the child rather than imposing my will on the family. Patients and their families do not have the medical training, knowledge, and understanding of the nuances regarding when to operate or not operate or what operative approach would be optimal in every situation. I have dealt with surgeons who would brag that they never had a situation where they didn't know what to do. Those surgeons were dangerous. The capabilities of our subconscious mind are profound, and we need to learn to use that portion of our intellect, a skill people of action do not find easy to develop. Physicians, and especially surgeons, do not deal well with ambiguity, yet ambiguity is part of dealing with complex systems. A former mentor always opined—for those whose tool is a hammer every problem is a nail. Surgeons, for example, are prone to propose a surgical solution to a problem even if there are other options.

We would like to think that the more primitive parts of our brains—the limbic system, brain stem, and amygdala—are often thought to be uninvolved from the portions of our higher cortex we use for decision-making, at least the highly rational and complex decision-making we encounter in clinical medicine. We fall into the trap of believing ourselves too intelligent, sophisticated, rational, and highly educated to be affected by our emotions. Good decisions require input from both the centers reason and of emotion. Patients with damage to their orbitofrontal cortex, a part of the frontal lobe in a location in our brain heavily involved in generating emotions, cannot make decisions even though their other cortical functions seem intact. From a neuroanatomical and humanistic standpoint, we are emotional beings—rational and reasoning—but our thoughts, though tempered by reason, are filtered through the emotional parts of our brains. An example would be our response to danger, where our reactions are processed through our amygdala milliseconds before we perceive the danger in our prefrontal cortex. If we are safely observing a caged snake and that snake strikes at us, we cannot control our instinctual response to back away.

Our brains have evolved to be able to make decisions rapidly. Our ancestors were not philosophers and theorists. They were survivalists, and survival required the ability to react to situations with minimal sensory input or information. Once we escaped danger, we could perhaps sit in the safety of a tree or a cave and reflect on our luck or our good actions but only if we survived. This is the advantage of the human species—to be able to process information gleaned from our experiences and reflect on what would be a better path to walk down to find our next meal or where it would be safer to sleep at night to avoid the danger from which we just escaped.

1.3 Thinking and Emotions

We can learn to suppress or minimize the fight or flight response, but we can never completely rid ourselves of our initial response to a situation. We will always react to finding a snake on a hiking trail, seeing a traumatic event, and meeting a loved one or an enemy.

The emotional brain is especially good at helping us make difficult decisions. It can process large amounts of data and break problems down into manageable chunks. Your emotional brain is constantly learning from mistakes, new situations, the barrage of social clues, and other bits of input from the environment involving all of our senses to include our intuition. This process takes time. Medical students and residents will complain that they are not being taught. What they are saying is that they are not being provided with a sufficient number of facts or isolated pieces of information that they can gather up like breadcrumbs. Crumbs need to be digested to be of any value, a process that takes time. The information must be processed in our subconscious and emotions. It is stored, organized, and available for retrieval and reorganization to address problems presented by new situations and new problems. There is no shortcut—one cannot be force-fed like a goose. The data must be sifted through and integrated. This should be a fundamental concern for those who propose shortening the medical school curriculum or deleting components that are deemed not critical to an individual's career goals or choice of specialty.

Shortening the medical school curriculum or period of residency training may impair the development of judgment and will diminish the exposure to the material necessary for establishing an adequate long-term memory. There is no question that not all experiences are equally valuable or even necessary. Medical care and medical education are constant battles of conflicting priorities.

As the following diagrams show, our emotional brains filter the data we collect and influence the decisions we make. When encountering a new patient or a new situation, we automatically consider factors such as a patient's race, dress, or social status without being aware of our initial conceptions—factors that may produce appropriate responses of caution, sense of urgency, or intuition that something about the situation is not quite right or more serious than others perceive.

What we notice about a patient is immediately entered into our decision-making as we work to put the narrative together. A surgeon meeting a patient who smells of cigarette smoke begins the search for information to answer questions such as is this patient a high surgical risk or is there any way to link her smoking habits to her present problem or do I need to start looking for underlying diseases such as cancer or pulmonary or vascular disease? A patient with stained, damaged teeth may trigger questions about methamphetamine or other drug abuse, hepatitis, or HIV. Our emotional brains can therefore be valuable in helping us to make nuanced and rapid decisions, and we ignore this input to our peril.

Our emotional responses can also affect our observations in negative or erroneous ways. We may dismiss aspects of the patient's history as insignificant, unreliable, or not worth pursuing. We may think the patient not capable of understanding their disease or the questions that may be put to them. To not be aware of our emotional reactions or snap judgments in these instances may lead to wrong

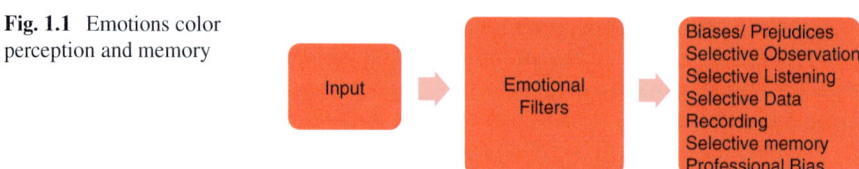

Fig. 1.1 Emotions color perception and memory

conclusions, misguided decisions, or management errors. We may assume a homeless person is not capable of caring for themselves or able to understand the rationale for a particular course of therapy. We may consider unfavorable outcomes we have experienced in similar situations and not include those options in our decision-making matrix (Fig. 1.1).

1.4 Bias and Prejudice

Biases and prejudices take many forms in medical practice. We bring professional or specialty-specific biases into the examination room. Specialists may subconsciously denigrate or downplay input from referring primary care physicians, and primary care physicians may dismiss input from specialists as being inappropriate, egocentric, or lacking in compassion or understanding. We are biased towards our own areas of expertise and comfort. Surgeons are likely to dismiss recommendations from oncologists or radiotherapists in favor of surgical management. Community-based physicians may be skeptical of input from an academic center and vice versa. A full professor may be immediately dismissive of a diagnosis from a nurse clinician or junior faculty member or a physician from an institution of perceived lesser stature. All too often those physicians will convey their distain to the patient verbally or with subtle nonverbal messages. Worse, our comments and behaviors as mentors have a lasting effect on the students and residents we supervise.

Our ego or practice habits may make us reluctant to consider alternate treatment options even if one of those options may be in the best interest of that particular patient. We may not offer a patient or his family the option of being treated at another institution, again, when that option may be in the best interest of the patient. We may take on a problem we have limited experience or expertise with when a specialist or expert in that area is readily available, but in another institution. We are likely to dismiss a particular course of therapy or surgical approach if we have had a recent bad outcome from that therapy or approach. We are likely to recommend a surgical or therapeutic approach if we have recently had a good experience or have seen data that is favorable towards that procedure.

Being smart does not always help us see faults in our logic. Indeed, intelligent and educated people may be more prone to errors of cognition because they are capable of developing arguments to defend their beliefs more rapidly and with greater assuredness than those who are less facile with their thinking. This ability gives them a blind spot to their own errors or lapses in logic and also allows them to find fault in the positions of others quickly. Our prejudices and strong opinions therefore hinder rational, analytical thinking.

We are likely to cherry-pick data or dismiss research studies or clinical observations that do not support the conclusions we have chosen to favor. We are also likely to dismiss opinions of colleagues or consultants we do not like or would like to undermine and are more willing to advance the observations and opinions of protégés whose careers we want to enhance or give us economic or professional incentives to support.

We would like to think we are immune to emotions and biases when gathering information, evaluating a problem, or making or carrying out a decision. As logical and as rational as we think we are, especially when making major decisions in life, we cannot ignore the fact that we rely heavily on our emotions when purchasing a house or a car, determining where we will take our next vacation, or choosing a favorite sports team, college, or mate. We do not lose our emotional filters when we graduate from medical school and are faced with making clinical decisions. *We ignore that fact at our peril and at the risk of our patient's welfare* (Fig. 1.2).

Avoiding Being Victimized by Our Emotions

We cannot ignore our emotions, and, as we have seen, our emotions provide valuable insights into our clinical practice. We do need to develop ways to avoid becoming victims of our emotions. We need a system to organize and categorize that information for later retrieval. When we recall information, we must accurately retrieve the relevant information. That information needs to be analyzed and put together in a coherent fashion for us to make a decision. All of these steps happen in different parts of the central nervous system. Some decisions require input from our higher centers, our prefrontal cortex, or executive center, and some decisions take the form of intuition, heuristics, and pattern recognition based on experience.

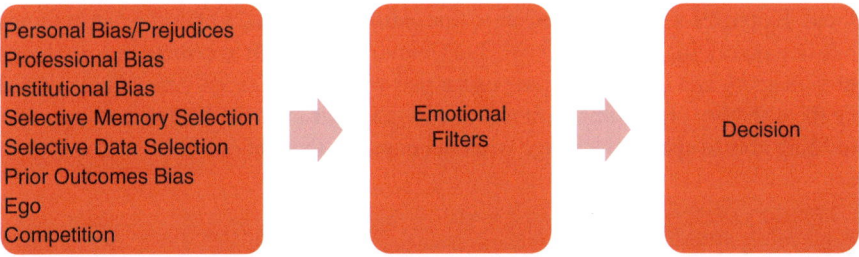

Fig. 1.2 Emotions color decision-making

The good news is that our understanding of how our brains work can be used to improve teaching, learning, and decision-making. The problem for teachers and practicing clinicians is to know enough about the brain to utilize that organ most effectively.

Most of our learning in the first 2 years of medical school is by rote or by association, and these are the least efficient methods of learning. Conversely, most of our learning in the clinical years of medical school and throughout or careers is learning by re-enforcement—learning by interacting with our environment and the situations we encounter every day (Schön 1987; Schön 1983). Learning by reinforcement is much more efficient and effective. Medical schools have done much to integrate clinical situations into the first 2 years of medical school to make the basic science information more relevant and alive, but, unfortunately, there is still no substitute for having to learn by memorization.

How our ability to think evolved does have implications in terms of how we approach problems today. Our attention is divided between conscious thought and the subconscious awareness of our surroundings. Most of our day-to-day perceptions are largely beyond our conscious. We may be intently chipping a flint for a new spear, but we are always assessing our surroundings, people, situations, and impressions, always on the lookout for danger. This trait has been called the *adaptive unconscious*—the ability to size up our environments, disambiguate them, interpret them, and initiate behavior quickly and unconsciously confers a survival advantage and thus was selected for (Wilson 2002). In the same way, we assess social situations and interactions with others, not always with our conscious, rational mind but with our emotionally driven subconscious. We would like to think we are always using the logical, analytical, executive decision-making portions of our cortex as we deal with events and make decisions, but it takes conscious deliberate effort to suppress the constant radar of our subconscious and be truly aware of the variables and elements surrounding a decision. Likewise, our ability to learn is profoundly influenced by the constant interaction between the conscious and subconscious brain. *Implicit learning* is a function of our adaptive unconscious. We can learn or perform complex actions or information quickly with a minimum of effort, much like when we drive an automobile or as a child learns their native language. *Explicit learning* or learning that requires activation of our conscious is more effortful and requires concentration and deliberate focus. Examples would be the effort to first learn the mechanics of driving an automobile or memorizing the Krebs cycle. Such learning is difficult to cement into our long-term memory and does not prepare us for real-world experiences. An example would be the difficulty of learning verb tenses and grammar in a new language as opposed to being able to speak a language without conscious thought or effort.

1.5 Thinking and Bias

Cognitive bias—cognitive bias is the natural tendency to favor solutions we are familiar with rather than risk a decision in a situation that is ambiguous. Cognitive bias can take many forms and can have major consequences for patient outcomes as demonstrated by

1.5 Thinking and Bias

one recent publication. Saposnik and co-workers (2016) screened 5963 case studies published between 1980 and 2015, using MeSH (Medical Subject Headings) headings of decision-making, and physicians, from the English-speaking literature. They found 20 studies that met their criteria of articles that demonstrated at least one form of cognitive bias to include overconfidence, lower tolerance to risk, anchoring effect (reliance on the first piece of information proposed—the anchor), or information bias (an error created by erroneous, mistaken, or misclassified initial observation) or availability bias (reliance on an immediate solution or the first one that comes to mind). In the judgment of the authors of this paper, some form of cognitive bias was associated with diagnostic inaccuracies in 36.5–77% of case scenarios reviewed in their meta-analysis. They concluded that physicians are often influenced by cognitive biases and that these biases might adversely affect decision-making and lead to poor outcomes. Example would be ignoring standard or evidence-based recommendations.

Saposnik also hypothesized that personality traits may also contribute to cognitive biases that produce diagnostic errors, tolerance to risk or ambiguity, framing effects (viewing situations in a narrow, usually specialty-specific orientation), overconfidence, and poor calibration, but found insufficient evidence to correlate personality traits with unfavorable outcomes.

In reviewing his conclusions, Saposnik noted that the lessons learned from clinical encounters were not consistent but influenced by biases and personality traits due to variabilities between specialties.

Dealing with biases, especially cognitive biases (bias due to fundamental differences or distortions in thinking), is difficult. We are rarely aware of the biases we are subject to, and it may be awkward for a colleague or mentor to point out those shortcomings to others. Many of our biases are driven by our personality or passively acquired from our mentors and associates. This list provides a few of the more common biases that can lead to errors in judgment or poor decision-making.

- *Calibration*—Physicians must learn to calibrate their decision-making—bring their perceived and actual diagnostic accuracy and outcomes into better alignment. Calibration is a problem-solving method used to assess our subjective ability to determine the probability of a given event. A few examples will, hopefully, put this concept into perspective; surgeons should know within a few per cent what is the incidence of injuries to the common duct in gallbladder surgery and, just as importantly, what their personal common duct injury rate is. Oncologists should know, within a narrow range, what the rates of side effects for commonly used chemotherapeutic agents are. Urologists and internists should know what the per cent resistance rates are for commonly used urinary tract antimicrobials which are in the settings they work in. It is possible to judge one's personal sense or facility to calibrate data or perceptions by taking tests designed to measure this ability (Hubbard 2007).
- When possible, use standardized approaches, such as SOPs, checklists, etc., which have been shown to reduce error rates.
- Play the devil's advocate, or assign a team member to play the role of the devil's advocate. This avoids "groupthink" and failure to consider less visible options.
- Use time-outs and the "prefrontal pause" to review your course of action, especially if there is doubt about the decision or if there are questions or uneasiness about the decision.

- Solicit input from consultants or peers—even if on an informal basis.
- Consider if the decision demands type 2 thinking, even if the decision seems obvious.

The processing of information obtained during any physician/patient interaction is unique to every individual and requires several levels of processing. Data is filtered through our emotionally driven centers before they are analyzed by our cortical centers. The information is also filtered by the memories of our past experiences and decisions. Decisions can, therefore, never be exclusively analytical or dispassionate. Our brains are not computers. Our brains are not programmed to handle data in a purely logical or analytical way. We have a bias towards events or situations influenced by our experience, failures, success, and prejudices. The calibration of probabilities and perceived results may be skewed by experiences with untoward outcomes with previous patients or inflated or exaggerated ideas of just how good our technical abilities or treatment results are for a given problem. We may be using the wrong data. We may think that the probability of a certain event or outcome is 10 per cent when in reality it is 25 per cent. We may think that the complication rate for a given procedure is 5 per cent *in our hands*, but our personal experience with that procedure may be inadequate to accurately assess or state one's own outcomes. Just because the complication rate in a published report is 10 per cent does not mean that an individual surgeon will have those outcomes. A junior or newly minted surgeon will not have had sufficient experience with any procedure to be able to truthfully tell a patient that: "In my hands, the incidence of this particular complication rate is 10 per cent." It may be years before a surgeon can legitimately make that statement, if ever. We all suffer from an overly optimistic bias towards our personal outcomes.

Imaging studies, for example, can be read differently by two equally qualified and experienced radiologists—there is an error rate: false positives and negatives inherent in any laboratory test and many physical findings are subject to interpretation and histories subject to listener or cognitive bias. Psychologists use the *Einstellung effect* to describe this type of a cognitive bias (Bilalic and McLeod 2014). The Einstellung effect is the tendency of even the most experienced experts to overlook better or more efficacious solutions in favor of the solution they are most familiar with or know has worked before. We are, therefore, often cognitively lazy and ignore opportunities to see a novel or potentially better approach to a problem. Some of the most brilliant developments in surgery are minor alterations in approach for a baffling or vexatious problem with an established technique rather than a major technical breakthrough. Approaches to avoid cognitive biases will be addressed in greater depth in Chap. 14 when we look at ways to manage errors in decision-making. The various biases we are prone to have been described by numerous authors (Saposnik 2016; Shiralkar 2011; Kahneman 2011; Johnson-Laird 2011).

Last Bad Experience

We're all creatures of what burned us most recently. (Kenworthy 1995)

Bad outcomes affect our judgment, especially when the complication or failure is recent. Surgery, for example, is a difficult craft to master, and even experienced surgeons can have a bad outcome from any operation they may frequently perform. It is natural to have doubts and be reticent to recommend a procedure, particularly a difficult or potentially morbid procedure when one is still emotionally raw from a recent complication or bad outcome with that same procedure.

In a study evaluating interpretations of chest radiographs, radiologists were 50 per cent more likely to recommend a patient undergo a biopsy after having recently missed been sued for missing a lesion on a mammogram (Potchen et al. 2000). In the same fashion, if we have had a string of successful outcomes with a particular procedure or approach, we are more likely to be enthusiastic about recommending that approach in spite of established data that does not support such optimism. This is also true for institutions that consider themselves as having noteworthy expertise in a particular area, and physicians at such an institution may overestimate the probability of a positive outcome, a particular problem, especially with today's intense marketing of medical products and services. This bias is really one of our confidence or ego overriding our ethics and sense of prudence and proportion.

Recency Bias

Recency bias is similar to last bad experience bias. We are more likely to draw upon information that we have recently encountered to make decisions. Our recent experiences are more powerful factors than events from our past. How many of us have encountered a problem that brings to mind an article we were just reading in the latest medical journal? If we attend a conference on a topic such as adrenal tumors, we are more likely to consider that diagnosis in a patient with headaches and hypertension rather than the possibility the patient has not been taking his medications.

Unpacking Bias

When faced with an abnormality or cluster of symptoms that are perplexing, we are more likely to expand the scope of our thinking and include less obvious diagnoses if we take the time to physically write down the less obvious or not immediately apparent possibilities. The simple act of writing diagnoses down forces our thinking to consider a broader range of options than we would if we just relied on a mental checklist. Making the effort to deliberately unpack our knowledge and experience may be time-consuming and not always appropriate but can help us find that one little item we packed and is hidden in the corner of our suitcase.

Confirmation Bias

Confirmation bias is the selection of a few selected bits of data and ignoring information that does not fit our hypothesis rather than considering the whole picture we are presented with. In common parlance, we call it cherry-picking.

We can be misled by selective hearing if we prematurely come to a decision even when facts do not support the conclusion. Confirmation bias and recency bias are especially difficult to avoid for those in academia who are engaged in research on a particular problem or are seeking patients with a specific set of findings in order to complete a series for a publication. Zebras are not common, but if we are thinking about zebras, it is hard not to imagine them lurking around every corner.

An example of confirmation bias is assuming that an elderly homeless man with dementia is an alcoholic rather than considering the entire differential diagnosis for dementia. Alternately one can exercise confrontation bias when one is committed to a particular decision and then selects findings or data to support that decision.

Representation or Anchoring Bias

We gravitate to aspects of a problem that are similar to past experiences and give undue weight to decisions we made in similar situations. It is easy to anchor or fix our arguments to a conclusion that is comfortable or has worked in the past without considering other reasonable alternatives. In the midst of flu season, it is hard to remember there are multiple other causes for flu-like symptoms.

Availability Bias

This is similar to representation or anchoring bias. We may consider a specific diagnosis because it comes to mind easily or is common or perhaps from a recent case or conference, lecture, etc. This bias is similar to the "red Volkswagen" paradigm. You may never think about red Volkswagens, but when considering purchasing a red Volkswagen, you are amazed at how many you see.

Sunk Cost Bias

This bias is the reluctance to abandon a course of investigation or treatment because all the effort and expense already invested would go to waste. This bias is also seen with medical students and residents who find they really do not want to pursue a career in medicine but have already spent so much time and money getting a medical degree. Investors have the same conflict when a stock they have purchased drops precipitously in value. Many investors are reluctant to sell because of the money they have invested in that stock even though their financial advisor might advise them to sell and cut their losses.

Hindsight Bias

This bias is the tendency to believe that one had reached the correct solution or predicted the outcome after the outcome is known. "I always thought that patient had that disease," or "I always thought that proceeding with that procedure would result in that complication." It can also be used to describe one's overly optimistic opinion of their outcomes. Surgeons tend to underestimate the risk of complications in their personal experience, and we all think our diagnostic accuracy is higher than it really is.

Framing Bias

People are fundamentally risk adverse and prefer options that offer a gain over a loss, even if the rates of gain or loss are identical or comparable. We are prone to accept a choice presented in a positive frame over data presented in negative terms. For example, if a treatment regimen is presented to a patient as having a 95 per cent probability of success, patients are more likely to accept that course than if it were presented as having a 5 per cent fatality rate. We are likely to state our recommendations in a positive light.

1.6 Thinking Fast and Slow

Two cognitive psychologists, Daniel Kahneman and Amos Tversky (Kahneman 2011), teamed up in the early 1970s to write a series of groundbreaking articles that explored decision-making. Their work challenged conventional economic theories about human judgment and behavior. They concluded that most decision-making is not fundamentally rational and that our perceptions of risk and probability are flawed—more often than not, we rely on heuristics (simple rules of thumb) and bias rather than deliberate analysis to make decisions. Specifically, they focused on the fact that people are not always logical or systematic in their approach to decisions. People look for patterns in events or behaviors, even when none exist. The Nobel Prize in economics was awarded to Kahneman in 2002 for this work. (Amos Tversky died before the Nobel Prize committee considered their contributions and was therefore not eligible for the prize.)

According to Kahneman and Tversky, when problem-solving, we use two systems for problem-solving—system 1, or *fast thinking*, and system 2, or *slow thinking*. Human beings, they argued, are intrinsically lazy when thinking about or solving a problem, with the fast system being our default, or primary approach. System 1 is autonomic, reflexive, involuntary, and intuitive, just like our Paleolithic friend who encounters a lion and reacts immediately. System 2 is rational, logical, effortful, and circumspect like our Stone Age ancestor who considers the best way to avoid or escape danger but only when he has the opportunity to do so safely. System 1 is heavily influenced by prior experiences and thought processes such as rules of thumb. System 1 relies heavily on heuristics, the use of mnemonics and pattern recognition, subjects that will be covered in depth later. System 2 is more selective and requires us to be more deliberate and calculative in our analysis of data and options before making a decision.

Both systems are useful and neither is intrinsically better or more valid. Due to the way our brains have evolved, we like finding patterns in our world and like to make associations even when no association if present—it takes work to shift into our system 2 mode. We want to believe that there is cause and effect in situations where the data does not support the conclusion; and we are quick to make conclusions based on a small amount of data or a small sample size. This approach is prevalent and not necessarily flawed in many medical situations.

Tversky and Kahneman used the term *heuristic* to describe this approach, and much of their subsequent work involved describing various heuristics. Kahneman lists at least 48 heuristics they identified during the course of their collaboration. Heuristics will be discussed in depth in Chap. 10.

The problem we face as decision-makers is recognizing which system is more appropriate for a given problem. Using system 1 in a system 2 situation may result in a hurried, sloppy, and flawed decision. Using system 2 in a system 1 situation is inefficient, wasteful of time and effort, and potentially dangerous in a crisis situation. In fact, most medical decisions are system 1 decisions. Situations that require

Table 1.1 Thinking fast and slow

Fast	Slow
Type 1	Type 2
Straight line	Imaginative
Active	Contemplative
Centripetal	Centrifugal
Defined problem	Complex problem
Tactical	Strategic
First best option	Deep thinking
Time-sensitive	Time independent
Pragmatic	Existential

system 2 thinking are generally complex or complicated situations and are usually situations that do not demand immediate answers. System 2 decisions often require input from consultants, often nonmedical consultants when, for example, social, ethical, or humanistic considerations must be taken into account. Some are better at system 2 thinking than others, and this orientation should be recognized early and given weight and deliberate consideration when choosing a specialty or career path. System 2 may be appropriate for long-standing or multi-system problems such as an internist would see, but that analytical approach might not suit for the patient with a cardiac arrest in the emergency department.

The terms system 1 and 2 or fast and slow thinking are applicable to several aspects of the decision-making or problem-solving approaches used in medicine but may be confusing for those not familiar with the work of Tversky and Kahneman. Table 1.1—thinking fast and slow—lists some of the ways the two systems can be looked at and will, hopefully, give a preview of topics that will be covered as we proceed.

1.7 Recognition and Elimination

The terms system 1 and 2 or fast and slow do not capture the essence of the thought processes physicians use to approach clinical problems. Physicians solve problems by *recognition* or by *elimination*. These terms describe the approaches used for the majority of medical decisions. When solving a problem by *recognition*, we choose the option or strategy we recognize as being similar to problems we have encountered in the past. Another approach is to develop a list of options as we do when we develop a differential diagnosis and then *eliminate* those options that do not match the data we have gathered about the problem before us. Recognition corresponds most closely to system 1 or fast thinking and elimination to system 2 or slow thinking. Recognition is used most frequently for solving routine or simple clinical problems. Much of medicine is simple pattern recognition. Most clinical conditions and management decisions are managed in an expeditious fashion using judgment born of experience and knowledge. Decisions that are complex or complicated or decisions that involve the consideration of multiple variables cannot be managed by simple, straight-line-type thinking but require collection of a much larger amount of data, development of alternatives, consideration of risks and benefits, and sophisticated judgment. These decisions correspond more closely to system 2 or slow thinking. This approach involves the judicious elimination of possibilities to identify the best option for a given situation. We will return to recognition and elimination later in Chaps. 10 and 12, but first let us consider other ways that thinking and decision-making can be approached.

1.8 Logic

We all like to consider ourselves logical and believe we apply logic in the course of making decisions. Logic is the use of formal reasoning to analyze a problem. Logic follows well-accepted rules, and its application is most rigidly developed in the fields of philosophy, mathematics, or computer science.

Clinicians do not use the classic principles of logic as they are taught in formal undergraduate courses. Instead, we rely on a more practical combination of experience, judgment, and intuition that defies formal description or codification into immutable principles. The rules of formal logic are not something we master or even use in everyday decisions, and formal logic is not a requirement for developing our clinical decision-making skills. Arguments based on the rules of formal logic are blind to content, and inferences are not subject to interpretation, perception, or variability. These tenants are very rarely characteristics of conditions in the human or biological world. Computers and other forms of artificial intelligence cannot negotiate these abstract, and for us, uniquely human nuances, severely limiting the use of computer-based algorithms for medical decision-making. We do commit errors in our thinking and can make decisions that would be considered illogical, so it is necessary to have an understanding of what logical thinking is and what we mean when defending decisions, but reason and rational are perhaps better terms to describe those processes than logic or logical.

Formal logic requires valid or true inferences, a context that is not generally available in medicine, as inferences in medicine are usually subject to interpretation, bias, beliefs (accurate or inaccurate), or theories that cannot always be proven to be true. Even an unequivocal finding, such as a forearm fracture, does not automatically dictate a set course of management. The decision for treatment may vary between practitioners and may even be controversial.

Few who teach clinical medicine have ever had any formal instruction in logic. Physicians usually take the attitude that what they teach their students, and the wisdom they impart to their fellows and residents is beyond the purview of current education theory or subject to critical analysis. This attitude is not unique to medical education. All educators in professional and graduate schools struggle with these issues (Kolb 2015). Good decisions result from the application of a process that requires a solid fund of knowledge, identifying the problem, gathering the appropriate data, analyzing that information critically, and then formulating and directing an appropriate plan of management. The initial problem may not be the problem that needs to be solved. Not all observations or purported facts are relevant or even true. Patient histories can be unreliable, laboratory studies are erroneous, and our observations on examination can be wrong or incomplete. Decisions are almost always somewhat time-sensitive, so knowledge must be stored and organized for rapid and accurate retrieval. Assets and limitations present must be objectively and realistically considered. Not every facility has the same resources or expertise. Finally, decisions must be governed by the unique ethical, human, and social concerns that define good medical practice and the unique needs of the patient and his or her family.

The discipline of formal logic does not deal with quantifiers: words that describe grades or quantities or degree. Logic deals in absolutes like a binary system that has options for either on or off like a computer. A premise is either true or not true, present or absent. Development of an argument using the principles of formal logic is also not an expedient or efficient way to analyze a problem—a disadvantage in most medical situations. Yet medicine is all about degrees of severity, response, certainty, or the level or certainty of the knowledge on hand at that point in time. Most medical situations are conditional and time-sensitive, requiring recognition and assessment of multiple, often conflicting factors, and a constant need to modulate decisions based on new or evolving factors.

Chapter 2
Ways of Thinking

> *You cannot enter any world to which you don't have the language.*
> —Ludwig Wittgenstein (1889–1951)
>
> *Words, words, words.*
> —Shakespeare, William, Hamlet, Act II, Scene II, line 194

Summary
Discussing or describing the decision-making process requires a defined, accurate vocabulary. We must differentiate between the decision-making process and the clinical outcome. Physicians usually focus on the clinical outcome and ignore the process used to obtain the outcome. The decision-making process and the outcome therefore need to be evaluated independently. The two are not necessarily congruent—a valid, well-thought-out decision is not guaranteed to produce the desired clinical outcome, and a good clinical outcome is not necessarily the result of a sound decision. This chapter discusses the fundamental terms and concepts used to describe or evaluate the process used to arrive at a given decision.

2.1 Words, Words, Words

To communicate accurately about thinking and decision-making, we must be precise in our use of words and have a common understanding of the meaning of those words. It is necessary to examine the terms and concepts used in a discussion of knowledge, thinking, logic, and decision-making. There is no way to accomplish this task in a logical or systematic fashion. One has to dive in.

A mentor once described an approach to this conundrum—I keep what I know to be true in my right hand and what I think is true in my left. The problem is to remember which hand you drew your information from. His point was that it is easy to confuse truth from belief and that to remain rational and analytical with our decisions, it is necessary to remember when we are operating from a basis of known facts and when we are using our experience which may be colored by emotions, by faulty memory, or by relying on medical dogma or myths which may be incorrect. That approach does not mean that experience, traditions, or dogma may not be valuable, but we must remain mindful of the source of our knowledge.

2.2 Empiricism

Empiricism or empiric thinking is based on observation and experimentation rather than theory or pure logic. True empiricism is practiced in the university or academic environment under the aegis of research. For that reason, the practice of medicine is not truly "scientific," even though decisions may be based on outcomes of research or clinical studies that have followed traditional scientific methods. Science and the scientific method employ empiric thinking. In medicine, empiric thinking is manifest in the systemic, prospective, or retrospective study of the nature and behavior of disease and the outcomes of treatments. This is not the day-to-day, patient-by-patient, type of decision-making used in clinical practice. Clinicians do not use the scientific method of developing a hypothesis and proceeding with experimentation when they care for patients.

2.3 Reasoning

Reasoning is defined as a set of processes that construct and evaluate implications among sets of propositions. This approach implies the use of mathematical modeling or of formal or algorithmic approaches. Humans do not learn the rules of formal logic in the course of their emotional, social, and intellectual development, but we do learn how to reason. Reasoning is not inborn or intuitive but is a skill that must be taught and developed. We interchange the words reasoning and logic, and I have done so throughout this book, but, in fact, the formal definition of logic and the practice of logic should be reserved for the practice of formal logic.

2.4 Deductive, Inductive, and Abductive Thinking

There are three basic approaches to formulating an argument or conclusion from any given set of data—*inductive*, *deductive*, and *retroductive* or *abductive* reasoning. These terms are frequently used interchangeably, but the methodology used to derive an answer is different for each approach. The distinctions may seem convoluted and of no importance to clinical medicine, yet an understanding and correct usage of the terms help to describe how a decision was made and whether the process was valid for the circumstances.

Deductive Reasoning

Deductive reasoning is the world of logic and mathematical proofs—the method of establishing a conclusion that is a valid inference based on given, established premises. A conclusion must be true if the premises were true. Thinking by deduction derives outcomes based on general laws or principles. One or more general and true statements are used to reach a logical and certain conclusion. Much of the education in the first 2 years of medical school takes the form of deductive reasoning. *Deductive reasoning* is *top-down reasoning.* It can also be thought of as *centrifugal reasoning* or reasoning from the center outward as will be explained when centrifugal and centripetal thinking are discussed in Chap. 6.

We teach top-down to give students the overall picture or classic presentation or behavior of a process or scientific principle. For example, if we have a law that states the circumference of a circle is twice the radius of the circle times pi, or $2\pi R$, and if we wish to know the circumference of a particular circle, by deduction, the answer can be obtained using the formula $2\pi R$. In this type of argument, general rules that are true over the domain governing the argument are applied, narrowing the range of possible outcomes until the one conclusion is left, and that conclusion, by default, must be true. If all premises are true, the terms of the argument clear, and the rules of logic are followed, the conclusion must be true.

Medical decision-making, is rarely based exclusively on absolute truths or universally accepted facts. We function in a world of interpretation and incomplete knowledge, relying on experience, heuristics, and intuition to fill in the gaps in the data and observations to complete the picture. Most clinical narratives contain too many variables for us to consider independently unless there is a glaring discrepancy between the data in our long-term memory and the narrative we are dealing with. If discrepancies or voids in information are present, we rely upon experience or our store of knowledge and, if necessary, acquisition of additional data, to reconcile the inconsistencies. This approach is necessary in the time-sensitive world of clinical medicine where obtaining more data may not be feasible or cost-effective. We fall back on our knowledge and experience, even though we may be relying on conjecture rather than a formal or analytical process. This type of decision-making is more consistent with *abduction*, another form of reasoning that will be discussed shortly.

Inductive Reasoning

Induction is the inference of a general law from particular instances. Inductive reasoning is bottom-up reasoning. Another way of thinking about inductive thinking is to envision it, as is *centripetal* or outside-in reasoning. Inductive reasoning relies on applying premises that are relevant or cogent to the problem at hand to supply strong, rational evidence for, but, importantly, not absolute proof of a truth or the validity of a conclusion. With inductive reasoning, it is important to remember that a conclusion reached by induction does not infer that the conclusion is based on absolute fact or truth such as the answer achieved by using the formula for determining the circumference of a circle (deductive reasoning).

A conclusion reached by induction is *probable* based on the evidence given. For example, if we take a trip to the zoo, look at the parrots, and note that all the parrots are green, we can infer that all parrots are green. This form of reasoning can be flawed, as we know that there are parrots that are blue, gray, or even white. Our sample size is limited by the number of parrots in the zoo and, therefore, too small to draw conclusions about all parrots. Clinical studies and one's personal experience are powerful factors in our decisions, yet our experience, no matter how extensive or vivid, can be very misleading, especially when colored by selective memory and our inevitable emotional bias. Basic science research and the generation of the initial clinical evaluation is the accumulation of knowledge by induction. The body of knowledge or medical truth is generated, over time, and with experience, by inductive reasoning. Some medical problems are rare or too uncommon to make valid general statements about their behavior difficult. One's personal experience with many problems will also always be limited to some degree, making absolute statements or predictions about the behavior of a disease or results a particular treatment, in our hands, subject to uncertainty, or speculation. In those situations, we have no choice but to rely on inductive reasoning. Much of the teaching in the clinical setting is in the form of inductive reasoning and can lead to erroneous conclusions. Even if the results of a research project or clinical study are statistically significant, the clinician cannot automatically infer that the outcomes of that study are directly applicable to or appropriate for an individual patient.

The differences between inductive and deductive reasoning are also analogous to the differences between the hard sciences such as physics and the soft sciences such as psychology or medicine. Much of medical knowledge is based on an incomplete understanding of the fundamental truths about the behavior of biological systems, systems that are prone to a wide variety of influences, not all of which can be immediately identified or recognized. The human organism cannot be reduced to equations.

Medicine decision-making is, therefore, not fundamentally deductive, even though we successfully use deductive reasoning to make a diagnosis in situations such as a radiograph that shows an unequivocal fractured arm. Many medical decisions are multi-faceted with few, if any, aspects being governed by deduction. We know that laboratory values, such as an elevated serum creatinine, indicate renal insufficiency or renal failure, but an improperly performed analysis or mislabeled blood specimen can indicate renal failure in a totally healthy patient. Large clinical trials will get us closer to the truth than an isolated clinical case report, but we approach truth in medicine asymptotically, never with the precision of mathematics.

Thinking by induction requires a broader range of knowledge and experience and a more analytical approach than deductive reasoning. Inductive thinking requires not only knowledge of the general laws in operation but also the corollaries to those principles and the anomalies or exceptions that require that the law not be followed. The fictional detective, Sherlock Holmes, was fond of stating that if you can exclude all but one explanation for a case, the remaining explanation must be true no matter how improbable it may seem. Medicine does not allow such a rigid approach. Rarely in medicine is a single premise or conclusion or solution present. There are always associated conditions and circumstances that confound even the most simple and straightforward of conditions. Because our decisions are time-sensitive, because some data such as patient histories and observations are intrinsically inaccurate or distorted, and because it is not economically, logistically, or ethically possible to obtain all data possible, we are compelled to make decisions based on a limited set of data and data we know may be inaccurate or is subject to interpretation and inference.

To quote Elizabeth Montgomery on this dilemma, "Because even the best scientific and clinical studies are inexactly related to any given individual, even the most knowledgeable and experienced physicians confront the problem of particularization with every patient in every clinical encounter." [This is the] "…ineradicable uncertainty of medicine" (Montgomery 2006). This statement highlights the tension that exists at the intersection of science and humanism or, stated another way, the shadow side of using best practice guidelines or evidence-based medicine in a rote or inflexible way.

Donald Rumsfeld, the former US Secretary of Defense under President George W. Bush, mused, "there are things that we know that we know, there are things we know we don't know, and there are things we don't know we don't know." This observation does contain a kernel of wisdom that underlies much of the problem in making decisions in medical practice.

An expert in a certain condition or disease cannot predict how that disease will affect a particular patient or exactly how that patient will respond to standard recommended therapy. Physicians are not mystics or fortune-tellers. Situations "identical to a case I once saw" will almost certainly not play out precisely like one's past experiences. This conundrum is complicated by the fact that no two patients will have identical expectations or wishes for the outcome of a superficially identical significant disease process. This is not necessarily a significant issue with an affliction such as the common cold, unless it precludes one's plans to fly to New Orleans for the Super Bowl, but a severed median nerve will have dramatically different impact on the life of a concert pianist.

In addition to discussing the differences between deduction and induction, it is worthwhile to mention other terms commonly used in the fields of knowledge and logic. These are terms Aristotle also used as he attempted to describe what knowledge and thinking were about (Aristotle, Nicomachean Ethics, translated by Ross 2009). Let us look at reasoning from a different and more modern, perspective. Thinking is not a seamless process. The process of thinking and decision is not deterministic or governed by natural laws or that events are caused by preceding events in a cause and effect or straight-line fashion.

Deductive and inductive reasoning are both used for clinical decision-making, but it is important to remember the differences between the two approaches and to realize that most clinical decision-making is accomplished by inductive thinking.

2.5 Prescriptive, Descriptive, and Normative Thinking

Thinking is a complex process and does not only involve sitting in a quiet place contemplating an esoteric or convoluted subject. It is an active, iterative process that can involve multiple steps. It should, therefore, be no surprise that thinking has occupied the minds of philosophers, creators, researchers, and individuals in a wide range of professions and disciplines, so it is appropriate to look at the processes used when engaged in thinking about medical or clinical problems.

How we think and how we approach solving a problem can be described by using models or approaches. Jonathan Baron, professor of psychology at the University of Pennsylvania and editor of books and journals on decision-making and judgment, has written and researched many of the facets of thinking and decision-making in his work (Baron 2008). He provides three models to describe approaches to thinking that can, for our purposes, also describe how physicians approach clinical problems. These models are *prescriptive*, *descriptive*, and *normative*.

Prescriptive Thinking

Prescriptive thinking is analogous to a prescription for a medication. A prescription specifies the drug ordered, dosage, and directions for the drug's use. We use prescriptive thinking when we follow rigid standard operating procedures, algorithms, or flow charts. Prescriptive approaches are often simple or rote and serve as checklists or guidelines for novice or inexperienced personnel or for emergency situations such as cardiac resuscitation. Non-physician providers can use for this approach to triage or manage routine problems. Prescriptive models can be thought of as the standard, most acceptable solution to a problem. Prescriptive thinking can also be described as the school-solution or best answer, usually given by an instructor for the solution to a problem in mathematics or physics. As we become more knowledgeable and experienced, we learn that there may be other ways to solve the same problem. Heuristics are also a form of prescriptive thinking or shorthand for solving a problem.

Descriptive Thinking

Descriptive models are founded on observation and assessment of a situation and development of solutions. It is on-the-fly decision-making, where we apply lessons learned from previous experience to a new problem, adjusting or fine-tuning our approach based on the results our interventions produce. Descriptive thinking includes the application of heuristics, intuition, and maxims or aphorisms. Descriptive problem-solving is not simple or elementary; it requires judgment, application of ethical principles, and comparison of potential with known or best practice outcomes. Descriptive models are not necessarily the best or most accurate models but are often the most efficient and prudent. Mathematical models are also descriptive in nature as they compare relationships, trends, and probabilities. Mathematical models may yield a more accurate solution but are not always as practical or expedient or even more accurate than other forms of decision-making for clinical problems, factors that will be discussed, in depth, in Chap. 9.

Normative Thinking
Normative thinking involves reflection and determination of optimal outcomes or desired goals based on personal experience, results, or outcomes. Evidence-based or best practice recommendations are normative approaches to decision-making. These approaches attempt to describe how goals can best be achieved based on standard or generally accepted approaches. Normative approaches form the basis for recommended optimal treatment methods that are taught in medical school and in residency training. Normative thinking is also the basis for questions on written or oral examinations. Normative thinking relies heavily on probability, based on the published or generally accepted incidence of diseases or events and outcomes of interventions. Physicians gather much of their academic or continuing education through normative approaches. With experience, the physician will consider normative recommendations and then modify them according to their personal experience, exigencies of a given situation, local capabilities, and available resources.

2.6 Optimizing and Satisficing

The study of decision-making owes much to Herbert A. Simon, an economist who was awarded the Nobel Prize for his research on rational decision-making in business organizations (Simon 1955, 1978).

In his Nobel memorial lecture, Simon stated—"...the classical model of rationality requires knowledge of all the relevant alternatives, their consequences and probabilities, and a predictable world without surprise" (Simon 1978). These conditions are rarely present in any decision-making situation today, to include medicine. Simon went on to point out that we do not have the luxury of time and resources necessary to ruminate extensively about a problem and probabilities. Simon was looking for more efficient approaches to solving problems and discovered that experienced decision-makers primarily use one of two methods in their decision-making—*optimizing* or *satisficing*. These approaches are also the most commonly used decision-making tools used by physicians.

Optimization is the use of a process or action taken to achieve the best or most efficient outcome for a defined situation. Optimization is used in many fields to include mathematics, economics, computer science, and systems or organizational management. There is even a journal for this discipline—*Optimization: A Journal of Mathematical Programming and Operations Research*. Optimization is not a term or concept familiar to most physicians, but our decisions are almost always designed with the goal of optimizing the diagnosis or management of a problem.

The solution to a given problem is called optimal if one can prove that no better solution exists. Optimizing is not about finding the best or ultimate solution. Optimizing assumes that an optimal solution exists and that a strategy exists to find it. Optimizing requires that the decision-maker be able to decisively and rapidly identify acceptable solutions, prioritize those solutions, and confidently pick the solution that is most likely to be productive. It is a tool for maintaining efficiency and momentum in situations that demand action. Optimizing requires the maturity to know when expediency and maintaining momentum in a given environment trump the risks of a more deliberate analysis and decision-making approach. Successful use of optimizing requires the decision-maker to have enough experience and knowledge to recognize the optimal decision, it, in the final analysis, is more desirable than conducting an in-depth, time-consuming, or costly analysis. To quote General George S. Patton: A good plan violently executed now is better than a perfect plan executed next week.

Simon also identified a more direct and reliable approach he described as *satisficing* (Simon 1978). Satisficing did not seek the perfect or ideal solution for a problem but a quick and efficient one that was "good enough." Satisficing is the process of accepting the first option that provides an acceptable, viable, and reasonable solution and not pursuing other possibilities, even though better solutions might be available. Satisficing sacrifices finding the best option in favor of selecting a good one. The decision-maker who opts for satisficing to resolve a problem is choosing efficiency over thoroughness. These solutions, could, with optimizing, be used effectively, avoiding the time, resource, and efforts required by formal and rigorous problem-solving methods. We all use satisficing, when making decisions. For example, when grocery shopping, if the shelf that usually contains what we consider the best brand of tomato sauce is empty, it may be best to select another brand than take the time to find an employee and ask her to rummage in the back of the store in the hopes that the delivery truck may have just unloaded a case of your favorite brand of tomato sauce. We are satisficing when we choose to save time over finding the optimal brand of tomato sauce. In medicine, we may choose to start an antibiotic for a patient with a suspected urinary tract infection and an abnormal urinalysis, rather than wait for the results of the urine culture. The finding of an abnormal urinalysis satisfies the requirement for making the diagnosis and justifies the decision to provide treatment.

2.7 Bounded and Unbounded Thinking

Simon's work was expanded upon by Leonard Jimmie Savage, an American mathematician and statistician, who also described two models for decision-making and used the term perfect knowledge to describe bounded problems (Savage 1972). In his work on decision theory, Savage introduced the concept of *small world decisions (bounded)* and *large world (unbounded) decisions* where—"...part of the relevant information is unknown or has to be estimated from small samples, so that the conditions for rational decision theory are not met" (Savage 1972; Gigerenzer and Todd 1999; Volz and Gigerenzer 2012).

We live in a world where even small deviations or influences can have a major impact on the outcome. The parameters under which a given decision is made will vary from situation to situation, but time and cost constraints do not allow us to exhaustively evaluate the parameters we may face in a given situation. We do not often consider limitations or parameters in the midst of evaluating options, but limitations are always there, if just beneath the surface. In decision-making, decisions that have established boundaries are called *bounded* or *optimized*.

Bounded problems may involve situations in which the variables are known and quantifiable. For example, if your company is in the business of making nuts and bolts and you want to determine production capabilities, the variables such as amounts of steel or other metals needed and supplies of ancillary products such as oil, solvents, water, and electricity can be identified and quantitated. The manufacturing equipment on hand, production times, and labor costs can also be quantified and formulas or mathematical models devised to project output over time. Those variables are bounded and generally readily identifiable In medicine, bounded variables might be patient age, race, drug or radiation dosing or toxicity or side effects, and complication rates. Such situations are optimal for a research protocol as the data is based on quantifiable variables.

Unbounded problems may contain multiple variables or may be qualitative rather than quantifiable, meaning that certain variables cannot be accurately assessed or identified. If the industry is plagued by labor unrest, material delays, or other non-quantifiable factors, you may not be able to accurately calculate potential output and costs. Such a situation is *unbounded* or *unoptimized*. In medicine, *unbounded* variables might include social factors or qualitative assessment of outcomes.

The concept of bounded and unbounded models is analogous to the difference between macroeconomics and microeconomics. Macroeconomics is the study of higher-level finance or economics—issues at the national or international levels. It is the study of how governments deal with each other in areas of trade and regulations. Macroeconomists are concerned with questions such as how whole economic sectors or industries deal with issues such as pricing and manufacturing of commodities, exports, and imports or what are the effects of a change in gross national product or new legislation on the general population, or workers in that industry.

Microeconomics is the study of the market behavior of individuals and businesses. Microeconomics encompasses the fundamental principles of supply and demand and how economic principles operate at an individual or practical or day-to-day level. It is about how individuals and small businesses manage and allocate resources or finances, how we act as consumers, and how markets function. It is what we study in Economics 101. Most medical decisions are bounded enough to consider them analogous to microeconomics. National or global health-care policy and oversight are more unbounded arenas and therefore more contentious and unpredictable.

One may suggest that mathematical models and careful analysis or probability theory could improve diagnostic accuracy, but experience has not shown that approach to be useful for managing individual patients in an active clinical situation. Certainly, the good clinician or surgeon must understand the statistical methodology and mathematical modeling relevant to medical practice and also be knowledgeable about the research and clinical studies relevant to his or her specialty, but this data is just one element in the multifactorial decision matrix that is developed when making clinical decisions. Mathematical models and complex decision-making matrices are perhaps more used in dealing with macro-medical situations such as public health or research protocols involving large groups of patients.

Mathematical models and statistical analysis of data on large numbers of patients may improve our understanding of the outcomes we can expect from chemotherapeutical regimens in a controlled study of a particular cancer in a specific group of patients. Their value diminishes the further one gets from the peak of the bell-shaped curve that describes the clinical course of a cohort of patients with the same affliction. The micro-medical clinical decision-maker is often operating at the extreme ends of the bell curve where the patient they are treating may not fit in the mean distribution of outcomes generated by a large cohort of patients.

The same analogy can be made for looking at microeconomics and macroeconomics. While economists, investment bankers, brokers, and financial managers pursue ways to make their analysis of financial markets more objective and quantitative, history has shown that the science of economics has a long way to go– forecasts in these fields are not very accurate. Just like medical research may provide information for the typical course of a disease or the most likely response to therapy, the economist is at a loss to be able to predict outcomes in most business, national, or international situations. If they could, we could all predict what will happen in the stock market and would all be financially stable and secure. Political scientists would be able to analyze international events and predict when a particular country might collapse, be invaded by a neighbor, or fall prey to a coup. Meteorologists would be able to predict the weather better. Again, this is a concept that seems remote to medicine, but it is highly relevant. We will return to this concept later when we discuss approaches to decision-making.

Being able to identify which mode of thinking is optimal for a given situation is a skill, but not a new idea. Economists, computer scientists, and mathematicians have used the concept of optimizing for years. We do not use the term optimizing in medicine, but it is a valid concept and helps us recognize which mode of thinking we are dealing with or the validity or clinical research data or mathematical models used for clinical decision-making.

Optimization requires making a decision with the knowledge or assumption that the problem at hand has boundaries or limitations. These boundaries can be fixed or bounded, meaning the relevant variables are identifiable and quantifiable.

Factors such as available resources (equipment, facilities and expertise, and consultants and ancillary staff) and situations that require certain ethical, social, or patient preferences which cannot be easily quantified are unbounded, creating problems that generally involve significant judgment, experience, or qualifications. By definition, such decisions are usually *complicated*, while bounded problems can be *simple* or *complex* (Gawande 2009) (See descriptions of these terms below).

Bounded decisions, decisions limited by cognitive limitations, data, and time available, can also be considered optimized, whereas unbounded decisions are often termed unoptimized. We strive to identify all quantifiable factors and develop methods to account for those variables. This may involve use of standard operating procedures (SOPs), checklists, protocols, or algorithms—all measures that help to identify potential problems, bottlenecks, or limitations on resources or personnel. Many of these variables are hard to predict or quantify. Medicine is also rife with other unquantifiable factors such as the unintended consequences of therapy, ethical or societal constraints, equipment or technical breakdowns, or material shortages or delays. An unstated goal of much clinical research is to identify and resolve aspects of a disease process or treatment that creates unbounded parameters. We can better approach risks and outcomes if we are able to identify and quantitate those individual parameters rather than just knowing that those risks or complications are possible. Such knowledge converts uncontrolled factors into controlled parameters that can be measured. We are always working to minimize or eliminate unbounded factors.

In medicine, unbounded situations pose a dilemma for clinical researchers as the unquantifiable factors limit one's ability to predict or analyze outcomes. There is a continuum between bounded and unbounded thinking. Some factors will always remain qualitative and unmeasurable.

Patients do not always present with straightforward problems. Patients often have situations that require advanced decision-making skills and consideration of the humanistic elements of patient care. These decisions rapidly become unbounded and not amenable to a linear problem-solving approach. Factors such as ethics, patient preferences, religious belief, or the availability of resources or expertise, create unbounded situations that cannot be converted into quantifiable variables. As the decision-making matrix becomes increasingly complex and qualitative, the variables to be considered become further and further removed from the unencumbered and reproducible world of bounded problems. Reliance on evidence-based approaches, mathematical modeling, or established guidelines is less and less helpful. Unfortunately, many patients and disease processes exist in an unbounded environment and require higher levels of experience and judgment.

2.8 Concepts of Knowledge

Not all knowledge—what we know or think we know—is the same, nor do we receive knowledge in the same ways. Knowledge can be acquired actively or passively. To be relevant to the user, new information must be processed both consciously and unconsciously before it can be integrated into one's individual practice or understanding of a problem. Not only does the data obtained need to be analyzed by comparing it with our existing fund of knowledge for relevance and believability, using our powers of reasoning, but knowledge must be filtered through our emotional and subconscious thinking centers before we are comfortable with changing our thinking, approach to management, or core principles. To be useful, knowledge must be verified by the user as relevant to their world view and experience before we invest in the process of incorporating that new information into our practice. The way we organize knowledge, evaluate, and incorporate new bits of knowledge and how we process the knowledge, we have to help solve problems shifts and become more streamlined and efficient as we mature during our training and as we gain experience throughout our career.

A Priori Knowledge

The knowledge we bring from the lecture room to the clinical world is *a priori knowledge*, knowledge that is known independently of experience, knowledge that is nonempirical or arrived at beforehand. First- and second-year medical school students receive a priori knowledge through sources such as lectures, reading, and conferences. Physicians receive a priori knowledge through their continuing medical education efforts, attendance at conferences, or journal reading. A priori knowledge can be abstract and without any anchor or basis for accepting given information. Consider the first-year medical student who is given information without any frame of reference as to the relevance, relative importance, or validity of one bit of information from another. Medical students lack the practical and real-world relevance to correlate the information they have learned in the classroom to patient situations. It is difficult to distinguish fact from supposition, reality from theory, and truth from belief. It is the memorization of data for memorization's sake.

A Posteriori Knowledge

Clinical rotations and all subsequent training and experiences are the vehicle for *a posteriori* knowledge. A posteriori knowledge is knowledge that is derived from experience. This type of knowledge is empirical or arrived afterward and is accumulated through clinical interactions and ongoing practice.

Blended or Mature Knowledge

Medical practice is ultimately the blend of a posteriori and a priori knowledge. Physicians learn from every patient encounter, every conference, every journal, and every interaction with another health-care provider. Approaches to diagnosis and treatment are constantly being revised as new information, and new ideas are analyzed. Are newly published data practical and commonsense? Do they jibe with one's experience and observations? This type of knowledge is achieved through having a good foundation of a priori and a posteriori knowledge obtained through on-the-job experience tempered with reflection and wisdom.

Clinical rotations and all subsequent training and experiences are the vehicles for a posteriori knowledge. The terms *blended or mature knowledge* better describe the working knowledge that all physicians rely upon. Blended knowledge also reflects the changes in education we have witnessed over the past few decades where adult learners can pursue their formal education outside of traditional educational environments.

2.9 Simple, Complex, and Complicated

Not all decisions have the same level of difficulty. Deciding to repair an inguinal hernia in an infant is usually straightforward, but the same condition in a child with unresolved congenital heart disease or an unstable home environment may require some consideration and judgment. Some decisions are *simple*, having a limited number of variables. Some decisions may be *complex*, composed of many interconnected parts or variables. Management of a patient with multiple system trauma or disease can try the skills of the most experienced physician. These problems cannot be reduced to an algorithm- or rigid evidence-based approach. Some decisions are *complicated*, composed of multiple, not necessarily interdependent or related variables. *Complicated* problems may be difficult to understand *but can be resolved*. Complicated problems may require extensive planning, consideration of multiple options, or preparation for untoward events, but they are, at least, amenable to being solved within a reasonable degree of certainty and risk. Sending a satellite to the moon, for example, is a complicated problem, but it is probably not complex with the level of experience and technology, available today.

Complex problems are those that we can never resolve with complete accuracy or reliability. Complex problems are analogous to predicting the weather. Assume, for example, a meteorologist who predicts that the current weather fronts indicate a 40 per cent chance of rain. Yes, there is a tremendous amount of data and experience with prior weather conditions that allow the models used to forecast that out of ten mathematical models built on previous similar weather patterns, it should rain 40 per cent of the time. With more data and better models, meteorologists will probably be able to increase the accuracy of their conditions to 60 or even 70 per cent, but the variables that influence the weather tomorrow are such that the science of meteorology will never be able to achieve 100 per cent accuracy. Medicine, medical practice, and the science of medicine are no different—we will never achieve perfect diagnostic accuracy or therapeutic efficacy. Our patients, lawyers, families, and any agencies involved in patient care must understand this fact—physicians are not wizards or somehow imbued with superhuman powers of divination.

Complex decisions often involve ethical issues, multi-system diseases, or concerns unique to the patient's family or culture. They may have outcomes that are hard to predict, they may be due to rare or anomalous conditions not discussed in standard medical textbooks, or they may require guidance from other medical resources, or may be beyond the expertise or capabilities of the individual practitioner. They may have no good solution or may be beyond the capabilities of even the most skilled practitioner. The magnitude of a complex problem may be easy to grasp, but the problem may be beyond definitive, ideal, or predictable solutions.

The concept of differentiating between simple, complicated, and complex problems is a concept that we do not articulate or teach well. We do not always convey these concepts and realities to patients and families in a transparent fashion. Nor do we make these distinctions in ways the public and the medicolegal establishment can relate to well. These failings result in unrealistic expectations and confusion about the outcomes that can be reasonably expected.

We must also be diligent about separating truth from belief or fact from fiction, always aware of decisions or actions based on tenuous or unproven assumptions. Medical practice is rife with myths, beliefs, and unsupported data. The data we use to justify a procedure or course of action is often tenuous or unproven. This does not make such data invalid, but we must keep facts and beliefs separate, a practice that requires diligence and persistence. Medical knowledge is not certain or rigid in the same way that the laws of physics or mathematics are. We base decisions on probability, prior experience and an imperfect understanding of human biology and behavior, and an incomplete and sometimes flawed interpretation of medical science. When making patient care decisions, there are correct and incorrect answers, but more often than not, there is more than one acceptable answer, and no answer may be the best.

2.10 Of Chaos, Butterflies, and Black Swans

> A system is defined as chaotic when it becomes impossible to know what it will do next. The system never behaves the same way twice. But as chaos theory shows, if we look at such a system over time, it demonstrates an inherent orderliness. (Wheatley 1999)

According to a Newtonian mechanics, small differences will be averaged out and ultimately converge. The world is linear. Heavily influenced by Sir Isaac Newton and the thinking that developed as a result of the Industrial Revolution, we look for a direct, straight-line predictable response when a system is perturbed or acted upon. That is not how nature always works. Outcomes of events in the physical world and in the world of medicine are rarely straight-line, predictable, without perturbation or deviation from the course we would predict based on our knowledge and experience.

The linear or mechanical view of the world persisted until the early 1900s when Einstein proposed that events could be viewed as being relative. The linear, direct cause and effect model has, to a great deal, also persisted in medical thinking. We look for neat, tidy, easily constructed models of how biological systems behave. We look for our interventions to have a direct and predictable effect. That type of thinking has permeated our decision-making processes. Even though human behavior and biological systems are unpredictable, linear thinking does suffice for thinking about most medical situations. Unfortunately, outcomes do not always reflect cause and effect thinking. We are constantly reminded that diseases can be perverse and that patients frequently surprise us with their ability to defy the commonly accepted wisdom of medical experience. As decision-makers, we must always keep in mind that biological events do not unfold in a closed system and that we can never anticipate all the variables.

The theories developed by modern physicists such as relativity, astrophysics, or particle physics do not directly touch the human condition or, at least, deal with events or concepts that relate to it (Gleick 1988). Chaos theory does. Not only that, chaos theory addresses events that relate to a wide array of man's concerns from weather to economics. Chaos also helps explain the primal condition of the human species in health and disease—we are biological creatures living in an uncertain world and can be affected by events that may seem trivial and can respond to our environment and the insults and events of daily life in unpredictable ways. Accurate prediction of a patient's response to a trauma or disease or forecasting the outcome of medical or surgical intervention are beyond the capacity of our current understanding of human biology or pathology. We often dismiss small aberrations in laboratory data or physical findings or discount minor events as unimportant or trivial or somehow capable of being averaged out in the course of a patient who has just undergone surgery or who seems to be having a routine, uneventful recovery from a significant illness. The good surgeon, or physician, has learned not to be so complacent or not to ignore subtle or seemingly minor events in a patient's course.

The human organism, like most systems, thrives when in a steady state, when all systems are functioning normally and synchronized. The steady state equates to good health. Disease is what happens when systems lose the steady state in which they are designed to function. Most aberrations in the steady state or homeostasis are self-limited, minor, or temporary, and correspondingly, treatment to reestablish the steady state is the medical equivalent of tweaking a few dials or readjusting settings that are askew. It is like having a car that needs a tune-up. Unfortunately, the connections between parts of a problem are not always immediately apparent, and like an experiment in particle physics, making observations or initiating treatment will alter the system in subtle or even dramatic ways that cannot be predicted.

Edward Norton Lorenz (1917–2008) was a mathematician and meteorologist working at the Massachusetts Institute of Technology on theoretical models of weather patterns. Commenting on the difficulties inherent in predicting weather patterns, Lorentz wrote:

> Two states differing by imperceptible amounts may eventually evolve into two considerably different states . . .If, then, there is any error whatever in observing the present state—and in any real system such errors seem inevitable—an acceptable prediction of an instantaneous state in the distant future may well be impossible . . . In view of the inevitable inaccuracy and incompleteness of weather observations, precise very-long-range forecasting would seem to be nonexistent. (Lorenz 1963)

In 1961, Lorenz programmed several variables for weather systems into his computer to study how weather patterns developed with changes in several basic variables. The calculations, although tedious, were not complex and would take time to run, especially given computer technology in the early 1960s. He decided that he needed to repeat the calculations he had just completed using one set of variables.

To expedite the process, he reentered the same data, but instead of using data to six decimal places, he rounded the data off to three decimal places. After all, minor differences created by rounding off numbers to such a minute degree should be evened out as the computer calculated the numbers. Lorenz then had his computer repeat the calculations while he walked away to get a cup of coffee. When he returned to his laboratory, he was baffled by the results.

The two runs were virtually identical, but as the calculations progressed, the differences in the data points began to diverge slightly and then deviate radically and unpredictably. The graphs created were initially virtually identical but with time, looked like they were produced by completely different sets of parameters.

Lorenz's first consideration was that there was some sort of computer malfunction. This was before microchips, when computers had banks of vacuum tubes and were notoriously finicky. An astute mathematician, however, Lorenz was quick to realize the significance of the outcome. Rather than being due to a technical malfunction, the outcome was because the two sets of data used to produce the graphs, although containing insignificantly different variables, were different enough to produce different and unpredictable outcomes. This observation was the seed of what would become *chaos theory*. Later, this phenomenon he was working on in the world of meteorology would be described as the *butterfly effect*—the idea that a butterfly flapping its wings in South America might cause a tornado in Texas.

Chaos theory is highly relevant in medical practice—aberrations or changes we cannot measure, visualize, or anticipate not only complicate decision-making but may render the process beyond the limits of traditional approaches. An example would be a major organ systems failure created by a rare side effect of an antibiotic or a congenital anomaly heretofore not described. In such circumstances, the best we can do is rely on experience with similar problems and then monitor the effects of any intervention closely to see if the patient is responding as we assume or theorize he should. Biological systems are not always predictable, and the outcome of therapy is not always logical or consistent.

The butterfly effect is analogous to another phenomenon described by Lorenz—the *strange attractor* (Grebogi et al. 1987; Taleb 2010). An *attractor* is called *strange* if it has a fractal or chaotic structure. A *fractal* is a mathematical or natural phenomenon where the initial conditions of a system are not fixed and produce a repeating or consistently evolving pattern. Systems that have a fractal structure would be snowflakes, a floret of broccoli, or the alveoli of the lungs.

In chaotic systems, small and unrecognizable differences, or strange attractors, in the initial conditions can cause a system to evolve in unexpected, turbulent, non-repeating, or unpredictable directions. In such a system, outcomes are variable and prediction of outcomes impossible. (To be complete, strange non-chaotic attractors also exist but are beyond the scope of this discussion.) In medicine, we often experience strange attractors. Unfortunately, it is not always possible to predict if we are dealing with a stable or unstable set of variables when we begin to manage a given problem or set of problems. Such is the nature of dealing with biological systems.

2.10 Of Chaos, Butterflies, and Black Swans

Black Swans
There are other ways of looking at potentially unstable or chaotic systems. Nassim Nicholas Taleb, an economist and broker working in the derivatives market, described such a chaotic event as *black swans*—events that are unanticipated or unaccounted for (Taleb 2010). A black swan produces a large impact on the outcome. Taleb points out that when asked what color swans are, the vast majority of responders would state—without hesitation—white. The concept of a swan being any other color is inconceivable to most. Yet, there is a strain of swans in Australia that is black. Black swans may exist, but they are not on most people's radar screens. We minimize the existence of the black swan or rationalize our failure to appreciate the black swan. Several observations can be made about black swans, all of which are applicable to medical practice.

Features of Black Swans
1. Black swans are hard to predict and rare events that are beyond the realm of normal expectations in science, technology, and medicine. How often are we blindsided by inexplicable or unpredictable events that, even though they can be overcome, have a habit of piling up and thwart our efforts?
2. Because of their rare and unpredictable nature, black swans cannot be included in calculations of potential results of outcomes. Even the most compulsive or thorough plans can be frustrated by events that one would never consider possible.
3. There are biases that make people individually and collectively blind to uncertainty and unaware of the massive role of the rare event in the most logical and well-intentioned plans. Not only are black swans impossible to predict, we are slow to recognize or accept their presence (Taleb 2010).

A black swan is more commonly thought of as an unexpected event that has a major impact on world events such as the black plague in the middle ages or HIV when it first presented. Black swans do make their appearance in medical practice with regularity. While some would consider such events to be outliers, Taleb argues they appear more often than appreciated and can have more devastating effects than the more common and often anticipated side effects or unfavorable outcomes we normally associate with medical or surgical procedures.

In medical practice, black swans may appear as a rare manifestation of a disease or an unexpected response to therapy. Biological systems are complex and are affected by interdependent and independent factors that are non-linear. Physicians therefore use shortcuts or heuristics to guide their decision-making and overcome the tantalizing allure of searching for black swans. They are taught that when you hear hoofbeats, think of horses, not zebras. This advice is usually correct, but we live in a world where there are black swans and zebras, and one where chaos reigns.

We strive to understand the human organism, the most complex biological system on our planet, and then intervene in a way that will produce a predictable and hopefully beneficial result, yet chaos theory tells us that medicine is also a world of black swans, a world where rare or unanticipated events or minor aberrations or changes can have major and unintended consequences. That shouldn't be a surprise—we are faced with these surprises every day. They are the banana peels we slip on when trying to care for patients in what we assume is a stable and rational world (Taleb 2012).

Physicians labor over evaluating probabilities of an event occurring in the course of a particular disease, its treatment, or the risk of a particular intervention. These considerations are often confusing for patients as they process the information the physician gives them about their condition. To tell Mrs. Smith that she has a 40 per cent chance of her breast cancer recurring in 5 years may be meaningful to a researcher looking at a large cohort of patients with breast cancer, and it may give her surgeon an indication of Mrs. Smith's prognosis in comparison to the many other breast cancer patient she follows, but what does it really mean to Mrs. Smith? Certainly, 40 per cent is much better than a 90 per cent chance of recurrence, and 40 per cent is marginally better than 50 per cent. In the absence of any markers or other relevant details, what can the patient do with that statistic? There is really nothing the physician can do except perhaps be more vigilant than she might be with a patient who has only a 10 per cent chance of recurrence. Does it change the calculus for the physician at all? Even the most vigilant or compulsive physician cannot hear the almost inaudible flapping of a butterfly's wings today—only to be devastated by the hurricane that has developed a year later when Mrs. Smith has metastatic disease.

Like the flapping of a butterfly's wings, the genetic, subcellular, or metabolic aberrations that allow a disease to recur can rarely be detected even with the most advanced of diagnostic testing or the most finely tuned intuition. We may improve the sensitivity or accuracy of our testing, but we will never be able to predict, with certainty, the course of a particular patient. Biological systems just don't behave that way. The butterfly may turn into a tsunami in one individual and fade to nothing in another. *The good physician hopes for blue skies but prepares for a stormy weather*. When going to New York City for a week-long conference, you are best advised to take an umbrella even if the weatherman predicts sunshine.

The possibility of black swans and the effects described by chaos theory should always be a part of our decision-making. The best clinicians are the ones who sense the appearance of a black swan or the impact of chaos before everyone else does. Black swans are obvious after the fact.

Chapter 3
Problem-Solving and Decision-Making

Summary

There are major differences between decision-making and problem-solving. The two entities differ in discrete and subtle ways and should be resolved at different levels within teams or organizations. Decision-making usually involves more experienced higher-order, process-dependent, and non-linear skills. The impact of decisions is usually more global, long-term, and less quantifiable and qualifiable.

3.1 Problem-Solving and Decision-Making Are Not the Same

Is problem-solving the same as decision-making? Many would not consider these actions to be different, but they are. The differences are not immediately apparent, and there is overlap between the two, so it is not possible to develop a simple answer to the question—it is necessary to spend some time exploring how the approaches are different and why the terms are not interchangeable.

Problems or issues that need a decision can be described using different terms—a dilemma, a conundrum, a crisis, a hurdle, an inconvenience, a stumbling block, or a problem. These terms convey a sense of the degree of severity, urgency, or magnitude of the event. It is not always easy to find the best word to describe a situation or classify the action needed.

Resolving disorders patients present with can be analogous to solving a problem in mathematics or a proof in geometry, but, just as frequently, the situation requires a more expansive and convoluted analysis than following your grandmother's recipe for apple pie. Decision-making can also be as simple as following a recipe, but more often than not, decisions require revisiting our observations and findings, reevaluating the patient's progress, or revising our diagnoses or changing course. This explanation still does not completely describe the differences between problem-solving and decision-making, however.

The distinction between problem-solving and decision-making is not just an exercise in semantics. Both skills require the necessary fund of knowledge, an understanding of the desired outcomes and potential pitfalls of an intervention, and the technical facility to effectively and safely apply that knowledge, but the processes require different levels of expertise and judgment. Problem-solving and decision-making usually have different goals and require different perspectives in terms of the impact those actions might have on the issue at hand and the individuals and resources that are involved.

Much of medical practice is linear and focused—simple problem-solving. Most patient problems or decisions do not require complex thinking, extensive judgment, or experience to establish an accurate diagnosis or develop a sound plan for management. Medical decision-making can rarely be reduced to binomial decisions like an on-off switch. This difference is analogous to the small world versus large world problem described in Chap. 2. Decision-making usually requires a broader and more sophisticated set of skills, skills requiring a greater fund of knowledge, experience, and judgment. Simple or straightforward problems are the staple of the novice, but decision-making is usually relegated to a more senior member of the management team.

Complicated problems, problems with more than one variable, or problems with ethical, social, or logistical considerations may require resolving a sequence of issues. Such problems may require more than a simple or unidimensional approach. Although the distribution of simple, complex, and complicated problems may vary between specialties and practice environments, we all learn to shift our thinking from problem-solving to decision-making in an almost effortless fashion.

For example, a laceration on the foot in a healthy young adult is not comparable to the same injury on a homeless diabetic patient. The management of these two patients may be very different, as the potential morbidity they face is quite dissimilar. For the first patient, the problem is straightforward—cleanse and suture the wound and provide instructions for care. For the patient with diabetes, this injury is not just a minor surgical problem but, possibly, the beginning of a lengthy and potentially morbid course. For this patient, decisions need to be made, decisions that require experience and judgment, and also consideration of the patient's social situation and need for aftercare. A simple laceration is a problem a student or junior resident may be able to manage. The requirements for decision-making beyond the obvious needs for the diabetic patient's initial wound management are likely to be elevated to the level of the senior resident or the responsible staff. There may be more than one acceptable answer with no one solution being the best.

The attributes of problem-solving and decision-making do not fit neatly into a rigid matrix—the characteristics of each approach often overlap. Problem-solving and decision-making are somewhat interchangeable and fluid. The distinctions between the two processes are often blurry—some decisions require solving a problem or series of problems, and at each step, the clinician may need to make decisions between two very different options. Complicated issues, such as those described above, are a different matter. Their management often becomes an

Table 3.1 Comparison of problem-solving and decision-making

Problem-solving	Decision-making
Content	Context
Method	Process
Limited scope of resources required	Need for resources, consultation, additional expertise
Training—experience	Education—judgment
Linear	Non-linear
If…then	Options
How to	Why, what
Orderly—identifiable components or components that are addressed sequentially or in an orderly fashion—capable of being broken down into discrete parts	Unstructured—not as orderly or neat
Lower-level authority	Higher-level authority
Unidimensional	Layered—values, goals, needs
Single, isolated considerations	Multiple, complex considerations
Short-term	Long-term
Focused	Holistic, global
Structured—algorithmic	Chaos—uncertainty
Analytical	Measured—calibrated
Independent	Interdependent
Single or best answer	Optimal solution
Sequential	Interdependent
Utilitarian	Translational
Quantifiable outcomes	Qualitative outcomes

exercise in decision-making and not just problem-solving. In these situations, there is no formula to distill the patient's needs into a chief complaint that will eventually be listed as a simple or single diagnosis code.

Table 3.1 compares the differences between the two approaches. Hopefully, this table will provide the reader with a good understanding of the differences between problem-solving and decision-making and avoid a lengthy and perhaps confusing explanation.

3.2 Learning Problem-Solving and Decision-Making: What Medical Education Is Really About

> Residency training is designed as a moral education, the purpose of which is to teach young doctors the standards of practice. (Bosk 2003)

One way to consider the difference between problem-solving and decision-making is to examine these processes in the context of how they are presented during medical education and training. The organization of our training system can be traced to the medieval university and guild systems, where the university student was exposed to the knowledge of the science and the arts available at that time and the apprentice initiated into the craft, customs, and closely guarded aspects of the trade they had chosen. Medical education and training can be thought of as a system of immersion in three distinct areas—*education, training, and acculturation. The objectives of each phase of medical education and training can be simply stated—education is the what of medicine, training the how, and acculturation is the why.*

Education
Education is the process of gaining foundational and theoretical knowledge—the science and language of medicine. The first 2 years of medical school expose the student to a broad range of material in a formal, systematic, structured way, generally in a classroom or laboratory setting. Students learn the science of medicine but little about the application or theoretical aspects of the normal human biology and disease. The concepts of problem-solving and decision-making are introduced during the first 2 years of medical school, but these lessons are abstract or hypothetical. The student has had minimal, if any, direct contact with patients or the settings in which medicine is practiced. Although not explicitly stated or formally presented, problem-solving is the cornerstone of the remainder of their training. The real work begins when the student starts his or her clinical rotations during the third year of medical school.

Training
The final 2 years of medical school are a transition between education and training. The student's time is no longer predominantly involved in didactic or passive learning activities. Instead, the student starts to apply the information and knowledge they received in the didactic phase of their education. The student will still spend a great portion of their time in lectures or other educational venues. Their education will never end; they will be attending lectures, reading, studying, and taking examinations for the remainder of their career. The third-year student must now start the process of ordering and refining their knowledge and skills that will be discussed later. Much of training is now skill development, learning by doing, education by reinforcement, practical application, and gradually narrowing their focus in preparation for their chosen field. The world of medicine, hospitals, and clinics is very much an "Alice-in-Wonderland" environment, with its own rules, conventions, participants, and playing field. This environment is unlike any other that the individual, wanting to pass through the looking glass that is medicine, could have experienced.

The change in focus from pure education to training also requires learning and ultimately mastery of the most critical, yet unspoken skill necessary to become a physician—learning to solve problems. *Medical training is initially learning to be a problem-solver, not a decision-maker.*

Students and residents start mastering this skill by dealing with simple problems—does this patient need an intravenous line, a urinary catheter, and laboratory studies, and if so, which studies? If an antibiotic is necessary, which one is best, by which route, what dose, and for how long? Gradually the trainee deals with more complex problems—determining the correct diagnosis, when to order invasive testing or obtain a consultation, deciding if it is best to admit the patient to hospital, and, if so, to what unit or service, when to discharge the patient, and on and on. Caring for a patient requires considering and solving a long sequence of problems, and, as one progresses through their training, one deals with higher-level problems—when to operate, when to transfer to a specialist or admit to an intensive care unit.

Developing one's problem-solving skills not only continues during one's post-graduate training but becomes one of the most important and closely scrutinized portion of this phase of the program.

Post-graduate training is not only a process of training in a particular domain of medicine; it is one of graduated responsibility and the development of judgment. As they progress through their training, the post-graduate physician also learns decision-making. Medical training also includes the gradual and progressive assumption of responsibility and independent thinking necessary for becoming a practitioner. With increasing responsibility and scope of authority, the more senior residents learn decision-making. Again, the fundamentals and nuances of decision-making are not formally taught; they are acquired by mentoring, by observation, and by example. They are acquired as a part of the daily discussion of difficult problems and actual patient scenarios that are part of the day-to-day responsibilities of patient management. As their skills and experience increase and as the resident develops the judgment and maturity necessary to make decisions, he or she is granted the freedom to make decisions and assume these responsibilities.

Acculturation
Like the medieval guild system, medical students and residents are indoctrinated into the culture of medicine in ways that extend beyond the mere accumulation of knowledge and technical expertise. The term that best explains this process is *acculturation*. The goal of acculturation is, to a great degree, to instill the qualities we recognize as the ideal attributes for practicing a profession. This is the moral education that is the soul of medical education (Pellegrino and Thomasma 1981; Montgomery 2006). This is the application of compassion, ethics, and humanism that are the basis of being a good doctor. It is not possible to become a good decision-maker without attending to these aspects of patient care.

3.3 Summary

The Differences Between Problem-Solving and Decision-Making
- Problem-solving is a more analytical process than decision-making.
- Problem-solving is more process-related, while decision-making is more contextual.

- Problem-solving is directed at a specific goal or discrete answer.
- Problem-solving and decision-making may have consequences that are not always predictable or sequential.
- Problem-solving is directed at a specific goal.
- Problems, once solved, may require no further action for that problem, while issues that require decision-making are more likely to carry long-term or unintended consequences or follow-on responsibilities or physician involvement.
- Decision-making requires a more global or inclusive understanding of the domain.
- Decision-making relies more on experience and judgment than problem-solving.
- Decision-making provides a course of action or final opinion—not the directions or steps to get there.
- *Problem-solving can be pushed down to more junior decision-makers and, indeed, helps them develop their decision-making skills. Decision-making is usually relegated to the more senior members of a team.*

Honing our problem-solving and decision-making skills does not stop once we finish our formal training—we continue to refine these skills throughout our professional lives. Much of the effort invested in keeping current through reading professional journals or attending conferences is driven by the need to be better at problem-solving and decision-making rather than learning about new developments in our field or expanding our knowledge base. We need to revisit the fundamentals again and again as we encounter variations or new situations, to fill in the gaps in our knowledge, or revise our understanding of principles if we are to provide our patients with the best problem-solving and decision-making skills we can offer.

In summary, approaches to problem-solving or decision-making in medicine can be looked at in several ways. The end result of our deliberations remains the same—caring for the patient. By caring, I am referring to caring with a capital "C" not just going through the motions. This chapter has wrestled with the concepts of problem-solving and decision-making from a detached and somewhat theoretical or existential view. Decision-making and problem-solving are interrelated. Like King Solomon, attempts to be as equitable or precise as possible risk sacrificing the essence of medical practice. A comprehensive or exclusive description of decision-making and problem-solving will often be blurred in the gritty world of medical practice. The concepts that will be presented in the remainder of this book are relevant to both decision-making and problem-solving, so as we turn to other facts of the subject and other ways in which we manage information, I will step back from the strict distinction between decision-making and problem-solving and use the terms interchangeably.

Chapter 4
The Decision-Making Cycle

Summary
Clinical decision-making does not follow vague or ill-defined principles. It is not just about finding the right diagnosis or prescribing the correct treatment. Decision-making must observe principles and guidelines that can be simply stated and formally discussed. Decision-making can be considered as a series of steps that form a cycle to be repeated over and over until the problem is resolved. Decision-making is cyclical—we may make a decision but rarely walk away from the patient—therefore our decision-making is evolving and always being refined.

We have looked at ways of thinking, types of knowledge, and how our thought processes may have evolved and what part memory plays in our thinking. We have presented some terms to describe knowledge and how we think and analyze information. These observations only scratch the surface of what are complex and difficult topics, topics that are not a part of normal medical education, nor are they limited to medicine. Before we consider the processes of decision-making, it is appropriate to look at what makes medical decision-making unique and also ponder the elements that are more basic or foundational than gathering and analyzing information and getting the answer right.

Let us step away from the more didactic, process-driven approach and consider the aspects of decision-making that are fundamental to humanistic and compassionate patient care. It is much more than the blind application of algorithms, flow charts, standards of practice, or evidence-based medicine. Other factors must be considered if we are to provide quality care, use the available resources and personnel in the most prudent way, and apply our technology and skills to the best advantage.

For most students and residents, the fundamental consideration is being correct. Students are taught that being right is good and whenever they answer a question correctly, they get positive feedback. It feels good to be right. Being right helps you pass an examination, look good on rounds, advance to the next level of training, and pass your board examination. Physicians love to be right and have spent their lives striving to be correct. Medical decision-making however is only partly and often, only superficially about being right. We revere those who can work their way through a difficult case presentation and come up with an answer, and we should. It is a remarkable skill. Unfortunately, making the correct decision is only one step in the process of caring for a patient, and the prize is not given for accuracy. Physicians are, above all else, moral agents, agents for the best needs of the patient and his or her family and for the community and society.

Accuracy in diagnosis is only the beginning. Decisions must be timely, practical, cost- and resource effective, and delivered with compassion. Decisions must consider the resources and expertise of the practitioners and support staff as well as patient and family preferences, values, spiritual concerns, and resources. The hardships and disruption of seeking care away from the patient's home may be overwhelming. Ethical considerations, local standards of practice, cultural beliefs, limitations imposed by funding sources such as insurance companies, or managed-care plans may require modification of treatment regimens or, in extreme cases, prohibit funding for tertiary, experimental treatment approaches, even if those approaches are what the family or patient desires.

As traditional, allopathic physicians, we rarely consider alternative, homeopathic, or non-Western approaches to treatment. Such a narrow or exclusive approach is no longer acceptable for many patients, creating new ethical considerations for medical decisions as well as requiring those trained in traditional Western medicine to be receptive to including nontraditional therapies in their decision-making algorithms.

Medical care requires, *but is never limited to*, good, skillfully applied techniques or knowledge. One can be artful in terms of how a procedure is performed, meaning technically proficient or having finesse. A surgical procedure performed with the highest skill and technical ability does not constitute quality medical care if it is delivered without attention to the other components of ethical medical practice or without compassion and concern for the patient and those important to him/her. Medical care must always be morally defensible and ethically sound and not just an exercise in technical prowess or knowledge. These skills are the tools of the clinician and, though not totally unique to medicine, define who we are as physicians and surgeons. Collectively, they produce *judgment*, the quintessential quality of the good surgeon or the good doctor.

Sidebar: The Principles of Medical Decision-Making
- Medical decision-making is an iterative and a cyclical process, never straight line, and rarely purely analytical.
- Decision-making is fundamentally a narrative process—listen first and then decide.
- Decision-makers are frequently forced to act on limited information and then review and adjust later.
- Experienced medical decision-makers rely on heuristics, maxims, and intuition more than analytic approaches.
- Medical decision-making is a highly orchestrated dance between inductive and deductive reasoning.

- Medical problems involve ambiguity and variables that cannot always be calculated or anticipated.
- Decision-making is inevitably accompanied by bias and emotions and beliefs.
- There is a limit to the volume of information and number of variables that can be considered in making a good decision.
- Decisions require understanding, buy-in, and good communication between all parties if outcomes are to be successful.
- Good, educated, smart, and well-intended people make bad decisions.
- There is a Zen to decision-making—you will probably have to deal with the parties involved in a decision at some time in the future.

The principles set forth in this sidebar summarize the observations and revelations I have made while thinking about this subject and developing my ideas about what decision-making entails for the clinician. The principles are not listed in any particular order, nor are these principles addressed in the text in a sequential fashion. I do think the list below is helpful to stimulate discussion about the decision-making process and especially how those principles may be highlighted in a teaching or academic environment. Any decision, whether good or flawed, can be analyzed through the lenses this list provides as a clinical event is analyzed in the course of a quality of care dispute or case presentation. The list can also provide the decision-maker a checklist or reminder to review in determining if a decision could be improved.

4.1 The Decision-Making Cycle

There is no one ideal approach to making decisions. Algorithms, standardized protocols, or best practice models are available for many clinical scenarios and in the chaotic situation of a major trauma or cardiac arrest are invaluable. These situations demand that actions be taken simultaneously or in the face of disruptive or conflicting problems. Some decisions require an intense analysis of a large body of data. Most decisions are not made with algorithms or after extensive, time-consuming analysis. Physicians do not use the scientific method as we learned it in undergraduate science courses or applied in the course of basic science research. It is rare for a medical decision to be made using the formal rules of logic, despite the belief that we are always being logical in our decision-making. Instead, experienced physicians rely on heuristics, instinct born of past experience, and pattern recognition to make the majority of their decisions. Unfortunately, these approaches require a great deal of experience, a process for which there is no shortcut. Intuition can, to a degree, be taught, but it is hard for the learner to follow the thought processes of an experienced physician and perhaps more difficult for the experienced practitioner to explain how he or she arrived at that decision.

The *decision-making cycle* is a methodical, organized approach that allows the learner to break a decision down into its component parts. The model can also be used to analyze decisions or identify where the decision-making process could have been improved. The decision-making cycle provides the framework to analyze and discuss clinical outcomes or problems within the context of traditional academic teaching venues such as morbidity and mortality conferences, preoperative conferences, or CPC (clinical-pathology conference) presentations.

If asked what the fundamental task of the physician or surgeon might be, the obvious answer would seem to be curing the patient. Not all patients can be healed, and not all patients seek medical advice with the objective of being healed. These facts make the first answer to this question simple to the point of being naïve. We don't always identify or define goals and priorities when making a decision in a complex situation. It is easy to focus on the most obvious symptom or finding. This is not to say that the patient's presenting complaint or the X-ray finding you can see from across the room is not important, but it is easy to overlook the patient in the excitement of dealing with the obvious.

The noted medical ethicist and physician, Dr. Edmund Pellegrino, described the three characteristic tasks of medicine as:

- Diagnose the patient.
- Consider the possible therapies.
- Decide what is best to do in this particular circumstance.

This is a succinct and accurate assessment of the basic task of the physician who is presented with a new patient. The first two tasks require a foundation in medical science and practice: the principal focus of the medical school curriculum. The first two tasks can be completed without a background in ethics or the humanistic side of medicine. We are taught to be inclusive and exhaustive in our approach to the first two tasks, lest a significant diagnosis not be considered or the patient given the benefit of the standard of practice for his or her problem and the options she or he needs to be aware of and consider. The third task is a different problem. Not only does it require knowledge; it requires judgment and an ever-present sense of humanism. This is the real task of the medical decision-maker and the implied goal of the medical student's clinical rotations and the soul of graduate training.

Let us break decision-making into its component parts and discuss how physicians integrate the parts to produce a decision. We need to understand how we gather, process, store, retrieve, and finally use the information available. Decision-making is not a straight-line process but cyclical and repetitive. We continue to refine and change our decisions as long as we care for each individual patient.

If you ask any professional how they learned to make decisions, most would answer that they were given facts, principles, and concepts and were somehow expected to put the information together in an appropriate way. No one is given a road map or process to follow. Decision-making in medicine is not different than decision-making in other disciplines, but there is one element that we can never avoid—*once a physician makes a decision, once he or she begins a therapeutic intervention, or once one commences a surgical or invasive procedure, it is no longer possible for that physician or surgeon to walk away*. The fiduciary and ethical responsibilities of medicine are just starting once a decision is acted upon (Fig. 4.1).

Fig. 4.1 The decision-making cycle

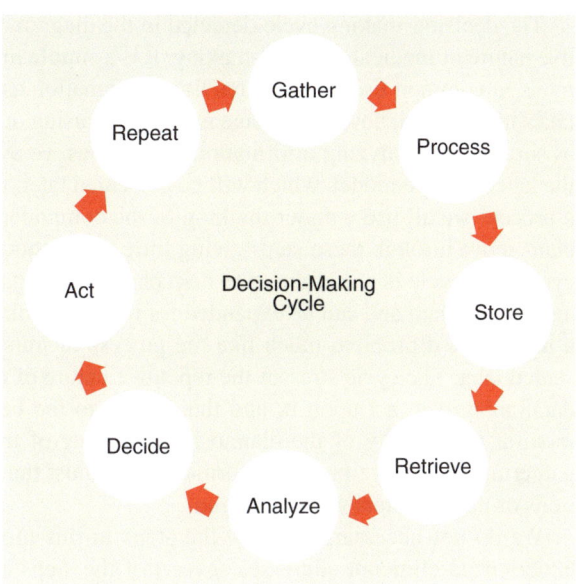

4.2 GPS-RADAR

Gather, Process, Store, Retrieve, Analyze, Decide, Act, Repeat.
Can we outline or identify the steps involved in making a decision? Is there a template that can be applied to medical decision-making regardless of the domain? I believe there is a simple, logical, and easily followed process, one that can be rapidly taught to students at any level.

The GPS-RADAR model is a useful way to organize our information gathering, thinking, and monitoring of the results of a decision. It is simple enough to teach rapidly and comprehensive enough to use when analyzing a decision or an outcome, and it can serve as an excellent teaching vehicle. Having such a framework such as the GPS-RADAR model in hand can help the novice physician or student learn the steps they need to take to formulate a decision and analyze a poor decision to determine where it went wrong. Medical educators at all levels should also be able to explain or teach decision-making in a more structured way than we presently use, which is learning by observation and osmosis, and a framework such as the one described here can aid in that process. Students and residents struggle with this problem, in large part, due to not having a firm grasp of how physicians or how specialists think. The surgery resident does not start his or her training knowing how surgeons think. Understanding these unwritten and mostly unspoken concepts takes time for even the most motivated or brightest resident. It is not a skill that is innate. What is even more frustrating for the resident is that the process changes in subtle and highly nuanced ways as one pursues higher levels of training such as a fellowship.

The decision-making cycle depicted in the diagram is based on a circular, iterative nature of medical decision-making. It is a simple mnemonic that uses two acronyms in common use and requires little explanation as to how it works. The cycle takes into account how we manage information using our long-term memory as well as sorting and analyzing information gathered as we evaluate a new problem. Like the kaleidoscope model, which will be presented later, the decision-making cycle is a process we all use without thinking of the component parts. Experienced physicians move through these steps giving little active thought to where they are in the cycle. The cycle is a useful tool to help physicians organize their approach to managing a problem and can be expanded for use in teaching or when working through a multifaceted problem much like the process of mind-mapping that will be presented later. The cycle stresses the repetitive nature of medical practice: We collect data, analyze it, act upon it, and then return to the beginning of the cycle as we monitor the validity of the diagnosis or efficacy of treatment. We are constantly gathering and analyzing new information to adjust the course of the recommendations or ministrations we have begun.

We do not necessarily follow the steps in this model in a rigid fashion. The experienced clinician addresses several of the steps at once, often shifting from one step to another as he or she refines the clinical problem or decides to intervene immediately for a life-threatening problem, such as establishing an oral airway or inserting a chest tube while continuing to evaluate the patient. Fluid and complex problems are the norm in clinical medicine, but for the purpose of teaching or evaluating the sequence of events that transpired in the assessment and management of a particular event, it is worthwhile to be able to consider what transpired in a logical and more formalized step-by-step fashion. After-action reviews used to analyze an untoward outcome rarely show that a failure was the result of only one factor—usually multiple problems or compounding events can be identified.

The decision-making cycle presents concepts that may seem obvious or overly simplistic. Some of the superficial or obvious components of this model are more sophisticated than they appear when placed in a fixed format as presented here. That is the risk of any attempt to break a complex and fluid situation down into its component parts.

Sidebar: GPS-RADAR

G-Gather

Any decision requires information. The information will be in the form of new data gathered from a patient history, current laboratory findings, and so on, as well as information we have stored in our long-term memory.

P-Process

After gathering information, the data must be prioritized as to relevance and applicability to the problem. Data such as patient gender, race, or social status may be highly relevant but not crucial for the decision. Gathering and processing information is a continuous process. These steps are not truly isolated or separate.

S-Store

The best decision-makers are those who have a good filing system for the information they already have. Medical school and residency training provide us with an abundant volume of knowledge, but it is up to the individual to organize and store that information in a fashion where it can be accurately and quickly retrieved. The issue of storage is introduced here as it is a part of the GPS-RADAR acronym and therefore a self-standing part of decision-making.

R-Retrieve

We have a similar problem with information retrieval. It does no good to have a large store of data in your long-term memory if it is not organized and available for accurate, rapid retrieval.

A-Analyze

Once we have the information available before us, the data must be analyzed. Analysis is a process that requires knowing what information is necessary and available or if there is sufficient information present and if the quality of that information is adequate. Here, the elements of decision-making considered previously must be brought into focus and also a decision made as to which type of thinking or approach is best for the problem at hand. We can be hindered by not having enough information, and we can be paralyzed by demanding more information that is necessary.

D-Decide

Finally, we get to make a decision. That decision may be only the initial or the definitive step to resolving a problem.

A-Act

Physicians act upon their decisions. It is only when we are asked an opinion or to provide a consultation that our work may end. Consultants still need to be available for future questions and more often have incurred the responsibility to continue being involved in the patient's progress.

R-Repeat

Once any medical therapy is initiated, the physician remains involved in the care of the patient. The cycle starts over with gathering information as the patient is reassessed as new laboratory data is available or as physical exams, vital signs, and laboratory studies are repeated. Is the patient responding appropriately or not? Is the patient's clinical progress in keeping with what your knowledge or experience would anticipate? What additional testing might be indicated? Was my diagnosis correct? Do I need to modify my treatment plan? All of the bases touched before need to be re-examined and adjustments made.

Chapter 5
The Elements of Medical Decision-Making

Summary
Decision-making is dependent on factors beyond the medical problem at hand. We must be grounded not only in the practical and technical aspects of the science and theory of medical practice but also the humanistic and ethical aspects of patient care. Quality of care is not limited to good clinical practice and goes well beyond the financial aspects of providing care and the outcome of an intervention as measured by success or failure. Decision-making must always put the patient first by having and maintaining appropriate clinical presence; communicating with the patient, family, colleagues, and staff; insuring and building teamwork; developing and exercising the skills of good leadership; remaining up-to-date on the development in one's field; acquiring and maintaining the appropriate technical skills and knowing the limits of one's skills; and being aware of the strengths, weakness, and changes in one's organization.

5.1 The Patient Comes First

The primacy of the patient is a constant in the physician's being and one that students must integrate into their behavior and value system—it is no longer about them. This virtue is developed over time as one goes about the processes involved in the care of patients which are the primary focus of the latter half of the medical school. Much of one's time is spent in non-educational tasks, which are a part of taking care of patients. Such tasks include gathering test data, coordinating appointments or procedures, running errands for the residents and staff, transporting patients, and so on. These are not welcome assignments and are derisively called SCUT or "some clinically useful training." These menial tasks are, unfortunately, a major part of the physician's responsibilities and are seemingly endless. More senior physicians can delegate much of these duties, but even the most accomplished practitioners need to perform some SCUT. If the professor needs a blood test urgently, sometimes she will have to take the time to draw the blood herself.

Our brains cannot be given a download of necessary information like a computer that needs a software update. We learn more from our mistakes and bad experiences than we do from any passive mode of teaching or from positive outcomes or a job well done. To quote Jacob Lehrer: "There is no secret recipe for decision-making. There is only vigilance, the commitment to avoiding those errors that can be avoided." (Lerher 2009). How can we as physicians avoid errors and sharpen our skills? In his book, *How We Decide*, Lerher (2009) discusses how flight simulators have dramatically reduced the number of airline disasters. Flight simulators allow pilots to practice maneuvers or learn the best course of action in a crisis situation. The initial or intuitively appropriate response may not be the optimal choice and may even be counterproductive. From a neurobiological standpoint, our subcortical centers, especially our amygdala, respond in a crisis situation before our prefrontal cortex analyzes the situation. From an evolutionary perspective, this is a positive and potentially lifesaving arrangement. A reflexive response may be counterproductive or dangerous in a highly technical, emotional or complex situation. For example, consider the police officer or soldier who is suddenly confronted with a potential enemy. That enemy could be a terrorist, or a child. The emotional response is to protect oneself and fire at the subject. The police officer or soldier must practice this situation to learn to override his amygdala and not fire at a benign target. Not easy. Military operations are discussed in detail at all levels before the mission is conducted, and if necessary, rehearsals or practice missions are performed. Practice and discussion allow flaws and potential problems in the operation to be identified and also allow input of opinions and observations from those participating in the operation. Military units and airline flight crews routinely conduct formal after-action reviews to re-enforce their training and learn from their mistakes and positive outcomes.

We use a more informal process in medicine than after-action reviews with preoperative case conference, mortality, and morbidity conferences and in grand rounds or clinical-pathology conferences. These conferences are used to focus on selected case-specific events that have teaching value, or are highly unusual, or situations where the expected course of events went awry. The best teachers are the ones who are experienced enough to anticipate problems that might arise in a particular clinical situation and can stimulate residents to anticipate adverse events and develop responses to unexpected situations. Simulation centers also allow physicians to practice techniques in an environment that is more vivid and realistic than the theoretical discussion in a conference room.

A surgery professor can also interrupt a procedure when there is a good opportunity to discuss options for dealing with a complication or problem. We should look for opportunities to engage in these discussions as often as possible. The introduction of preoperative checklists and time-outs before starting a procedure has reduced error rates, but the infinite variability and complexity of human biology and hospital environments require that we find ways to improve our efforts to reduce complications and untoward events with techniques such as processing improvement surveys and in-depth review of significant or recurring adverse events. This type of thinking should be an integral part of one's training.

It is impossible to make a complex decision de novo without prior preparation such as study, reading, research, or consciously developing a plan. History is filled with examples of individuals who have prepared for years for their moment of fame.

When considering famous figures throughout history, individuals such as Dwight D. Eisenhower, George E. Patton, Winston Churchill, and Alexander the Great come to mind as leaders who spent years of study and quiet consideration about how to respond to a hypothetical crisis or problem. Patton, a larger than life figure who is frequently characterized as gruff and unlettered, owned a massive personal library, the books in which were heavily annotated during the course of his studies. He had spent a lifetime preparing for his role in the Second World War.

5.2 Virtue and Ethics: The Good Doctor

The most revered physicians are not the ones with the greatest store of scientific knowledge or the most highly developed technical skills but those who demonstrate the greatest degree of humanism and compassion towards their patients. A good physician is one who has high moral character classically defined as *virtue*. It is this quality that requires years to perfect and is the true art of medicine.

Writing about the concept of the good doctor, medical ethicist Wayne Shelton states:

> "We must rethink and debate with renewed interest what it means to be a 'good doctor'. This will include some non-negotiable expectations of all students who have committed themselves to the profession of medicine." (Shelton 1999).

Shelton continues:

> In the contemporary health care system, these procedural values are reflected as the capacity and courage to function professionally in environments in which moral ambiguity is pervasive, to tolerate moral differences and uncertainties, to develop thoughtful individual moral positions, and to respect and understand various cultural traditions. (Shelton 1999, page 673)

We all aspire to be virtuous, to be known as a "good doctor." A good doctor is not necessarily the esteemed professor with international stature, or the physician or surgeon who has the largest practice, earns the most money, has written the most papers, is president of the most societies, sees the most referrals, or takes on the most difficult cases. It is the doctor that other doctors go to, the doctor one thinks of when describing the physician who demonstrates the highest degree of professional behavior. Some would call him/her the doctor's doctor. It is the person other physicians turn to when there is a problem with a family member or if they have a patient in the hospital that has a particularly unusual and agonizing problem. It is the physician whose guidance is sought when there is a question of ethics or professional misbehavior. This admonition is not excessive or rigid: it is a modest request to develop a sensible and measured system of values. This is no different than the many medical schools that teach courses in *physicianship*—the intangible, yet essential qualities of being a physician or surgeon, not just a doctor of medicine. The concept of and training in physicianship were begun at McGill University (https://www.mcgill.ca/physicianship) (Boudreau et al. 2011).

The Greeks called this quality *arête* and the Romans *virtue*. In their cultures, the development of virtue was a lifelong pursuit and the mark of a superior citizen and human being. The Greeks and Romans believed virtue was not a natural state of being but that it could be taught. The role of ethics was not to teach people to live a good life but rather demonstrate what a good life was and how one might set about developing a life and practice that embody this goodness. Doesn't that sound old-fashioned! Yet, there is wisdom and value in emulating the approach of the ancients.

As educators and mentors, we have a profound influence in the lives of our students and residents and have an opportunity to help them develop these traits. We may be temporally remoted from the concerns of Greco-Roman societies, but the requirement that physicians be men and women of virtue is no less important.

Aristotle argued that the *intellectual virtues* were taught by formal instruction (Aristotle, *The Nicomachean Ethics*). This is the purpose of undergraduate education and the first 2 years of medical school. *Moral virtues*, on the other hand, were acquired by habit and practice: what transpires in the second 2 years of medical school and continues throughout one's career. Medical education is, therefore, a blend of the moral and intellectual virtues with the primary focus of the first 2 years being the acquisition of a sound basis of knowledge and the principles of medicine. The remainder of the training process is heavily weighted towards the moral virtues—knowing how to exercise knowledge with judgment and care and learning how to act in the arena of medical practice.

Patients want a good doctor: one whose judgment, ethics, and humanity are above reproach. To that end, mentors and physicians have a duty to pass these values on to students and young physicians. Development of a personal value system and ethic is an individual process, but as Wayne Sheldon noted, all decisions and interactions with patients and families must be framed suing the value system of "the good doctor." Aristotle called this concept the "virtue of the mean" which, today, translates into a flexible, considered balance between the needs of the patient and the precepts of good medical practice. Medicine is an interpretative practice—it enables physicians to combine scientific information, clinical skill, and collective experience with similar patients to make sense of the particulars of one patient's illness and to determine the best action to take to cure or alleviate it (Shelton 1999). The biological cause of the disease and what can be done is just the beginning of what a patient wants to know.

5.3 Ethics

Of fundamental importance for the virtuous physician is an abiding sense of ethics. The principles of biomedical ethics may sound remote or complicated, the stuff of ethics committees. The fundamental principle is simple and does not require remembering terms that may seem arcane or stilted. Philosophers love obtuse and convoluted language, and the principles of biomedical ethics, although only recently formalized, have been debated for centuries. The difficulty with the corpus of philosophical writing is that philosophers have been unable to develop a consensus as to what is good and what is moral. Physicians cannot wait on philosophers to answer those questions (MacIntyre 2007).

Philosophers do not take care of patients; they are not in the trenches like the practicing physician or surgeon where individuals with immediate, often life-threatening problems demand immediate answers. Reliance on science and rationalism alone does not resolve ethical dilemmas, so decision-making cannot be purely pragmatic, or based on scientific truths. Likewise, art or technical excellence applied without wisdom and humanism is innately egocentric or self-gratifying. Aristotle emphasized that laws and morality are not separate, a distinction that is not universally held today. Hippocrates summarized the fundamentals of ethical decision-making in medicine over 2000 years ago: first, do no harm. That statement should suffice for the vast majority, if not all, of medical actions.

Injecting the ethical and humanistic dimensions into making decisions is more difficult when we use formal or structured approaches. While these considerations are always present, they do not fit neatly into a formula. It is possible to ensure we put the requisite consideration of the humanistic aspects of a patient's management into perspective at the outset, and not just as an afterthought. Such an approach is the kaleidoscope model that will be presented in Chap. 8.

5.4 Quality

Much ink has been spilled attempting to define what quality medicine looks like and how the quality of medical care should be measured. The concept of quality in medical care is recent, and such debate is necessary and proper. These arguments are also consequential in our efforts to make the best decisions we can. The definition of quality, when applied to the provision of medical care, is not fixed and to a great degree depends on the position you occupy in the debate. Patients interpret the quality of the care they receive from one perspective and physicians from another. Further, the definition of quality is often subjective or, as we have learned, even biased. Quality of care is often interpreted as the speed or efficiency of care, cost, or the more entrepreneurial aspects of health-care delivery. Defining quality with these parameters overlooks the ethical and humanistic side of patient care and undermines efforts to develop more innovative or creative care.

The process of determining quality is not rigid or always reproducible. Quality can be evaluated from the standpoint of process or outcome, as well as by different values or perceptions used by observers looking at the subject from differing orientations or backgrounds. Benchmarks for quality such as standards of care or evidence-based recommendations are quickly outdated. Standards for treatment evolve rather than arise by design, requiring that we continually review our decisions in light of processes, outcomes, and patient and system factors (Eddy 1990, 2000).

Avedis Donabedian, a physician who conducted seminal research in quality in health care and outcomes, described two ways of looking at quality. He argued that quality could be defined *empirically* (outcomes verified by experience, usually from two or more settings), using standards that rest on demonstrably attainable levels of care in settings that are similar, or defined *normatively* (the ideal or standard), using standards from sources that set the standards of knowledge and practice (Donabedian 1996).

With this model, outcomes from community hospitals would be empiric if compared to outcomes from similar community hospitals. In the case of normative standards, outcomes would be compared to the outcomes in the published literature provided by subject matter experts, usually those individuals practicing in academic centers. Clinicians look at quality in medical care from both empiric and normative viewpoints. We have a refined sense for recognizing good medical care empirically through our experience, and we know from our training and continuing education what the normative standards for treatments and what anticipated treatment outcomes are. This is the world we live in— experience and knowledge. These are also the sources we draw upon to make decisions. We often use data from each side of the equation indiscriminately, with little or no conscious consideration as to whether it is empiric or normative, relying rather on how applicable or similar the observations are to the situation we are assessing. This approach may be acceptable for the experienced and discriminating clinician but may lead the novice or ill-informed practitioner astray.

Quality Is Also Evident in Its Absence Former colleague would describe an unacceptable event or situation as—this is not chocolate cake. We know chocolate cake when we see it, and if it isn't chocolate cake, we all know it. It is like the Supreme Court Justice Potter Stewart, who, when trying to define pornography, stated—"I can't define it, but I know it when I see it." Quality in medical practice is elusive and not as easy to define as one would think. What is the desired outcome? Is one outcome preferable to another? Does the process and outcome meet humanistic, ethical, and moral standards? Was the process and outcome considerate of the patient's expectations, desires, and personal needs?

For example, let us assume your Uncle Joe, a retired gourmet chef in his mid-70s, has had extensive surgery, radiation, and chemotherapy for cancer and was considered cured. If the therapy depletes the savings Uncle Joe has set aside for the education of his grandchildren, renders him unable to enjoy his passion for a game of golf or walk his dog, and destroyed his enjoyment of a good meal, was the treatment really a success? Was quality care provided? The team that cared for him may congratulate themselves on having performing a medical miracle. The hospital administration may point to the outcome as a shining example of the expertise of their institution, and the quality assurance committee may look at Uncle Joe's hospital stay as having met the parameters they have chosen to monitor. All of these measures of quality do not consider that their ministrations have taken what little quality of life for the years he has left. This outcome, as far as Uncle Joe sees it, was not chocolate cake, and anyone would be justified in questioning if Joe's care was really the quality. The care he was given may not have been the best decision for Joe and his family.

The issues involved in determining what quality in health care looks like, and how it can be determined, are beyond the scope of this book, but it is worth considering the interface between quality of care and decision-making.

Donabedian also considered the relationship between individual physician performance and the quality of care rendered. He noted that the physician is at the center of this process, not only in terms of the care he or she provides but also in terms of wider reaching decisions such as the patient load each physician feels comfortable with managing and the utilization of institutional resources (Donabedian 2000). The expertise of each physician includes mastery of their specialty, appropriate use of consultations, ancillary staff, laboratory and radiographic resources, good medical record keeping, participation in teaching and continuing professional development at all levels, as well as interpersonal relationships with staff. Hospital personnel and patients all contribute to the quality of health care an individual patient receives. All of these factors are considered, to some degree, in the decision-making process. This matrix is complex and difficult to articulate as we deal with teaching students, residents, patients, and families.

In addition, medical decisions usually involve consideration or management of multiple and often conflicting recommendations, opinions, or expectations that may conflict with the optimal clinical recommendations or approaches. For these reasons, medical decision-making requires flexibility. Physicians examining the same radiographs, pathology specimens, or clinical findings will not always agree. Not only is there a significant degree of interobserver variability; the conclusions of the individual physician will not always be consistent depending on multiple personal and intuitive factors.

5.5 Clinical Presence

Good decision-making requires presence, a laser-like concentration on the problem at hand, and total immersion. A coach cannot direct his team from the locker room, nor can a general assess the progress of a battle from the comfort of the rear lines. Just being there is not enough, however. Some have the ability to walk into an operating suite or a hospital room and intuitively know that there is a problem. It may be that the family is anxious or distressed, the patient is "not right," or that the nursing staff is flustered. The surgeon may think all is in order and that she can start, but the anesthesiologist may not be comfortable, or the instruments may not be organized or even all there. Experience helps us develop this sense of something being out of order, but not all experienced clinicians have an awareness of the tension or disorder around them. I have termed this skill *clinical presence*, realizing that there is some unspoken or unrecognized disturbance in what should be a calm, professional, and controlled environment, and the ability to know when a patient is not responding appropriately or may be developing a complication. It is this sense that separates the outstanding from the merely good physician. There is probably no way to teach this skill. It certainly is not learned in the classroom. I suspect that the individuals who have this almost extrasensory perception of their surroundings have that skill in their DNA—it is just a part of their personae. Not all of us are good at being intuitive, reflective, and contemplative. We do not all analyze what is going on around us. Some of us are the archetypal, absent-minded professor who may be thinking about serious and complicated issues but is unaware that it is raining and that he has no umbrella. Albert Einstein was known to lose his way home when he was deep in thought about a problem he was working on. Such lapses might be acceptable for a genius in theoretical physics, but medicine does not permit such lapses when looking after patients. Lack of attentiveness can harm people. Why mention this shortcoming in the context of decision-making? If that skill does not come naturally, the clinician is obligated to work at overcoming this blind spot. A good decision requires that one be physically present and engaged in the problem at hand, aware of all that is going on in the immediate environment. It also requires that the physician seeks input from all those involved in the patient's care. It is the wise physician who talks to the nurse who is just finishing her shift, the resident who was on duty last night, the respiratory therapist who has been treating the patient, and the family members who know the patient better than anyone. This intelligence should be gathered before approaching the patient and making new decisions or changes in management.

5.6 Communication

Students must also learn to communicate with physicians and staff, as well as patients and lay persons. They have already acquired a medical vocabulary larger than the average person's working vocabulary. This vocabulary will grow exponentially as they progress through their training. They learn to communicate with (and listen to) the non-physician members of the health-care team who do not have the sophisticated vocabulary or level of knowledge they are trying to master. This also includes the monumental and lifelong task of learning to communicate in an ethically appropriate, understandable, and compassionate way to patients and families and other lay persons who are involved in the patient's care.

Students must learn to take the information they gather from the patient's history and examination, and the results of any laboratory and radiographic testing, to formulate a cohesive meaningful narrative in order to arrive at a diagnosis. They are learning to sift through the information about a particular patient and then relate that to their already significant but unorganized and inefficient knowledge base—the overwhelming number of facts, concepts, and principles they learned during their first 2 years.

This skill is the pattern recognition that so many researchers in the fields of learning and expertise have described as being the principal way that most of us use to recognize situations and develop a defense or strategy.

5.7 Teamwork and Leadership

Physicians, especially junior physicians, do not often think of themselves as leaders, but by virtue of the position they have in the medical hierarchy, no matter how menial, they are viewed as leaders. These skills are just as important as the ability to make a correct diagnosis or tie a good knot, but are rarely taught directly or explicitly. Indoctrination into the guild of medicine and learning the way a physician should behave is done more by osmosis and passive learning rather than by more directed or overt means. Unfortunately, this passive approach teaches students and residents that socially inappropriate, mean-spirited, or abusive behavior is acceptable if senior physicians are allowed to act inappropriately and not checked. As has been demonstrated in many domains, a good teacher is a good mentor and role model, constantly on display and at risk of being emulated by his charges whether his behavior is admirable or not (Reynolds and Blickensderfer 2009).

It is often possible to determine what attending physicians the residents have been with recently just by listening to their speech, the words they choose, or the attitudes they have towards their patients. It is amusing to hear them incorporate aphorisms that are specific to one attending physician into their conversations as a way of showing that they see themselves as a part of the society or group they wish to join. The responsibilities of senior physicians run deep, and the effect of their actions persists long after their didactics have been forgotten. We all use aphorisms and pearls of wisdom from the residents and staff from which we learned.

5.8 Developing Management Plans

Students and house officers must also learn to formulate effective and appropriate plans of management based on the individual patient's story and what they have learned during the first 2 years of medical school. This is a process they will refine throughout their training and beyond. They learn that patient management is not a cookbook process, followed like a recipe for apple pie, but a complex melding of ethical, social, scientific, and clinical factors unique for each patient. Some will be dismayed by the apparent uncertainty and chaotic nature of the process. It is an exercise in judgment, not science.

5.9 Technical Skills

Finally, students begin developing their technical skills: how to write orders, how to tie knots, how to draw blood or start an intravenous drip, and how to perform a lumbar puncture or place a urinary drainage catheter. Even in a discipline where technical expertise is highly valued, choosing residents for a surgery program must place great emphasis on the candidate's communication and leadership skills.

The most important ingredient in any discipline requiring great expertise is knowledge (Ericsson 2009). The mere acquisition of technical skills is not the goal. Top performers are better organized and have consolidated their knowledge. This allows them to approach problems in a different, lateral, or more effective way. The approach is from higher-level principles. While we teach the principles of medicine, the student must integrate those principles into his or her thinking, a process that requires experience, contemplation, and deliberate thinking about those fundamentals. It is one thing to be able to recite a principle but another to really understand and integrate the principle into one's problem-solving ability and thinking.

I have always been impressed at how much a good clinician can remember about a patient. This includes patients that were treated years or decades ago. The master clinician may remember the name or situation that made the case unique. With a few facts, the master physician can often reconstruct the case recalling minute and intimate details. This encyclopedic memory should not be surprising—medicine is case-based. We do not remember random facts or specifics of a disease process in isolation. This is why medical students have such a problem with remembering details about a patient—they have not developed the extensive framework required to integrate and categorize information into a useful framework. We require medical students to remember details such as the patient's hemoglobin or serum creatinine at admission, a difficult challenge for the novice clinician to manage. The master clinician automatically and effortlessly gathers this pertinent information and also is able to recall the patient's creatinine from the last admission or last year.

5.10 Organizational and Operational Awareness

I was once asked to develop a plan for establishing a comprehensive maternal-fetal-neonatal unit at a large university medical center. The center had a complete complement of specialists to include obstetricians specializing in high-risk pregnancy; the necessary fetal, neonatal, and interventional services; as well as the capability to provide those services in a comprehensive and first-class fashion. The concept required having the center's helicopter services transport women with maternal or fetal problems that needed high-level care to the center from small hospitals scattered around the state. There did not appear to be any hurdle that would preclude establishing this service.

After a few meetings with the administration and care providers to ensure their support, I began to develop a business plan. There was great need for such a service in the region, and it seemed to be very easy project to organize and implement. The project was totally dependent on the availability and capabilities of the air transport system; however, and before investing any further time, I contacted the chief of the air transport services. His response for the project was enthusiastic. They had the capacity to take on the additional flights, and their service range was even greater than the first estimates we had been given. Additionally, there were no other centers in the region providing such a service, and the referral hospitals were relying on ground transportation with no established referral patterns. In spite of all of the optimistic information I had gathered, I was still unsettled.

I did not feel comfortable that the air transport service fully understood what we were asking for. My next call was to the flight nurses and pilots. I then learned that their helicopters were not sufficiently pressurized or equipped for transporting these fragile patients over long distances, and even more to the point, their patient bays could not physically accommodate a patient in the final weeks of her pregnancy. They had no capability to reconfigure their helicopters and no funds to purchase a helicopter that would meet the requirements of a pregnant patient and potentially a newborn as well. I relayed this information to the medical director and advised him that there was no benefit to pursuing this idea further.

Just as the coach must be on the sidelines and plugged into all phases of the game, the medical decision-maker must also be aware of the capabilities, limitations, strengths, and processes used in any organization or team he or she is working with. Just as the combat commander must know when and where his supplies are coming from, the good physician must be knowledgeable about the personnel she will be calling on for help in the operating room or intensive care unit, whether the intensive care unit has a shortage of beds or if the laboratory is having to send specific assays out rather than doing them in house. Obviously, knowledge of all of the facets of an organization as complex as a hospital or even an operating room are beyond the scope and concern of the individual physician, but the physician caring for complex patients must have a sound understanding of the capabilities and services available in the institution he or she is contemplating using for the care of such patients.

We have all had similar experiences. How many times have you needed a specific size catheter, drug, or suture and discovered that "we no longer order that style or size or use that vendor" or that "the product is on back order?" Physicians are not involved in the mundane aspects of running an organization or a facility, but it becomes our responsibility when such deficiencies and decisions impact the care of one of our patients. A visit to the nursing supervisor or person responsible for supplies in the operating room may be necessary if you are anticipating having a patient with requirements beyond the norm or a problem that may stress the limits of the institution's capability or personnel.

Chapter 6
Information: Gathering, Storing, and Retrieval

Summary

Decision-making begins with our ability to develop a cohesive narrative of the patient and their personal and environmental background, their family and resources, and their desires and expectations. We must develop the arts of listening to a patient's narrative and observing the subtle clues that each patient and each disease process exhibit.

Medical education is two-pronged—first, the acquisition of the necessary technical knowledge and, second, the ability to process and apply that knowledge towards the care of a patient. These skills must be developed within the moral, ethical, practical, and humanistic context of honorable medical practice. To that end, our education can be thought of as being centripetal and centrifugal. Centrifugal thinking describes the process of learning and organizing the core knowledge primarily learned during the first two years of medical school or in the course of other didactic activities such as lectures. Centripetal thinking is the skill required to gather information, observe, interpret, synthesize, and prioritize the data we gather about a particular patient or case and use to make a decision and develop a plan of action to address the needs or a particular patient or a particular problem or set of problems.

Learning involves the ability to gather and process information in a specific, logical, and neuroanatomically based manner. This process can also be depicted as a cycle as outlined in this chapter.

6.1 Narrative Thinking

> Patients do not always come to be healed—sometimes they come to be heard.

All humans love a story, and it is through stories that we are able to understand ourselves and interpret the natural and supernatural world. All patients have a story. Patients are anxious to tell their story and the best physician is the one who can listen carefully and compassionately to that story. The physician who is a good listener easily gains the patient's trust and quickly establishes the relationship necessary for providing good care. By definition, this is a retrospective process. The scientist, on the other hand, develops a hypothesis and then proceeds to prove or disprove the hypothesis. Science is a prospective business. A master physician does not merely interview the patient. She does not just ask predetermined or formulaic questions. Rather, she asks the patient to tell a story—a narrative of their disease and their life.

Humans have always been narrative beings. Stories have allowed us to document important events, explain phenomena in the world, and maintain traditions and history. All humans love a story, and it is through stories that we are able to understand ourselves and interpret the natural and supernatural world. All patients have a story. Patients are anxious to tell their story, and the best physician is the one who can listen carefully and compassionately to that story. The physician who is a good listener easily gains the patient's trust and quickly establishes the relationship necessary for providing good care. Attention to the patient's history, guided by thoughtful, pointed questions about that history, allows the astute physician to construct a cohesive, meaningful narrative that explains the patient's complaints and then develop a plan of management.

Our knowledge is context dependent. Learning a string of facts about a disease process one has never seen is hard. It is interesting though that we can recall, with minimal prompting, minute details about a case we dealt with decades ago. The trick is to always be cautious and remember that our memory is selective and imperfect. We remember in the context of a story. Our knowledge base and ability to make decisions grow with adding to our repertoire of stories we have learned. The resident more likely wants an immediately applicable pearl that will allow him to proceed with managing the patient or help with a board or in-service examination. Nothing wrong with that, but reflecting, over time, the impact of a patient's story is, ultimately, what produces clinical judgment.

The construction of a good clinical narrative requires mastery of many skills, to include taking a good history, performing a skilled physical examination, knowing how to fill in the gaps with pointed questions, and, if necessary, going elsewhere—to include sources such as old records, interviewing family, talking to previous care providers, or asking for observations from nursing and ancillary staff.

Establishing a diagnosis is primarily an exercise in taking a good history. At least 75 percent and possibly as many as 82 percent of patients can be accurately diagnosed by history alone (Montgomery 2006). The corollary to those statistics is that between 5 and 25 per cent of patients require imaging studies or more sophisticated or invasive testing to determine a diagnosis (Hampton, et al. 1975, cited by Montgomery 2006, page 223). Obviously, many patients will need imaging or invasive studies to plan therapy, establish the extent of the disease, or confirm the history, but these data underscore how important communication and effective listening are to patient assessment. How reliable is the patient's own history? Again, there is no firm data to answer that question, and it takes great skill and experience to know how to extract an accurate history and to detect when the patient is not providing truthful or complete answers. Many patients are, by nature, evasive in their responses, either from embarrassment, ignorance, or failure to understand the question. Patients may think the doctor should know the answers anyway or are, in a conscious or subconscious attempt, not ready to cooperate.

6.2 Observation

Tell me to what you pay attention, and I will tell you who you are (de Madariaga 1989).

Physicians and Sherlock Holmes
A clinician is more like Sherlock Holmes than a scientist. An expert clinician is a keen observer of humanity and the patient, noticing details and starting to make connections about the patient that may have been missed before one question is asked.

Good medical practice, and good decision-making, begins with observation. Not just seeing what is in front of you but really observing what you are seeing. Observation is the most fundamental skill that the student and young physician must learn. Unfortunately, many are more likely to first sit at the computer terminal and review what others have noted or review the results of a CAT scan and then examine the patient. Physicians must become expert observers. A physician should be able to walk through the clinic and make diagnoses about several patients with a quick glance—not an easy skill to master. We all know of the professor who can listen to a case presentation by a student or resident and then go into the examination room, ask one or two pointed questions, and extract that one bit of information that sheds light on the diagnosis. This is the master detective at work, what Sherlock Holmes would do to solve a case that has everyone else baffled.

Medicine is highly sensory. We use all of our senses to evaluate patients, make diagnoses, and evaluate progress. Subtle visual clues, smells, touch, changes in a patient's speech or heart sounds—all are noted by the experienced physician and may be of more value in decision-making than the results of highly technical studies or laboratory reports. Good decision-making demands that we be attuned to the subtle aspects of a patient's narrative, and this is a skill that requires constant effort to develop and is easy to neglect in today's world of electronic medical records and virtually instant laboratory and imaging study results. If the consultant notes that a patient has a specific complaint or physical finding, we are still obligated to question or re-examine the patient to verify that finding and cement those details into our own narrative.

One evening, when I was a junior medical student on my surgery rotation, I had the opportunity to play Dr. Watson with a budding Sherlock Holmes: a mid-level surgery resident. The institution where I went to medical school had separate emergency areas for OB/GYN, pediatrics, surgery, and medicine. The surgery and medical emergency centers were on opposite ends of the hospital. It is made for interesting problems, as patients were not always accurately triaged by the ambulance crews bringing the patients in.

Patients who came seeking emergency care generally walked into the first area they could find, unaware that they may be on the wrong side of the hospital. Patients with non-specific complaints were sometimes directed to one emergency center or another based on the impression of the admitting clerk. Chest pain or shortness of breath triggered transport to the medical side of the hospital. This was problematic if the cause of the chest pain was shortness of breath was due to a gunshot wound. The quickest way into the hospital was through the waiting room for the medical side of the emergency department. As we walked through the crowded room, my resident noted a distinguished, elderly African-American man who was calmly sitting by himself. It was summer in Virginia, hot and sweltering, yet this man had a winter scarf wrapped around his neck. He was also smoking a cigar, nothing unusual in the days before smoking was banned in hospitals. What was unusual though was the smoke that rose from the folds of his wool scarf as he puffed his cigar. I noticed the gentleman but did not put the obvious discrepancies together. My surgery resident did. He was walking at a very brisk pace but stopped abruptly in front of the cigar-smoker. The resident asked the man why he was there, and the man replied that he had shortness of breath. This complaint was all the man had uttered when asked by the admitting clerk why he was there. No one had bothered to gather any additional information. The resident asked if he could unwrap the scarf around the patient's neck, and the gentleman obliged. The resident proceeded to gently unwrap the scarf revealing a large transverse laceration across the patient's neck that had lacerated the trachea. It was almost bloodless. A head and neck surgeon could not have done a neater tracheotomy. The man had been assaulted by a man with a straight razor who cut the gentleman's neck when he refused to hand over his wallet. The poor man went home, wrapped a scarf around his neck, and walked to the hospital. The resident took the man by the hand, and we escorted him to the surgery emergency area where he was assessed and quickly sent to the operating room. He recovered uneventfully.

How many others saw this man? How many had talked to him when he was triaged, and how many walked past him as he sat in the waiting room? Certainly, other physicians walked by him. The fact that this man was wearing a wool scarf in heat of the summer should have been of interest, and the smoke curling up around his head and neck should have caused some alarm. Yet, there he sat, patiently waiting and being ignored. How could anyone, myself included, overlook such a bizarre situation?

The author of the Sherlock Holmes mysteries, Sir Arthur Conan Doyle, was a physician and surgeon. The character of Sherlock Holmes was based on his mentor from the University of Edinburgh, Dr. Joseph Bell (Liebow 2007). A gifted surgeon and teacher, Bell was a member of the clinical faculty. Bell, a very popular instructor, taught what he called "the method" based on keen observation of the patient, his dress, mannerisms, accent, general appearance, and the subtle findings about his person. Bell was able to tell a person's trade, recent activities, and chief complaint by observation and by asking a few key questions. Bell admonished his students to first observe and gather facts and then make a diagnosis, not formulate an opinion and then look for data to support one's preconceived diagnosis. Bell was enlisted to use his skills in forensic medicine, helping the police to solve crimes, and would recommend that this method also be used in police training. Bell's ability to accurately diagnose medical problems and a patient's background was uncanny and would later provide Doyle not only the physical characteristics and mannerisms for his literary hero but also the method Sherlock Holmes made famous in solving his cases. Bell's clinical cases also provided the material for many of the characters and plots in the Sherlock Holmes mysteries.

Doyle distinguished himself from his classmates by his fastidious and diligent note-taking in an attempt to record every observation or comment Dr. Bell made. Later in life, Doyle wrote:

> I felt now that I was capable of something fresher and crisper and more workmanlike. Gaboriau (Emile Gaboriau was a French writer of detective fiction) had rather attracted me by a neat dovetailing of his plots, and Poe's masterful detective, M. Dupin, had from boyhood been one of my heroes. But could I bring an addition of my own? I thought of my old teacher Joe Bell, of his eagle face, of his curious ways, and his eerie trick of spotting details. If he were a detective he would surely reduce this fascinating but unorganized business to something nearer an exact science. (Liebow 2007)

Perhaps *The Adventures of Sherlock Holmes* should be required medical school reading (Konnikova 2013).

6.3 Centripetal and Centrifugal Thinking

Learning to manage information is a skill that does not come naturally. The practice of medicine requires ingesting, understanding, analyzing, categorizing, and organizing a large volume of data. Not all information is immediately relevant. A fact learned today may not be useful until years later. Not all we learn is true or valid over time, and new information is always being presented. Acquiring a large volume of data is of no use if that data is not kept in the neurological equivalent of readily identifiable and accessible files. We have learned how the principle of *seven plus or minus two* applies to our short-term or immediate memory, yet we also know that the storage capacity of our long-term memory is virtually limitless (Miller 1956). Most clinical situations demand we access and consider many more than seven bits of information. The diagnosis of pneumonia or pancreatic cancer can often be made with a high degree of certainty given a few facts or parameters, but the complete assessment of the patient, planning for management, and all the other factors involved in caring for a patient require consideration of a host of disparate and seemingly unrelated variables. We learn to juggle such data with experience, but the learning curve is steep. Mnemonics, chunking, and algorithms can help, but we need techniques that are more flexible, capable of handling large quantities of information, and are able to be altered or expanded depending on our needs and our ever enlarging and more sophisticated store of data.

Absorbing a large number of concepts and bits of data is almost exclusively what medical school is about for the preclinical years. Having a large base of data to draw from is of little benefit if we do not have the contextual framework to categorize and prioritize information we are given. We start as passive learners. We will always, to some degree, remain passive learners as we read, attend conferences, workshops, and other educational events during our careers, but experience provides the mental scaffolding necessary to rapidly assess and retain or discard new information.

Once we enter the clinical portion of our training and are challenged with applying the data we have accumulated, we are no longer passive learners. We must convert data into knowledge. That process not only requires a radical change in how we think but also requires us to develop ways of organizing and prioritizing information as well as looking for connections between what we may have perceived as being unrelated facts or concepts. We must learn to be qualitative in our thinking and consider that not all the facts or theories are correct, relevant, or immutable.

Experienced clinicians move from the passive to active consideration of knowledge effortlessly and seamlessly, but the novice can find that process intimidating and confusing. It is analogous to learning to drive a car with a standard transmission—one must consciously choose the right gear or end up grinding the gears or stalling the car many times before the process becomes natural.

One way to visualize this process is to consider that we use information in primarily a *centripetal* or *centrifugal* direction. These terms that you learned in high school physics may require reintroduction. Centripetal and centrifugal refer to the forces acting on an object moving in a circle around a fixed point or center. *Centripetal* describes the force that pulls the object to the center (Latin derivation: centri—center and petere—to fall), and *centrifugal* is the force on that same object pulling it away from the center (Latin derivation: centri—center and fugere—to flee).

The first 2 years of medical school are all about centrifugal learning. Think of a wagon wheel with the subject as the hub and the details about that subject being the spokes that radiate outwards. If a lecture is about pneumonia, then pneumonia is the hub, and all the characteristics and facts relating to pneumonia become the rim of the wagon wheel, which is connected to the hub by the spokes. Once you construct your basic pneumonia wheel, any facts you subsequently learn become additional spokes, and facts about the facts on the rim become ancillary spokes and wheels.

A medical student will have a rudimentary understanding of pneumonia represented by his wheel, but the pulmonologist or infectious disease specialist will have developed a large, comprehensive, and complex wheel. The wheel developed by the pediatrician based on her clinical experience and knowledge base will look quite different from the wheel that meets the needs of the pulmonologist (Fig. 6.1).

This model works to learn about pneumonia but does not help one to diagnose the patient who presents with pneumonia. The spokes radiate outward, and the physician needs to reverse his or her thinking and start from the rim and work towards the hub to establish a diagnosis and initiate therapy.

6.3 Centripetal and Centrifugal Thinking

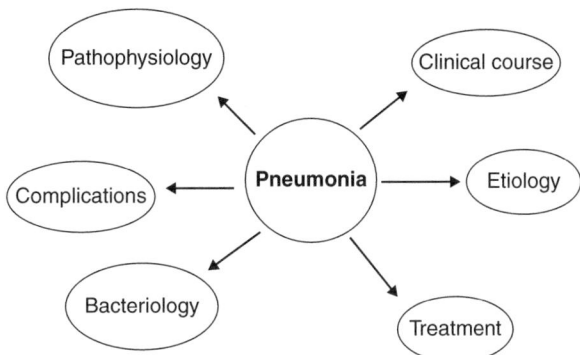

Fig. 6.1 Centrifugal learning

The student who finally faces a patient after having had information delivered in a centrifugal manner must now reverse his or her thinking and think centripetally. They must work *from the outside* or rim of the wheel by identifying the patient's presenting symptoms and pertinent physical and radiographic findings to establish a diagnosis which lies at the center of the wheel. The diagrams used to illustrate these concepts are generated using mind-mapping or concept-mapping techniques. Mind-mapping, a technique that will become integral to optimal learning and information management, will be described in the next section (Fig. 6.2).

The third year of medical school is, therefore, a world turned upside down. Students who have spent the last several years in a class with one teacher learning passively and in a centrifugal fashion must now reverse their thinking in an active way that requires them to have the information they have learned organized in a readily accessible and logical format. It is not possible to sit in the back of the lecture hall and be passive or receptive. They must now uncover the facts, analyze them and come to a conclusion, and stand before their peers and mentors and recite the history of a patient they have interviewed and examined. These bits of data must be organized to point to a diagnosis at the hub of the wheel. Talking to the patient, performing a physical examination, and reviewing radiographs and laboratory studies produce a mountain of data. This data must be sifted through and the pertinent pieces assembled to form a coherent snapshot of the patient, what brought him to the hospital, and what the relevant signs and symptoms discovered during the examination are. The thought processes required have been turned around 180 degrees from what the student has been doing for the past 2 years. They are now thinking *from the outside* to the center.

Putting It All Together

Centripetal and centrifugal thinking is the push-pull of medical practice—knowing the principles and then applying the appropriate ones to a specific case versus identifying the effects of a disease process on a patient and then determining the underlying cause. It is the shifting of gears we go through when we transition from centripetal to centrifugal thinking, and we are thinking by reduction or elimination—evaluating several options and eliminating those that do not meet the search criteria.

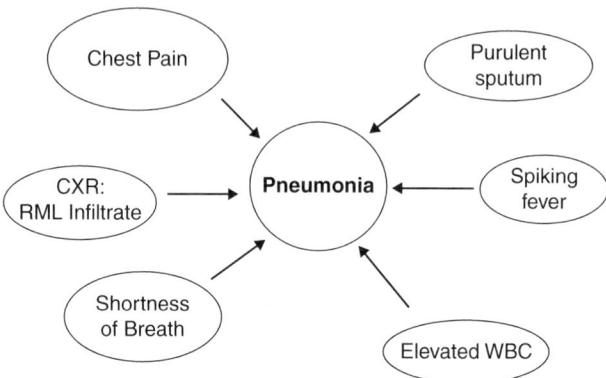

Fig. 6.2 Centripetal learning

Problem-solving using algorithms is also centripetal but directed by predetermined criteria not necessarily selected by the decision-maker. Approaches based on algorithms are common in medical decision-making, especially in time-sensitive or acute situations such as trauma management or cardiopulmonary resuscitation. They are also used in situations where decision-making is performed by non-physicians to manage simple, straightforward problems that do not need immediate physician input. Such algorithms are used in triage and acute minor illness clinics where many of the presenting complaints can be handled by following a decision tree.

This is also the world of the practicing physician—she must shift from centripetal thinking when managing patient problems and back to centrifugal thinking when learning a new treatment, the latest research, or new findings about a disease. This back and forth way of thinking is the yin and yang of medicine, learning to shift from one gear to another. It is knowing how to take the new data on the rim of the wheel and apply that knowledge to generate a solution that is in the center. Centripetal thinking requires judgment, experience, and introspection. Not all new data is good or useful, and some new data may challenge and change established solutions to a problem. Observations and new data must be analyzed in the context of one's own practice setting and capabilities. The potentially useful data and techniques need to be tried out before being adopted. It is difficult to change one's practice, especially if what you have been doing has worked. The process of developing a visual map for pneumonia makes this process much easier. Not only are we visual learners and able to better remember information when organized like a road map, but a well-organized road map is easy to reproduce and can be expanded to include a massive amount of data in a readily accessible and logical format. An approach to developing such a road map is mind-mapping, a concept we will turn to next. Visual tools such as mind-mapping make learning, critical thinking and decision-making much easier than relying on or reproducing a list of bullet points from a PowerPoint slide, one's notes, or a textbook.

6.4 The Learning Cycle

To understand how we make decisions, it is useful to know how we learn. Learning is not an abstract process. Learning is the result of the logical, sequential, and neuroanatomically based way in which we gather and analyze and ultimately use information. We use all the areas of our brain in the process of learning. Many theories have been proposed to explain the process of learning as researchers have slowly deciphered this process. If we understand this process, we will become more efficient learners and consequently better teachers and better decision-makers.

The *learning cycle* is a model based on current theories of optimal learning and is a useful way of appreciating how medical students, residents, and practicing physicians process new information and then incorporate it into their own practice and ultimately how that information is used to solve problems. The learning cycle is based on the theory that we learn best through experience, not the passive learning that transpires in a lecture hall. David Kolb, the researcher who, building on the work of his predecessors, described this theory, called this process—*experiential learning or deep learning*—and describes the phases of the learning cycle as *concrete experience*, *reflective observation*, *abstract hypothesis*, and *active testing* (Kolb 2015) (Fig. 6.3).

This cycle represents how we learn surgery or procedures as well as how we learn about diseases or physiology and then put that information to use in our daily practice. We take in information through all of our senses. As we are exposed to new information, data, or techniques, (*concrete experience*), we think about what we have seen, analyze the experience, and decide if the data is applicable to our practice or knowledge base. We then critically examine that information and determine if the

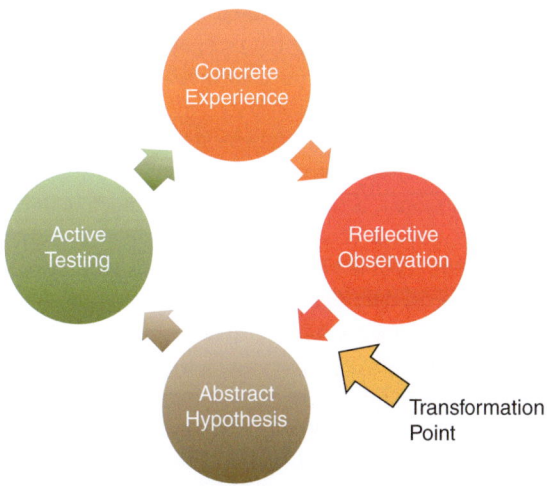

Fig. 6.3 The learning cycle. Used with permission. (From Kolb (1983), with modification by Zull (2002)). Modified and used with permission

approach or data can be expanded upon or needs validation or improvement (*reflective observation*). We then develop an approach that reflects our assessment and individual needs (*abstract hypothesis*). This point is designated the *transformation point* on the diagram. It is the point where we convert information or data into knowledge or theory. This is the point in the cycle where information is transferred from our posterior cortex to our frontal cortex. Looking at it another way, this is the point at which passive learning becomes active testing or active learning. This step requires time, as our brains must evaluate the new data, reorganize it so that it becomes useful to the individual, and integrate it into our long-term memory. New neuronal connections need to be established, and these connections will become more sophisticated and complex as we add to the memory we have and relate that data to the data we already have stored. When we challenge our abstract hypotheses with active use of the new information and then observe the results and modify our thinking as needed by repeating the cycle as many times as necessary we truly "own" the information–it has become hardwired into our memory.

A fact by itself is meaningless and probably will not become incorporated into our long-term memory unless we have other related information to attach it to. Cementing data into our long-term memory is also more time-consuming for abstract or new concepts, as we have nothing to hook that information on to for better recall. This is a particularly beneficial aspect of mind-mapping as mind-maps create visual links in the form of images or models between bits of data. Such visual images allow us to expand our computational or working memory. Data by itself is rarely useful. The data needs to be transformed from external sources into knowledge that can be effectively called upon and used. In other words, we don't own new information until our brains have pondered and personalized the data (Zull 2002).

There is a limit to how much data we can process in a meaningful and lasting way. This fact begs two questions—first, how long does one need to comprehensively and critically analyze a new experience? This process may require churning the information in our subconscious to make sense of our observations. It is why we often need to sleep on a problem rather than respond immediately. It also takes time for new information to be integrated into our memory: We need to rehearse options, identify optimal ways of achieving success, and consider possible outcomes. Second, there are limits to the amount of information we can effectively process from any given experience. As we know from studies on one's ability to remember numbers or a series of objects or words, there is a limit to how much data we can be exposed to and remember. How much information can a resident absorb from one lecture, demonstration, or operative procedure? Can a resident hold their concentration and learn continuously during a procedure that lasts several hours and meaningfully process and retain the data that they are taking in? We do not learn optimally from participating in a procedure that takes several hours. In fact, once information overload has been reached, the educational benefit is lost by laboring on. Would it not be better to divide a long procedure into discrete segments and have the resident operate for that portion of the case and then act as an assistant for the next steps of the procedure? This approach is a departure from traditional surgical thinking and is not always practical. Is it better to have one resident perform the entire case or break the case up into multiple parts and

6.4 The Learning Cycle

have a fresh resident perform each segment? Rather than having one tired and perhaps overwhelmed resident perform the entire case, is it not better to have two or three residents benefit from being intimately involved and learning a critical portion of an operation? Utilizing the information is important as the learning is enhanced by engaging your motor cortex. Learning a new technique or procedure or management approach is not solidified into one's memory until you actually perform the activity. This is accomplished by performing a task such as an operation or technical procedure and also by writing the orders for the institution of chemotherapy and explaining it to the patient and those around you. These tasks all involve activation of the motor cortex, an activity that reinforces and cements learning.

An important part of the learning cycle is reflection. *Reflection* helps to further integrate data and ideas and deepen the learning process. Reflection is augmented or reinforced by sidebar discussions with fellow residents or staff surgeons, conferences, reading, or watching videos. Such activities provide ways of developing hypotheses or insights into the experience. Learning is also enhanced by performing or participating in additional, similar procedures, conferences, lectures, seminars, research projects, or practice using models. Simulation centers or other similar training aids reinforce this portion of the cycle.

The next step for deep learning is the *abstract hypothesis* or *active testing* phase. Many of the activities just listed help with this phase as they allow the learner to apply and further develop the concepts she has been exposed to in the reflection phase. These activities reinforce the relevance of the learning experience as well as help the student to be in control of their learning. We learn much more efficiently when we feel we have control of our learning rather than being passive recipients of knowledge. It converts what could be a purely extrinsic experience such as a lecture into something that is intrinsic and a real part of one's knowledge and experience.

At this stage, the hypothesis is abstract in the sense that it is the initial mental picture of the observation: what happened? How was the problem identified and approached? and most importantly: What can I do to replicate the lesson or the movements I witnessed or tried to perform? Development of this hypothesis may also involve further reading, research, or discussion. The fruits of the learning experience are not realized until one is able to test the hypothesis-active testing. This may take the form of practice or repetition of the procedure, but it must involve active pre-motor and motor output. We need to test the validity of our hypothesis. By looking at the learning activity just completed in the sense of an abstract hypothesis, we consider how we can better position our hands to place a certain stitch or how we can better explain what we are doing to a patient. We are now taking ownership of what we have learned and reconfiguring it to meet our needs and talents.

This produces *concrete experience*, which is more refined and nuanced than our first evolution through the cycle. With this new experience, the learning cycle starts over again. If we bypass these steps, we will never truly learn and will never truly understand and master a task. We will never be able to improve on our hypothesis or our motor skills, and we will never own the concepts presented by the experience. The knowledge will never be imbedded in our long-term frontal and motor memory. One remains a bystander who merely watches a performance. Learning requires not only input into the sensory cortex but also transformation of the information in terms of reflection, the development of concepts and plans, and finally understanding and being able to put those concepts into practice.

Emotionally charged or stressful events affect our memories and ability to learn in both positive and negative ways. The rush of hormones secreted under situations of stress or fear activates primal reflexes such as the fight or flight reflex and narrow our field of vision to what is directly in front of us rather than what is happening in our peripheral vision. We remember minute details about such events *and must always guard ourselves against the fact that our memories may be inaccurate.* I have been impressed at how, with little prompting, physicians can remember extensive histories to include trivial details about patients they cared for years ago. We are trained to maintain distance between ourselves and our patients to minimize how our judgment is affected in our decisions. Yet, the admonition to keep objective distance between you and a patient, particularly a patient you have known for years, is asking us to disregard human nature and the inevitable, if subtle, emotional attachments we subconsciously make about other human beings. This is especially true if we are personally invested in the decision or outcome either through ego-driven and selfish motives or if we have a vested interest in the particular problem a patient presents with. We are less likely to remember details about a patient who comes to us with a minor illness such as a cold or simple skin rash, unless that complaint was somehow caused by or exacerbated by recommendations that we gave and that went awry or if we missed recognizing a major illness.

Traditional methods using lectures, formal talks, PowerPoint, etc. are not the best method to teach a topic, yet this is how most information is presented in our education and our careers. Because of our training, physicians can probably focus longer than the average person, but we are not superhuman and need to appreciate that we cannot maintain our focus for extended periods of time. For this reason, it is probably unreasonable to have a conference that lasts over an hour without a break or expect a resident to maintain their attention and absorb the maximum amount of information when they are performing a procedure that lasts more than an hour. Even an experienced surgeon cannot maintain optimal focus for more than that amount of time before benefiting from a break. It is not humanly possible. We often undertake procedures that take several hours, so how can we provide the optimal care and the continuity our patients expect? Surgeons perpetuate the myth that they are able to stand at the operating table for many hours without a break and bear our endurance like a badge of honor. All research concludes that this practice does not produce optimal results, is unhealthy for the surgeon, and is potentially dangerous. We can concentrate with the laser-like focus required for only short periods.

Chapter 7
Mind-Mapping

Summary

Using graphic, written models is an invaluable way to capture data, insights, and options as we collect and outline our thinking and develop our decision-making. Many models and processes that use visual or written methods to capture, refine, and organize our thinking have been developed. The approach most applicable to clinical practice is mind-mapping. Mind-mapping is a simple, easily mastered approach to help organize our thoughts, identify and prioritize problems, uncover where we need more data, and convert our thinking from a centrifugal to a centripetal mode. It is an excellent decision-making tool. Mind-mapping cannot only help us develop a differential diagnosis but also define a management plan and assign tasks and responsibilities for a team. Mind-mapping is also an excellent tool to organize a talk or written product such as a lecture or case summary.

7.1 Mind Mapping: An Overview

We have all experienced the ordeal of "death by PowerPoint." How many lectures built around computer-generated slides have we endured? How many thousands or tens of thousands of these slides have we seen with their pastel backgrounds and bullet after bullet of data? *PowerPoint may be an easy way for lecturers to present their information, but it is an inefficient way to teach or to learn. Unfortunately, we continue this mode of thinking and looking at problems in our clinical practice. There is a better way of organizing and analyzing information. It is called mind-mapping.*

Our brains are not configured to remember lists on PowerPoint slides or to connect the points that are being made and, more importantly, to store or develop a functional information retrieval system. Our brains do not store information slide by slide; our brains process, store, retrieve, and process information by patterns and relationships. Our brains have an unlimited capacity to handle information in this way. The beauty in this process is not that mind-mapping helps us store information but that mind-mapping can improve our ability to manipulate data and create new relationships, insights, and ideas and, most importantly, for our present concern, make decisions.

The first 2 years of medical school are analogous to trying to memorize the listings from a telephone book for a large city in a foreign country. Not only do students have to become facile with a new language, but also, they have to memorize fact after unrelated fact without having a good framework to organize them. To further complicate the task, memorizing facts is of no use unless the student can see the relationships between the facts and develop solutions to problems or create new ideas. If our brains are created to handle information in this unique and individualized way, why don't we teach in a way that allows students can take maximum advantage of this capability?

As we start medical school, we all must master the same fundamental fund of knowledge, the common language that will allow us to communicate with colleagues and understand the basic scientific and conceptual basis on which any medical practice is founded. The orthopedic resident may think that renal physiology is of minor importance for her future, but she must still learn the fundamental concepts of kidney function. Once having a basic understanding of renal physiology, our future orthopedic surgeon is at least able to pass the examinations and certifications necessary to obtain a license. That may be the end of one's need to know about what the different parts of the kidney's collecting tubule do. The budding nephrologist, however, cannot stop once he has a fundamental understanding of the renal tubule. He needs to continually, and over the course of a career, build a greater and greater understanding of the renal function. Both students need a framework to organize, tailor, and retain the knowledge about renal physiology that they learn throughout their education.

Learning by repetition or rote memory is slow and does not make use of what knowledge we already have. Learning may be hindered by our emotional or sensory response to experiences of the past with the sterile and lifeless, if not intimidating, environment of the standard lecture hall or similar passive learning environments. We remember best when we are active participants in the learning process and when we can relate new information to a construct we have already established in our long-term memory.

Medical educators should look for more engaging and memorable alternatives to teaching than the standard classroom lecture or PowerPoint presentation. We also need to provide students with a framework that will allow them to create an organized, coherent framework for the information they are presented with. Having such a tool makes it easier to draw upon whenever information is needed to study for an examination, analyze a clinical problem, or add to their knowledge base. It also helps our decision-making.

Learning techniques that engage the whole brain, the right and left hemispheres, and as many of the senses as possible are the most efficient waysof processing, sorting and storing new information. Mind-mapping engages the whole brain to include the right and left hemispheres as well as our most important sense—our vision. Mind-mapping is, perhaps, the most efficient way of processing, sorting and storing new information. Many creative thinking techniques are available and are taught in management and leadership courses where information gathering and creative thinking are necessary. We do not teach these skills to medical students or residents, but learning how to think more creatively is just as important for medical practice as it is in business, management, systems analysis, organizational development, strategic planning, and any number of situations where complex problems need to be analyzed and solved.

Numerous systems for organizing and managing information, or for thinking out loud, or for thinking on paper have been developed. Individuals learn differently, and medical educators assume that every student, by the time he or she enters medical school, has a good approach to learning new information. Unfortunately, even the best undergraduate student may have a very difficult time adjusting to the pace and volume of information presented in medical school. Medical school is not graduate school, and medical school is not a continuation of undergraduate basic science courses. Medical school is hard not because the concepts are overwhelmingly abstract or inaccessible but because information is frequently not presented in a coherent and logical way. This is not to condemn medical educators or the process; it is an observation on the frustration that both the teacher and student must deal with as they go about the task of imparting or absorbing the massive body of knowledge, unrelated facts, data, terminology, and difficult concepts required to understand the human body in health and disease, much less to diagnose and manage patients. An excellent technique for capturing and organizing information is *mind-mapping*. Mind-mapping (also called concept-mapping) was developed in the 1970s by Tony Buzan to help students take lecture notes more effectively (Wycoff 1991).

The technique has several uses beyond note-taking. It can be used to develop a case conference on a blackboard with a small group of students or residents. It can be used to get ideas from a group that is brainstorming ideas to solve a problem, as a thinking tool to work through any problem where one needs to capture ideas or options, to capture ideas in preparation for a formal or informal talk, lecture notes, or a manuscript. Mind-mapping or concept-mapping is but one of many fun and useful tools to improve our thinking and stimulate our creativity. We are visual creatures and learn best by using our visual cortex as much as possible. A mind-map is a powerful tool to take advantage of that ability.

Mind-mapping is deceptively powerful and easily dismissed as too simple to be useful. Once learned, many find it the default or go-to tool for solving a problem or organizing their thoughts. The beauty of mind-mapping for students is that it creates a visually and easily remembered skeleton on which the information from any subject can be depicted for easy recall. Mind-mapping can be taught in a few minutes. There are numerous books and websites about mind-mapping, as well as sophisticated software programs that can be used to build mind-maps that have stunning detail and visual effects. (www.illumine.co.uk and https://blog.iqmatrix.com/how-tomind-map).

7.2 How to Mind-Map

Creating a mind-map or concept-map is an easy and informal process. The key to starting a mind-map is not to start with the end in mind but to keep one's mind open and start with simple or fundamental ideas. Structure can be added to a mind-map, and a mind-map can become very detailed and complex. A large topic can generate several mind-maps. Mind-mapping can be used in group settings with all members able to contribute to the creation of the end product. I personally use mind-mapping to approach many problems and have taught the concept to residents and students as a study aid and method to organize a talk or paper or make a decision, develop a treatment plan, or organize their work. (I have not formally studied the outcomes of residents who were taught mind-mapping, but residents who used this technique were able to improve their scores on annual in-service examinations by as much as 20 to 30 percent—a profound result that deserves further study.)

Developing a mind-map to address an active clinical problem is an excellent vehicle to teach small groups in a clinical situation. Several references are listed in the end notes for those who want a more in-depth treatment of mind-mapping. There are also excellent programs available for those who want to create mind-maps on their computer (Fig. 7.1).

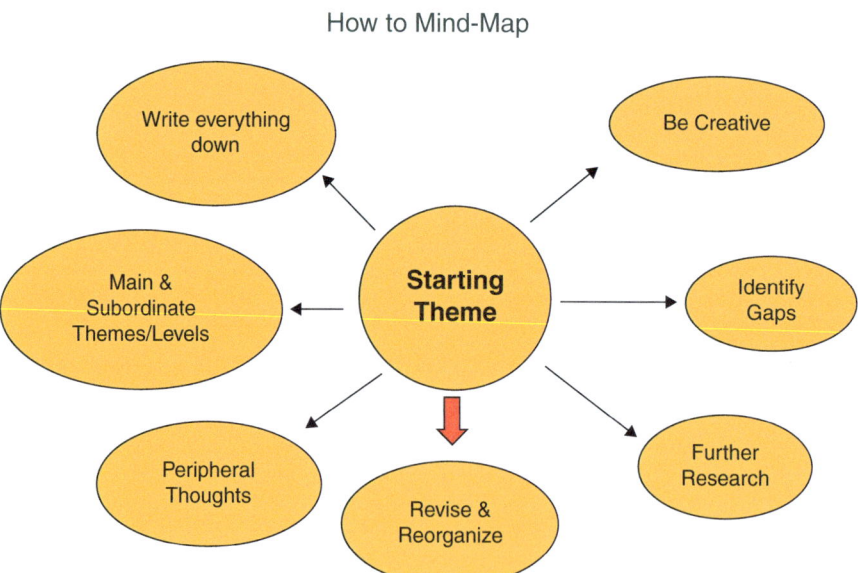

Fig. 7.1 A basic mind-map

Start with a Theme

To start a mind-map, first identify a central or basic theme from which you can develop your thinking. (See: https://wikihow.com/Make-a-Mind-Map). The theme should be one or two words and very generic. This allows your thinking to be very broad and allow generation of a maximum number of ideas. Suppose you are the attending in the medical intensive care unit and you want to discuss with your residents and students a patient that presented last night to the emergency department with a high fever and hypotension, and infected urine. You would want to start with a basic and generic theme such as urinary tract infections (UTIs) rather than a more specific diagnosis, even if you know your goal is to consider a more focused topic such as febrile UTIs. You can immediately proceed to thinking about febrile UTIs, but starting with a more generic topic keeps your mind open to all aspects of UTIs rather than prematurely focusing or omitting aspects of UTIs that may be relevant to the concept you want to develop. The starting theme may not be your final theme, and the mind-map you create may evolve into several interrelated mind-maps about UTIs as you develop your ideas. You may find it necessary to create other mind-maps to handle the information you generate (chronic UTIs presenting with a fever, UTIs with stones and fever, UTIs with fever in an ICU setting, and so on). Each of these secondary themes can be expanded at a later time into an informal or even formal learning setting (Fig. 7.2).

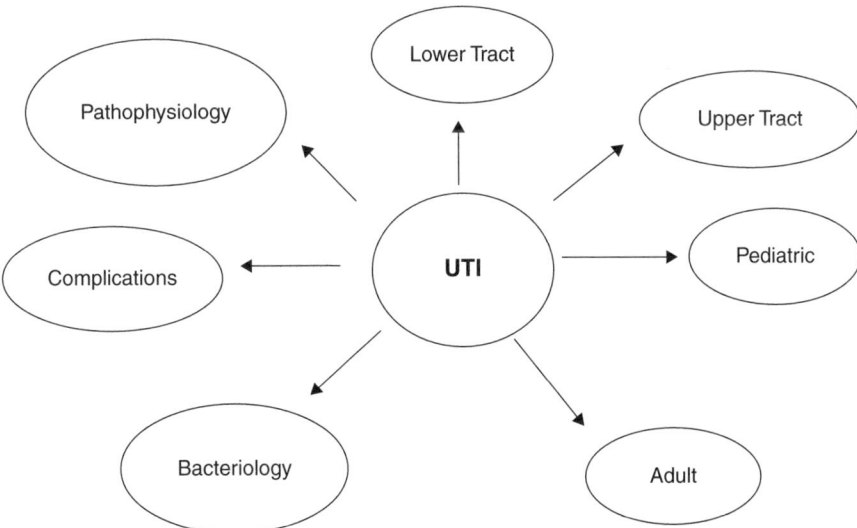

Fig. 7.2 Possible format for a mind-map about UTIs

Put Everything Down
Once the starting theme has been recorded, secondary themes should also be written down. These secondary themes could be discarded as the mind-map is developed or put aside and developed later. The key point here is to not limit the scope of one's thinking prematurely.

Be Creative
You are thinking on paper, so any device you can use to help stimulate your thinking may be helpful. You can add graphs, mnemonics, symbols, colors, different shapes, pictures, or drawings, anything that will make remembering the mind-map easier or stimulate your memory.

Capture Peripheral Ideas and Thoughts
Your mind-map may be created for a specific purpose, but you or members of your group will invariably think of closely related topics. Put those thoughts down rather than dismiss them at this stage. Any peripheral ideas may be deleted when you revise and reorganize the mind-map, but a peripheral thought may stimulate you to consider another related problem later or even develop a new mind-map. For example, using our UTI example, someone may bring up perinephric abscesses or papillary necrosis, topics you do not want to delve into now or are not pertinent to the patient you may be discussing but topics worthy of coming back to at another session to develop a separate mind-map.

Identify Main and Subordinate Themes
We started with a very generic theme and are now putting down secondary and even tertiary themes that relate to where we started. One of these secondary themes may become the pivotal or primary theme once you get all of the ideas down. For example, we started with UTI (primary theme), but, with further analysis, it may be obvious that the real topic is febrile UTIs (secondary theme) or febrile UTIs in the emergency department (tertiary theme). Addition of major branches and subordinate themes by any member should be encouraged when creating mind-maps in a conference or team environment. As each theme that more closely focuses on the problem at hand, the mind-map will become more purposeful and focused on a train of thought. The tertiary theme then becomes the primary theme, and the primary and secondary themes may become subordinate entries. The problem you want to discuss (febrile UTIs) becomes primary, and the fact that the patient has a history of UTIs is a secondary theme. The fact the patient is now in the ICU becomes a subordinate theme you can use to discuss issues such as when admission of a patient with a febrile UTI is necessary and when an ICU admission may be required, as in this patient who had hypotension. You are now putting this patient's problem into the greater context of the presenting problems of UTI and fever.

Identify Knowledge Gaps
The mind-map graphically identifies weaknesses in one's knowledge base, showing areas where further reading, study, or attention is needed. For example, it may become evident from the discussion that the students do not understand the clinical manifestations of upper versus lower tract infections—a knowledge gap that the

leader could address as a part of the discussion or the students could be assigned as a topic for library or Internet research in the form of a short presentation or for discussion the next time the team meets. This approach is a win for everyone in terms of increasing knowledge and providing a visual or graphic image that they will easily be able to remember.

Identify Areas for Further Research
Look for subjects to develop into a lecture, case presentation, or even a formal research project. A mind-map can be as simple or as complex as one needs. The sub-topics can be changed or more added as needed. The sub-topics can be further refined into sub-sub-topics or sub-sub-sub-topics as one's information base expands and deepens. The patient we are considering may require surgical intervention and that outcome could easily become the subject of a grand rounds presentation on when severe UTIs require surgical intervention. The mind-map provides the initial outline and focused thinking necessary for such a project. The inertia required to start such a project has already been overcome by putting the scattered thoughts and ideas of the group into visual form.

Review, Reorganize, Revise, Redraw
Once the initial map has been completed, it may be appropriate to reorganize and prioritize the themes that have been recorded. At this time, key words can be reorganized, clustered, and juxtaposed to help provoke new ideas and discover missing elements or find better ideas (Fig. 7.3).

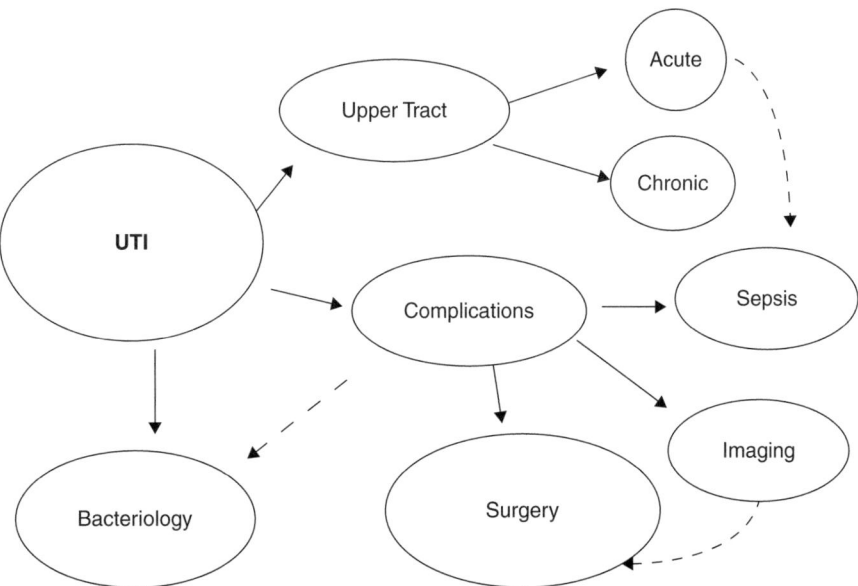

Fig. 7.3 Urinary tract infections in the ICU

7.3 Clinical Application

The internal medicine resident might wish to expand her knowledge of UTIs in the ICU environment in preparation for a rotation there. This expanded mind-map could then serve as a road map to management of patients in intensive care situations and fill in information gaps for problems she is likely to see there.

The pediatric resident might want to develop a mind-map that addresses the areas she needs to learn to pass her pediatric boards or deal with patients admitted with a urinary tract infection. That mind-map might look like Fig. 7.4. The urology resident who is asked to give a quick lecture on pediatric urinary tract infections to medical students rotating on pediatrics might develop a similar mind-map to identify the major points she wants to make to the pediatric service. She can pick the sub-topics she feels are most relevant and expand them quickly and easily using the mind-map to help organize the knowledge she already has. This process will also identify areas where she might need to do some reading before the talk.

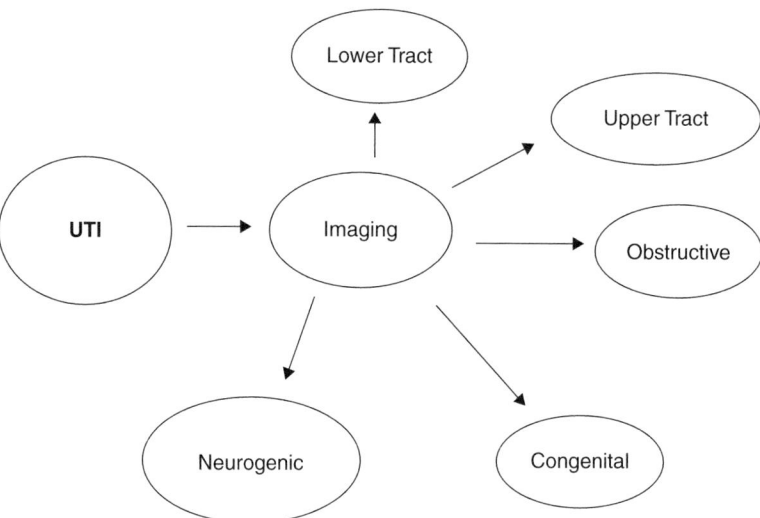

Fig. 7.4 Pediatric UTIs

7.3 Clinical Application

Let us look at another way of using mind-maps. Mr. Smith presents to the emergency department with shaking chills. He is 76 years old and has been admitted before. In addition to a fever, he also appears somewhat confused. He is admitted to Dr. Kelly's service for evaluation and treatment. Kathy is the senior medical resident on Dr. Kelly's service, and after Mr. Smith has been admitted and examined by Bill, the intern on the team, Kathy, gathers her teams which include two medical students into a conference room on the ward and has Bill present his findings. As Bill presents Mr. Smith's history, Kathy uses the blackboard to develop a mind-map that captures all of the pertinent data. That mind-map, depicted in Fig. 7.5, is then used to discuss the information necessary to think about the management of an elderly man with fever.

The team can add to the mind-map as information is gathered and start to think about possible diagnoses. More importantly, they can now organize their efforts and develop their initial plan for Mr. Smith's care. That plan might look like Fig. 7.6.

Kathy, the chief resident, can now start to prioritize what the next steps in Mr. Smith's management are and assign tasks for each team member. A major concern might be whether Mr. Smith's mental status changes are new, so Fred, one of the

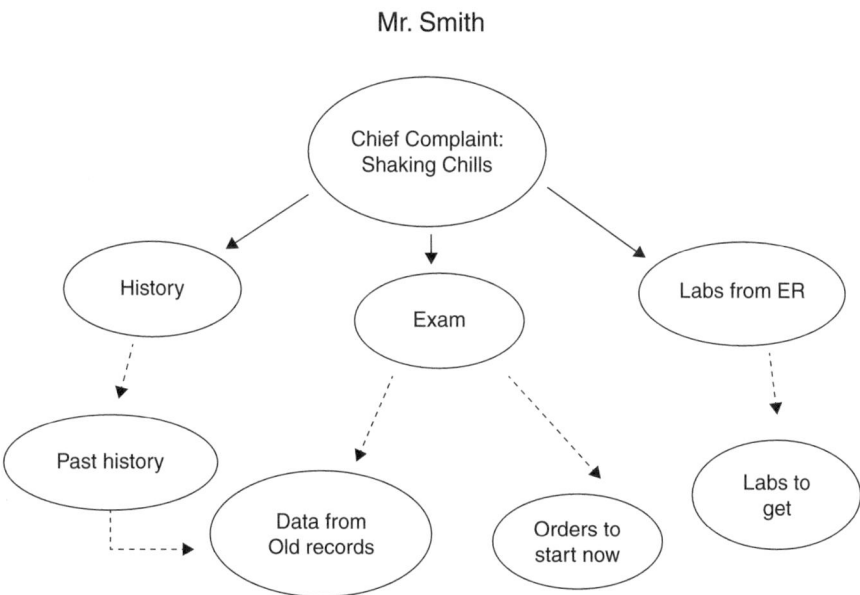

Fig. 7.5 Mr. Smith's initial evaluation and management

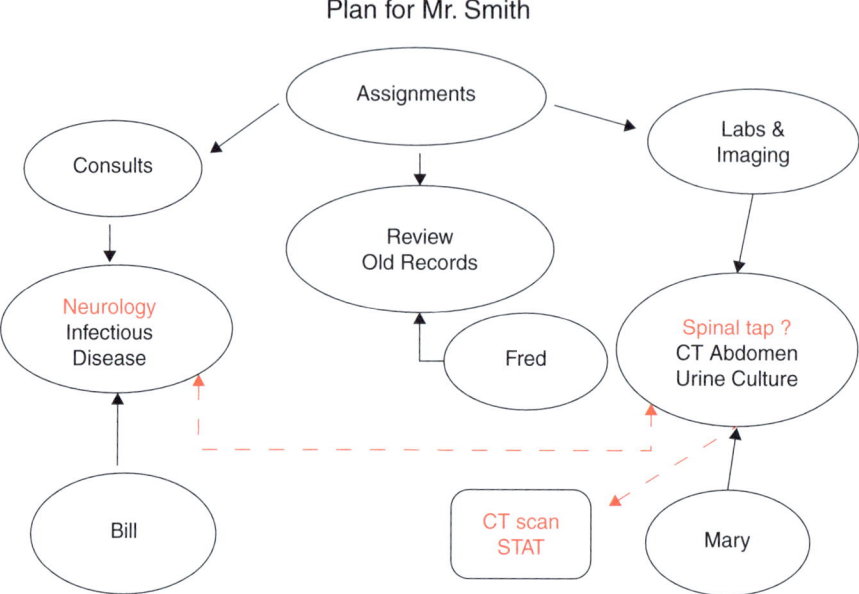

Fig. 7.6 Plan and team assignments

third-year medical students, is tasked with looking up the information available from prior admissions to help answer that question. Kathy is concerned that the mental status changes and fevers may be related and needs to consider if a spinal tap is indicated. Before making that decision, however, she wants to obtain a neurology consult. She tasks Bill, a first-year resident, with that assignment, contacting the services she feels are needed to placing a high priority on talking with the neurology service. Mr. Smith has some abdominal discomfort and has been too uncooperative to examine well. She also decides that an emergency CAT (computerized axial tomography) scan of the abdomen is necessary along with other initial laboratory testing and assigns Mary, the other medical student available, to make those arrangements. These maps can also be used when the team presents Mr. Smith's case to the attending physician, Dr. Kelly. Dr. Kelly can then use the maps to guide any teaching points he wants to make or show where the decision-making by the team was noteworthy, inefficient, or ill-advised.

This process may seem to be a lot of work or pointing out the obvious. Experienced clinicians may intuitively think this way and have no need for resorting to a visual representation of how to manage a patient like Mr. Smith. Students and residents, however, do benefit from thinking out loud in a group and seeing how a clinical problem can be approached and how the management and decision-making are organized. It shows the attending that his residents are thinking clearly and logically and gives them a framework from which to work when they are presenting the case of Mr. Smith. The team leader can now see where information gaps or lapses in

7.3 Clinical Application

management occurred, pick up on that problem, and tailor their guidance accordingly. Students benefit from the exercise as they can develop a personalized mind-map, tailored to their needs, such as in Fig. 7.7. This mind-map can show where they need further study and how they can approach the problem the next time they see a patient with similar problems.

Mind-maps establish a visual image of the facts we would like to remember. Keeping the topics limited to a number our brains can easily deal with allows us to create an image we can easily recall and use to fill in the circles on the map. For more detailed information on a specific aspect of the main topic, we need to create a separate map with the second-order information. The degree of detail we are able to capture on maps is virtually limitless as we dig deeper into subsets of information on the main topic.

The internet is a good resource for finding other thinking tools as well as organizations that promote creative and advanced thinking skills.

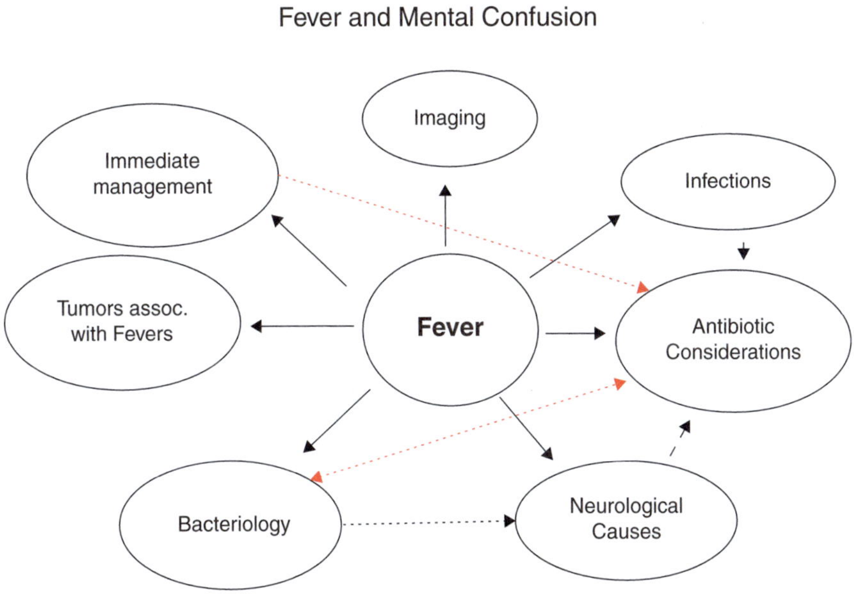

Fever and Mental Confusion

Fig. 7.7 Mind-map for evaluation of elderly patient with fever and confusion

Chapter 8
The Processes of Decision-Making and Problem-Solving

Summary
The good decision-maker must be able to define the elements inherent in a particular situation to include identifying the real problem as well as what aspects are not immediately apparent. Other factors include, but are not limited to, identifying major or critical variables and comparing the present situation with one's experience with past similar problems. Addressing each of these elements in a systematic manner is a critical part of utilizing the decision-making cycle presented earlier to its maximum effectiveness. The practice of medicine is filled with risk and uncertainty—elements that physicians do not relish. Achieving the optimal outcome for the patient is not always possible, and assuming risk is unavoidable but is part of being a busy clinician subject to distractions and constraints on our time and concentration beyond the problem at hand. Considering only the scientific and technical aspects of any clinical problem is not adequate. The humanistic elements ethics, family dynamics, patient desires, and expectations must be balanced and tempered with our technical knowledge, skills, and judgment. The kaleidoscope model presented here integrates these elements visually and can be used as an aid when seeking the optimal decision or discussing the outcome of a decision in a forum or teaching situation.

8.1 The Elements of Problem-Solving

After having considered the softer and often more subtle and unspoken elements of analyzing a problem, let us now focus on the more quantitative and readily identified facets of the decision-making process, those factors that more easily lend themselves to being enumerated or outlined as steps to be followed in a more or less rigid or fixed fashion. Every decision, from the simple to the complex, requires that we consider the components listed in the sidebar.

Activation of these components is heavily influenced by our *intuition*, a critical component of decision-making for the experienced decision-maker. (See Chap. 10 for a discussion of the role of intuition in decision-making.) In such situations, our intuition provides a barometer or sense of what the problem is, the urgency of the problem, what additional data or knowledge must be obtained. All of these elements provide an initial formulation of priorities and resources that will be required. These aspects are not considered sequentially or in an ordered fashion but flood our consciousness as we grapple with a problem. We do not deliberately review our experience or knowledge base unless the problem demands an orderly, analytical approach.

The novice decision-maker, or the individual faced with a problem that requires a great deal of reflection, are not served well by the intuitive, less structured approach. In such situations, the decision-maker may be faced with the need to analyze a large amount of data or multiple issues. These situations require breaking the problem down into several steps and explore each facet in an orderly and thorough fashion.

This structured approach is an excellent way to teach problem-solving, allowing the learner to assess the available data, review their experience, identify gaps in knowledge, and examine the need for further information gathering and identification of goals and desired outcomes in a more logical manner.

The sidebar provides a list of the steps one may take in solving a problem. This list is analogous to, but more detailed than, the previously presented circular or GPS-RADAR concept.

Sidebar: The Elements of Problem-Solving
1. Identify, define or describe the problem(s) according to the patient history and examination.
2. Ask— what is the real problem–it may not be obvious.
3. Identify the accompanying and relevant variables.
4. Recall analogies or similar problems encountered in the past.
5. Recall stored knowledge in the form of pertinent technical or subject-matter expertise, observations, or experiences.
6. Evaluate the validity or relevance of the various elements, data, or findings.
7. Identify the desired outcome(s).
8. Apply of observations or knowledge using inferences or comparison of options based on previous outcomes.
9. Describe potential solutions.
10. Evaluate the advantages and disadvantages of each potential solution.
11. Determine the best solution.

8.2 Identifying the Problem

As mundane and as obvious as it may sound, we are frequently led astray in our thinking by our tendency to jump to a diagnosis or definition of the problem prematurely. This is natural. We want to fix problems. It is the analogy of the hammer and the nail. When we see a problem that looks like a nail, we know we have a hammer

8.2 Identifying the Problem

in our toolkit and are quick to use it. It is easy to focus on a presenting problem or chief complaint. It is easy to make a diagnosis and immediately apply our knowledge and skill to fixing that problem without consideration of what may be more serious but less obvious issues or patient concerns. We have all seen situations where a patient with a non-specific complaint such as shortness of breath would be triaged for medical care, only to discover that the cause of the chief complaint was a gunshot wound.

I recall a patient I cared for as a senior resident who had advanced bladder cancer. He was an otherwise healthy and vibrant gentleman who was a retired minister living in Ashland, Oregon, the home of an annual Shakespeare Festival. His love was going to the festival and watching the plays held every summer in the parks of Ashland. His other passion was fishing with his two young grandsons. He presented with anemia due to severe, gross hematuria, and also intractable urinary frequency and painful urination. He was miserable, and his disease too advanced to cure by surgery alone. This was in the early days of chemotherapy, and he was not willing to go through with treatments that would leave him further debilitated and weakened with little prospect of prolonging his life in a meaningful way. All he wanted was a good summer to see his plays and spend time with his grandkids. After being given options for treatment, he chose to have his urine diverted into an ileal conduit, a safe, relatively simple operation that would relieve his symptoms and allow him to sit through a play or go to the stream. We could also instill formalin into the bladder under anesthesia in an attempt to stop or minimize the bleeding. He had his surgery and was out of the hospital quickly and back to Oregon. I last saw him that autumn when he was admitted for terminal care, thoroughly content with his decision and grateful for the quality of life he had that Summer.

Focusing on the medical or surgical treatment might have produced an outcome that would have denied this gentleman what was really important—pursuit of his passions. Aggressive treatment would probably have deprived him of the activities that were meaningful to him in the time he had left.

How you define or perceive a problem determines how you solve it. A term for this precept is *framing*. We usually think of the problem as the chief complaint or, later, the primary diagnosis, and move forward in a directed and focused way. We need to be careful with this process, as tunnel vision created by honing in prematurely on a specific solution may limit our thinking, resulting in our being blinded to the correct diagnosis or what the patients primary concern might be. Our first impressions may be wrong. For that reason, physicians must be ever on guard that their decisions and recommendations are always evolving and a work in progress. Formulating a diagnosis and treatment plan is always a retrospective, iterative and circular process.

We learn early in medical school to begin our interaction with the chief complaint—what brings you here today? or, how can I help you today? The patient may be having headaches, losing weight, or having trouble with heartburn. We are then taught to have the patient relate, in his or her words, if possible, a narrative of their symptoms and the history of their present problem. This information usually is translated into a statement we can write down in a few words such as—Mrs. Jones presents today with complaints of headaches for the past 2 weeks. We have established 'the problem,' and, off we go, chasing headaches. The chief complaint may be obvious and not need much elaboration like the patient presenting with a superficial laceration that needs cleansing and sutures. Unfortunately, focusing on the problem too early and closing one's mind off to other possibilities or viewpoints can lead us down the wrong path.

The history begins with letting the patient explain his or her assessment or description of the problem, interrupting only to get clarification of a point. The questions asked are open-ended, inviting the patient to reveal as much detail and personal observations as possible. After only a few minutes of allowing the patient to speak in this undirected and narrative fashion, the clinician has usually settled in one or two diagnoses that are most probable.

As the interview proceeds the nature of the questions change to very pointed and directed inquiries as the clinician tries to fill in the gaps with the small details that will hopefully complete the picture of the patient's problem. Here the clinician is asking key questions to help him exclude certain diagnoses or possibilities, and a simple yes or no is sufficient to tick off certain diagnoses or direct the trail of inquiry down one path or another.

What started out as questions such as—What can I do for you? or What kind of trouble brings you in today? shifts to very specific inquiries—Do you smoke? or Have you traveled out of the country in the past 3 months? or Is anyone at home sick like you are?

This way of gathering information is analogous to the submarine movie where the battleship hunting the submarine uses sonar to find the enemy submarine. As the battleship gets closer the "pings" get louder until the submarine is finally pinpointed. Such questioning requires intuition and pattern recognition on the part of the clinician, just like the grizzled submarine commander who is trying to outwit his foe. Sometimes the pings are in response to responses the patient has given, and sometimes the pings are random in an attempt to find hidden clues or resolve suspicions or fill in details. This type of questioning is particularly evident when we take a review of systems. Questions there will become precise and directed if a positive response is elicited or if the information is critical to management decisions. The surgeon who is considering surgery for a patient's problem will ask very general questions about one's neurological history but may ask pointed questions about one's cardiac or respiratory status. The specialist will, within his or her area of expertise, ask fewer questions than the non-specialist to get the critical information. The trick is to avoid narrowing one's diagnosis too early and risk overlooking a significant co-morbidity or anomaly.

Although it may take time to identify the problem, we must always ask ourselves— what is really the problem here? It is not enough to make a diagnosis, even a correct one, if that decision does not fulfill the needs of the patient and his or her family. The problem or problems may ultimately be non-medical. Doing the right thing from a medical standpoint may not be the right answer for the patient seated before you. Making a decision in such a situation may be an iterative process, one in which the ideal solution may need to be negotiated or made, not by the physician, but the patient.

8.3 Out with the Old and in with the New

Clinicians are inherently conservative. They are interested in new developments or new research findings, but are pragmatic when considering new techniques or drugs, or accepting possibly unsubstantiated theories. Clinicians do not want to be the first to use a new technique or treatment, nor do they want to be the last. An advance must be considered by the individual clinician in the context of their daily practice. Does this new data make sense in terms of my experience, or is it just another journal article? Much of what is published under the guise of scientific research is intuitively obvious, if not the common-sense of an experienced clinician. Would my current practice or outcomes benefit from a new addition or approach? Is incorporating this new approach into my practice worth the risk to my patients and to me if what I am doing now is working well? Information that is preliminary or advances in the basic sciences is of little value to the practicing clinician other than intellectual interest—it rarely will affect clinical practice immediately or even in the near future, and by that time, the impact of the information will certainly change from the initial predictions.

New basic science information or therapeutic breakthroughs are handled somewhat differently in the world of academic medicine. New findings may directly impact ongoing or planned research. Such information is often the coin of the realm, and important to be aware of and discuss with trainees who are expected to be aware of the latest research in their specialty. Such information can make or break a career in academic medicine if you can be the first to capitalize on it.

In the non-academic world, implementation of new technology or new approaches may result in the clinician being branded as foolhardy or cavalier if the early promises of a breakthrough produce more disasters and complications than cures. An example of this in urology was the introduction of cryotherapy for treatment of prostatic obstruction. Freezing the enlarged prostate could ostensibly be done in a minimally invasive way that did not require the time or expertise involved in standard transurethral resection of the prostate. It also promised an approach for management of prostate cancer in the patient who was a poor candidate for major surgery, and would avoid the risks, time and expense of radiation. The device was not expensive and many looked at this approach as a bonanza for their practice and jumped on the cryotherapy bandwagon. Then the complications started piling up. The procedure was nothing short of disastrous.

Most problem-solving is accomplished without any conscious attempt to break down the problem into the steps enumerated above. Argumentation, rhetoric and logic are well-developed disciplines that are concerned with using these elements to determine the best solution for a problem or to test the validity of an argument, but medical decisions rarely involve a formal assessment as described above, nor are most medical decisions made with conscious consideration of these elements. Many of the variables are considered on a subconscious, rather than in a deliberate, analytical, or methodical, way.

8.4 Risk and Uncertainty

We deal with risk and uncertainty every day. Medicine is a risky profession, and we ask a lot of our patients when they put their trust in our hands. A mentor used to tell me *there are no brave surgeons, just brave patients*. Both risk and uncertainty are unavoidable, but there are major differences between risk and uncertainty. Risk and uncertainty are a part of the decision-making equation, and it is important to distinguish between the two.

Physicians and patients accept that there is risk associated with any intervention or decision, even though the risks may be formidable. For most conditions, the risks have been identified and the probability of those complications defined. We know, from published data and our own personal experience, the risks from a particular procedure or therapy. Such data is usually bounded in that the risks can be quantified allowing both the patient and the physician to make decisions in an analytical and informed manner. Most physicians and patients feel comfortable with this approach and are able to make a decision with confidence even if the risks are high. Patients understand this and accept risks as a part of medicine and of life.

What patients and physicians really do not like is uncertainty. Uncertainty is an entirely different matter. Uncertainty is also a part of medicine, and both physicians and patients are more uncomfortable with uncertainty than risk. Uncertainty is unbounded. Uncertainty cannot easily be articulated or quantified. Uncertainty makes decision-making more difficult for both the physician and the patient. Being asked to make a decision in a situation with uncertainties or unknowns creates an entirely different dilemma, both for the patient and the physician.

These observations may be obvious, but it is worth pausing and thinking about the differences between risk and uncertainty as we go about decision-making, counselling, and making arguments rational and coherent. We should remain humble and honest about the risks and uncertainties to which we expose our patients and outspeak about our efforts to minimize those factors in our practice. Risk cannot be avoided but with effort can be minimized. Uncertainty is a more formidable enemy (Evans and Trotter 2009).

Recognizing the difference is a part of our duties to provide informed consent and objectively review and improve our practice (Fig. 8.1).

Fig. 8.1 The decision-making dilemma

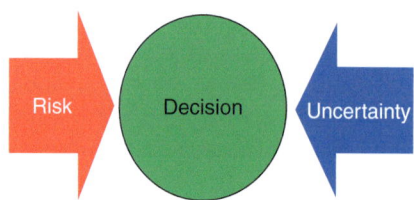

8.5 Multitasking: The Shadow Side of Decision-Making

Medical problems do not always provide the luxury of contemplation. In a medical emergency, a decision must be made, and a diagnostic and therapeutic approach must be developed if the patient is to have a successful outcome. The physician is faced with problem after problem in the course of a normal workday. She does not have the time or the mental or emotional energy to deliberate or agonize over each decision. Decisions are made and executed, and the physician must move onto the next patient. The world of the physician is not like the chess player who sits across from an opponent and waits for the opponent's next move and then has the luxury of thinking how best to respond. The physician's day is more analogous to the chess master who plays a dozen or more games simultaneously.

Multitasking can lead to poor decisions. We cannot focus on more than one task at a time. The physician who cannot successfully manage this degree of multitasking and takes each problem individually leads to frustration, burnout, or worse. Certainly, multitasking is not a good environment for decision-making and is not an environment for making certain decisions or contemplating certain problems. Unfortunately, multitasking is the reality of medical practice, but we must always be on guard against such intrusions into our decision-making and maintain the focus and presence necessary to serve our patients in the manner which we would want for ourselves whenever making decisions.

8.6 The Kaleidoscope Model

How does one integrate the distinct, yet overlapping, concerns between judgment, knowledge, expertise, ethics, and humanism as we approach decision-making? No model that relies on artificial intelligence such as mathematical formulas or computer programs can integrate these aspects into the decision-making matrix. No two patients have the same mix of medical, ethical, social, or family concerns. I propose a simple model to show how these concerns overlap and change in relation to one another as we consider the needs of each patient or situation. This model uses the image of the kaleidoscope, which, depending on how one rotates the wheel containing the fragments of glass of different colors and shapes, produces an unlimited number of images for the viewer.

This model gives us a simple, easily visualized way of reducing these variables into a manageable approach that can be used to teach and discuss the humanistic, ethical, and practical aspects of making a clinical decision. Like mind-mapping, the kaleidoscope model can also be applied to management or systems-based decisions. Consideration of the ethical and social components of issues that are broader in scope is critical in today's medical and social climate where patients have access to more health-care information and demand greater input and participation in health-care decisions (Fig. 8.2).

Fig. 8.2 The kaleidoscope model of decision-making

Medical decision-making involves considering variables in widely different, but for patients and physicians, related domains. They are the concerns of the physician or surgeon, and all of the nuances, subtleties, and finer points of medical practice are contained in these four circles of responsibility. These domains are represented on the diagram which looks like a kaleidoscope. It is expected that the good physician will have the appropriate degree of *knowledge* and *technical skills* to manage the problem he or she is faced with. Those domains can be considered as bounded or quantifiable.

The other two domains are *professionalism* and *judgment*, areas that are qualitative or unbounded. For this reason, especially complicated and complex problems are generally unbounded, and, although it may be possible to measure outcomes for these patients, the skills we designate as belonging to the art of medicine cannot. This is a serious limitation of statistical analyses or rigid recommendations from outcome studies or even evidence-based medicine.

The kaleidoscope model places quality at the center of medical care and, by extension, at the center of decision-making. This model is unique from most approaches to measuring quality as it ensures not only the analytical but also consideration of our moral and ethical responsibilities.

In the diagram, the circles overlap and are equal in size. Each decision is unique, however, meaning that the circles are not fixed in size but, like a kaleidoscope, the configuration, size, and intensity of each sphere change as the decision-maker focuses on the unique elements of each individual clinical situation. Every participant in the process may have a different degree of involvement and a different vision of what quality should look like, but none of the participants can ignore the concerns and constraints of those in other spheres. The focus may be simple and crisp for most decisions, but, with problems of increasing complexity, problems that require addi-

8.6 The Kaleidoscope Model

tional personal or resources, social, technical, and ethical considerations may demand dramatic alteration of each sphere. These four disciplines can be represented as a Venn diagram, placing each discipline in a sphere and considering the degree of overlap for them as shown in the diagram. Even if a physician has the requisite technical skill and knowledge, some decisions or options offered require alternate or even unconventional solutions. This is especially true in severely compromised or terminally ill patients or situations in which there are overriding ethical considerations. In these situations, judgment and professionalism become paramount.

The model is actually quite simple. Quality is at the middle in the context of the majority of decisions involving patient care. The kaleidoscope can be refocused to fit the parameters of a specific case, but no circle can be overlooked. Quality may lean more towards cost containment or efficiency of health-care delivery. In another situation, quality of an outcome may be more driven by the skill of the caregivers. The scope of consideration within each circle can certainly be expanded or changed to meet the needs of a particular situation. The skills circle, for example, may need to consider the risks and benefits of acquiring or applying new technology, the level of support and expertise within a given institution, or the training and experience of the involved staff. The hospital staff may include surgeons highly skilled in surgery for complex cancer problems, but if the hospital does not have adequate intensive care or blood bank support, the level of knowledge and skill present should be superseded by the considerations in the circles of judgment and professionalism.

A procedure performed with the utmost of skill and technical expertise may not meet the definition of quality if any one of the circles is ignored or minimized. Likewise, a plan that fails to address any technical limitations in an institution cannot be considered as having quality no matter how much attention is given to the other circles. Decisions incorporating each circle of concern are made intuitively by experienced clinicians and well-organized teams, but the considerations in such situations may not be apparent to the student, resident, or even a junior staff physician.

The kaleidoscope model is useful for making decisions in the classroom and the boardroom. For some decisions, quality does not need to be at the center of the model. For decisions in an organization or clinic, it may be necessary to substitute other goals such as market share, new construction, personnel reorganization, and so forth. Having a clear concept of what represents quality and keeping that concept in the center of the matrix are never inappropriate. Hopefully, visualizing the elements of making a caring decision within overlapping, omnipresent, yet ever-changing factors can help both the novice and experienced decision-makers insure that a complex decision was made with equipoise and balance.

The kaleidoscope model can also be used to examine health care from the perspective of the individual provider, an institution or clinic, or a health-care system by focusing these circles on the subject of interest.

Chapter 9
Towards a Unified Approach

Summary
No decision-making process can ever consider all of the information or data it is possible to gather about a given situation. There will always be a level of uncertainty or information gap. These variables can be displayed graphically to define what can be called a decision threshold—the point in the process when one moves from gathering and analyzing information to committing to a course of action. This point will be different for each individual depending on one's experience, training, knowledge, and level of comfort with uncertainty and risk. The decision threshold will change with experience. We learn to search for information in a logical and organized fashion as we gain experience. Researchers in the field of decision-making have identified systems and strategies that can be used to aid in making a decision to include tally systems, strategy selection, and information hierarchy models. These models can be cognitive or formulaic. These models reinforce the concept that decision-making is a continuum and cyclic and not a one-time process or isolated event.

9.1 Approaches to Decision-Making

Concepts such as optimizing, bounded and unbounded problems, and the difference between simple, complex, and complicated problems are ways of looking at problems. Induction and deduction are approaches to reasoning. The decision-making cycle presented earlier gives us a way of evaluating a problem in an organized or methodical way, but we have still not addressed the fundamental problem of making a decision. These approaches serve as a preamble to the fundamental purpose of this book—how do we make decisions? Those who have hoped for a quick recipe or a formula may, so far, be disappointed, and some may find their patience wearing thin, wondering if the definitive or reassuring answer will ever be given.

There is no one simple or universal approach to decision-making in medicine, but I believe there are only a few practical and clinically useful approaches.

This chapter will attempt to put the many observations and definitions listed so far into a context that will, hopefully, provide a simple, rational answer to the question of just how we make decisions.

Approaches to decision-making in different domains or professions, to include the different specialties of medicine, are not very different. Even though medicine is a field that is grounded in science and one that requires a thorough understanding of scientific and research methodology, the physician is ultimately faced with the dilemma of translating science into a practical solution that includes a compassionate consideration of the patient.

Models, flow charts, diagrams, algorithms, or complex mathematical formulas can be used to make decisions. These approaches, while useful in some situations, have limitations, as the premise underlying a formal model or the models created to explain a particular problem or process may be flawed or incomplete. Premises taken for granted may be too limited, assumed causalities may not be present, and modulators are difficult to factor. This is especially true when we incorporate deeply entrenched beliefs into the decision-making process. Formulaic approaches alone do not provide the insight necessary to understand the fundamentals of how to arrive at the optimal decision.

In medical practice, most decisions are made without the benefit of formal conferences, models, or formal analysis. We rely heavily on intuition, judgment, and experience, but there is still a need to be able to recognize and explain the rationale for such approaches.

In the training environment, clinical events are the primary vehicle used to impart the skills of decision-making. These interactions range from informal discussions between patient visits or discussions in the lounge between surgical procedures to formal settings such as morbidity and mortality conferences, preoperative case conferences, or grand rounds. Conferences are at the heart of how we teach clinical decision-making. These discussions rarely consider the actual steps taken to make a given decision or whether the approach was appropriate or could be improved. Conferences, informal or formal, are most often focused on teaching facts or principles, analysis of data or findings, or critique of approaches or outcomes. To teach decision-making, we need to focus less on outcomes and more on process. Many industries and organizations to include aviation, nuclear power plants, primary responders, and the military accomplish this objective with after-action critiques that focus on process improvement rather than the results of missions.

9.2 Decision-Making Strategies: A Conceptual Model

Uncertainty is a large part of the physician's world. We rarely have all the information it is possible to gather or information we would like. Information is also not always accurate or complete, but we still have to make decisions. If we have no

9.2 Decision-Making Strategies: A Conceptual Model

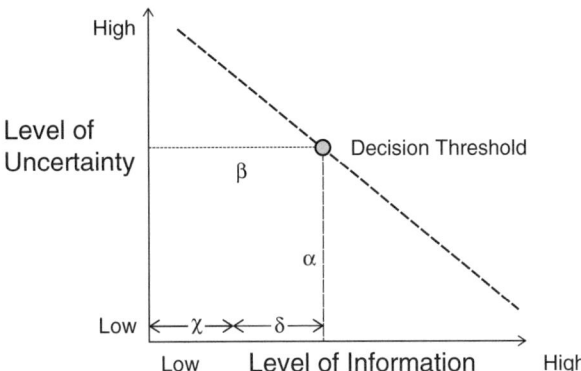

Fig. 9.1 A conceptual model for decision-making

information, our reluctance to make a decision should be high, and the judicious person would consider it foolhardy to even consider making a decision. It is much easier to make a decision if we have all of the information possible, a situation that is rarely practical or possible.

The model shown in Fig. 9.1 demonstrates this concept. Decisions are fundamentally the convergence of the knowledge needed or desired and the level of risk or uncertainty involved in making that decision. The level of information available (represented by χ) plus the additional information needed (represented by δ) establishes the level of information desired (β). If the level of information is adequate to offset the degree of risk or uncertainty (α), the intersection of these two variables—the *decision point*— is the point where one can reasonably and comfortably make a decision. The additional information needed can be called the *information gap* (δ). The size of the information gap is dependent both on quality and quantity of information desired and the experience of the decision-maker. A novice clinician will feel comfortable only with a greater amount of additional information, while the experienced clinician will want limited, specific, or focused bits of information.

Reducing the information gap may require more testing or data, procurement of additional consultations, an increased fund of knowledge, or greater experience. A large information gap creates more patient discomfort due to testing and invasive procedures, is more expensive, and takes more time. We will never have 100 per cent of the information possible yet must learn when enough is enough— a skill developed only with experience and thoughtful application of knowledge. Having a larger knowledge base, by itself, does not reduce the information gap or improve the decision threshold— it may even prolong the interval between gathering of information and being able to reach a good decision. The information gap is not quantitative; rather, it is qualitative— the experienced clinician knows what information is critical, and he/she knows what bits of data will truly make a difference in terms of being able to make a decision and what bits of information, if missing, must be obtained.

9.3 The Decision Threshold

Experienced physicians and surgeons handle this concept easily. They have developed the skill, sense of their abilities and limitations, and judgment necessary to assess a problem and determine the risks and benefits of intervention. We all know of the professor who can listen to a case presentation, go into the examination room, and ask one or two pointed questions that provide that one bit of information that sheds light on the diagnosis. This is the master detective at work, what Sherlock Holmes would do to solve a case that has everyone else baffled. Experienced physicians have a finely tuned sense of the information gap.

Another way of looking at this skill is the *decision threshold* graph in Fig. 9.2. This graph depicts the relationship between the data required by the decision-maker, as represented by the horizontal or x-axis, and the perceived degree of risk or uncertainty involved in making the decision, as represented by the vertical or y-axis. The point where these two variables intersect is the decision threshold. An inexperienced clinician will feel less certain in the accuracy of their decision and will require more information before making a decision. For the clinician with well-developed skills, the decision threshold is shifted downwards and to the left—he or she need less information than the novice and is more confident in their decision-making.

Having the information required to make an accurate diagnosis does not exempt decision-makers from acquiring the additional information necessary to exclude a potentially life-threatening problem or considering potential complications unrelated to the primary diagnosis or proposes intervention that could have untoward consequences. Examples of the need for additional information might include insuring that a woman is not pregnant before she undergoes surgery, or excluding the presence of a consumptive coagulopathy in a patient with a severe infection and no obvious hematologic disorders.

With experience, one progresses slowly down the curve. For the novice, the upper portion of the curve is flat as their knowledge slowly accumulates. As the

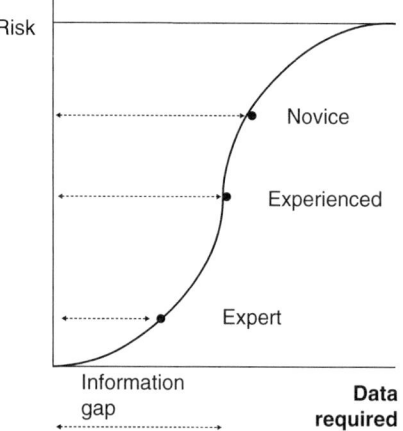

Fig. 9.2 The decision threshold

novice develops the knowledge to function effectively in that domain, the curve becomes steeper until competency is reached. Decision-making rapidly becomes more and more comfortable. Having the knowledge or experience to graduate from a training program or pass a certifying examination does not confer mastery—only the competency to work independently. Improvement beyond the level of competency may progress rapidly, but, as one develops a high degree of competency, the curve becomes flat. Even the expert will be shadowed by the specter of risk and uncertainty. The information gap never vanishes.

9.4 Decision Support Systems and Search Orders

Any method used to aid or organize the act of making a decision can be defined as a *decision support system*. Such systems can be formal or informal, simple or complex. Simple systems include pattern recognition, heuristics, and algorithms. More complex systems tend to be more analytical and dependent on extensive cognitive input or mathematical or computer-based resources. Simple systems are desirable for their efficiency, overall accuracy, and ease of use. All decision support systems rely on some form of a search order—an organized, logical, sequential, and orderly strategy used to evaluate the available data or cues. These steps have been defined as a *search order* (Dieckmann and Todd 2004). The efficient use of search orders requires clinical experience. The novice, even the novice with extensive knowledge, will not be able to formulate an effective search order efficiently and confidently. With experience, decision-makers become better at knowing which strategy is optimal for a given problem. We also learn from our mistakes, and we learn which variables to use or discard. With time, our decision-making becomes more accurate and more efficient (Rieskamp and Otto 2006; Rieskamp 2008).

We are taught to evaluate patients using a rigid order starting with chief complaint, history, past medical history, family history, review of symptoms, and so on. Such formal types of search orders not only help us focus our thinking but also prevent us from omitting crucial questions or steps. When we move past our initial assessment and start formulating a diagnosis or plan of management, we become highly selective in considering what variables, or pieces of the history, physical examination, or laboratory test results are important. It is now to the process of sifting through the information we have gathered in almost rote fashion that we now turn. Decision-making is, to a great degree, an exercise in considering and prioritizing information—we now look for what variables are critical and what are not, where we need more information, and where we can be comfortable with the data we have. The most basic or reflexive decision and also the most complex decision can be broken down into these steps. Every decision requires that we choose an appropriate strategy—a certain definable and demonstrable processes to guide us through making and implementing that decision.

We cannot properly weight more than a couple of cues, and those weights cannot be tallied in an additive fashion—we can only seek configurational or relative relationships between cues. *One cannot consider more than the number of cues that can be numbered on one hand without risking the creation of a poor decision or confounding the decision with information overload.*

Search orders follow a few basic rules. (Adapted from Dieckmann and Todd 2004).

- First, they assume that all options or pieces of cue information are not laid out all at once but that each option, step, or variable has to be considered one at a time.
- Search orders should consider the fewest number of variables necessary to make an accurate decision.
- Variables should initially be formatted in a qualitative fashion (a laboratory value, e.g., should be viewed as either present or absent) and only quantitatively (the degree of abnormality of a given variable) in the secondary or follow-on or refined analysis.
- The ranking or order of variables is dependent on the situation.
- Variables should be prioritized rather than weighted to simplify the search and minimize confusion or ambiguity.
- Search orders tend to be self-organizing. We do not consider variables in a random fashion but, often subconsciously, order the variables or cues in a logical or progressive order.
- The relative importance of the variables is not known before the search is initiated.

The experienced clinician can rapidly identify erroneous or nonproductive search orders—he or she can usually recognize when the decision-making process has taken the wrong path or when the chosen strategic approach is inappropriate. Good decision-makers recognize quickly when they are going down the wrong rabbit trail.

With experience, we are able to differentiate the usefulness of cues or variables. This is especially true when the number of cues is limited. This learning is, in part, dependent on the memory and computational requirements of those cues. Learning goes on in the context of decision-making without exhaustive review or search of the information. With experience our cumulative accuracy or ability to work with cues increases beyond heuristics which rely on minimal number of cues.

9.4.1 The Search Rule

Most clinical decisions are not made by proceeding through a formal model as one would when using an algorithm or decision tree. Instead, we conduct a search of the data before us and make a decision based on an ordering or analysis of that data, searching through cues in order of their validity such a search may use criteria that are arbitrary or qualitative. We search through cues in what we consider the order of their validity. Validity is defined as the proportion of correct decisions made by a cue out of all the times that cue discriminates between pairs of options, but, more often, we rely on our experience and judgment to determine which variables are valid or most important in a given situation. The goal of our efforts is to select the option for which the discriminators or variables used are most likely to be associated with the best outcome.

We rarely consider an exhaustive list of possibilities in our initial differential diagnosis. Instead, we are more likely to settle on a diagnosis that seems the most probable. This process may appear quite simple, but, in reality, we are considering many options or variables without any discernable effort. Examples in our daily activities include catching a ball, hitting a moving target, or knowing when to brake our automobile safely or comfortably. We rely on our intuition when performing such tasks.

We stop the search and make a decision when an option meets the search criteria we have, usually, subconsciously, chosen or considered mandatory. Brand name marketing and advertising exist primarily to influence or convince consumers to purchase their product based on this principle. Our grocery list may include a can of tomatoes, but when faced with the myriad choices of canned tomatoes, we do not evaluate each brand or option but probably choose the first brand we recognize. We stop our search as soon as we find a solution that, according to Simon, satisfies the conditions of that search or allows us to discriminate between options. This is known as the *stop rule*. Research supports several observations about this process. Studies have documented that we have a good ability to select search systems (Bentley and McGeoch 1985; Marewski and Gigerenzer 2012).

Heuristics often use search orders to help us make decisions, a quality that helps to explain why heuristics are used so much in medical decision-making which will be discussed in depth in the next chapter, but as some search orders are based on simple heuristics, so it is appropriate to point out now. An example of how search orders are used to make decisions is found in *take the best* (TTB) heuristic which is discussed in the next chapter. In this heuristic, we may consider many good options but settle on the one that best fits our criteria.

9.4.2 Tally Systems

How do we mentally process, rank, or grade a list of variables when considering a diagnosis?

We often consider the variables in a decision by the total or tally of past outcomes produced by those variables. This may be done subconsciously or by recording the tally directly. Using a tally system gives the decision-maker the ability to view the variables in a comprehensive way. Such an overview provides the user with a way to discriminate between and to order the variables. A tally system works because we are very good at remembering how frequently we have encountered similar events in the past (Dieckmann and Todd 2004).

If we consider the results of several variables, such as a particular imaging study, laboratory test, or physical finding, and realize that a variable was particularly useful or accurate in establishing a diagnosis, we will subconsciously advance that variable in the overall rank order we use for that particular problem. If that variable is not helpful or not necessary, it will be placed lower on our mental priority list and, with experience, may ultimately be discarded.

Dieckmann and Todd (2004) proposed that such discriminations can be manipulated in three ways:

Validity Rule This method reorders cues based on their applicability or validity to the current situation. The outcomes for each variable are reordered according to the number of correct against the number of incorrect decisions produced by the cues in the past. This approach requires a great deal of memory and ability to record the cues in use.

Tally Swap Rule This method moves a cue up (or down) one position if the tally of correct or positive outcomes for a variable minus the number of incorrect or poor outcomes is $\geq$ the next higher cue. This approach requires a great deal of memory, computation, and moderate degree of recording.

Simple Swap Rule This method moves the cue up one position if it has made a correct decision and down if it has made an incorrect decision. This method requires a minimum of effort in terms of remembering past outcomes and the least amount of effort in terms of recording the data necessary to reorder variables.

Search orders like those described above work. We are good at discriminating between cues or variables in terms of their usefulness. We are good at remembering the frequencies of events and do so almost automatically without particular attention or intention. Unlike computer models or clinical decision systems, we remember and rank events without needing to compute or tally events so that outcomes can be compared.

9.4.3 *Strategy Selection and Learning (SSL)*

Strategy selection is essentially a *cost-benefit analysis*—we informally calculate the costs and expected benefits of the strategies under consideration and choose the strategy that has the least cost while providing the optimal benefit (Beach and Mitchell 1978).

9.4 Decision Support Systems and Search Orders

The ideal strategy requires the least amount of information and cost. The ideal strategy also produces the greatest yield in terms of diagnostic and therapeutic efficacy, accuracy, and minimal risk.

Strategy selection is achieved by learning—we learn from the successes and failures of the strategies we choose. We most frequently choose strategies to manage a problem based on the strategies that have worked for us in the past.

Initial preferences for strategy selection:

- Prior success or failures with similar situation
- Training/education
- Evidence-based medicine
- Outcomes or actuarial data from published studies
- Institutional or departmental bias
- Institutional capabilities

Other authors (Rieskamp and Otto 2006) proposed that we learn to select strategies on the basis of reinforcement learning. We learn to choose which decision-making strategy is best from the successes and failures of our past experience with those strategies. We select a strategy based on whether that strategy has worked in the past. Rieskamp and Otto called this theory strategy selection learning (SSL). As novices, our initial strategies are modeled by our training and education, institutional biases, and the examples set by our mentors. As we mature, our strategies evolve to reflect our individual outcomes, continuing learnings and understanding of the science of medicine, as well as the capabilities of our current practice environment and our own individual preferences and biases. Selection is based on the simple equation of benefit minus cost, based on known outcomes. For clinical decisions, that analysis is generally made informally based on the physician's knowledge of the behavior of a disease, the risks and benefits of a particular treatment approach or surgical procedure, the outcomes that the physician has had with that therapy, and any other relevant factors that can be loosely quantitated. Costs may include patient inconvenience, pain, risk, or emotional stress, actual monetary costs, hospital stay, side effect, or risks associated with a procedure. The physician may also rely on data produced by studies in the literature or from a meta-analysis performed in the context of a multicenter trial or an evidence-based approach. The clinician uses this method to evaluate strategic options contingent on whether they are likely to be of high or low net benefit and chooses the option that putatively will yield the optimal benefit at the lowest cost for the situation under consideration (Fig. 9.3).

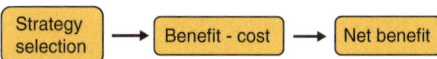

Fig. 9.3 The cost-benefit equation

9.4.4 Search Restrictions

Physicians do not think in terms using search strategies that are as streamlined or frugal as possible. Physicians do not calculate the minimimum or optimal number of variables necessary to make a valid decision of this construct. We are often cavalier in ordering additional tests or requesting more information. Increasing the number of variables to be considered may have several negative effects on the search to include, increasing the real and hidden costs of the decision-making process, increasing the complexity of the decision-making matrix, and increasing the risk of misleading information, to name a few.

Potential costs of decision-making strategies:

- Patient considerations for additional tests, procedures, inconvenience, risk, pain, and stress
- Risk of false negative or false positive results from additional tests
- Risks of omitting additional testing
- Monetary costs of proposed intervention
- Side effects of additional testing or procedure(s)
- Treatment delay from options that require additional testing, consultations, etc.
- Prolongation of hospital stay

The ideal strategy requires the least amount of information and cost and produces the greatest potential yield in terms of diagnostic and therapeutic efficacy, accuracy, and risk. To some degree these goals are conflicting as physicians are pushed to insure their evaluations are data rich to avoid potential diagnostic or therapeutic errors and simultaneously frugal in their cost and resource expenditures.

Let us consider the following example:

Let V_x = a variable chosen in the matrix used to establish a strategic option. If $V_1 + V_2 + V_3 = X\%$ probability of accuracy of establishing a diagnosis or achieving a desired outcome,

then $V_1 + V_2 + V_3 + V_4 = (X + Y)\%$ yields an increase in % probability of Y.

The question created by this example is how significant does Y need to be to warrant the inclusion of the additional variable V_4? Although SSL does not provide a quantitative answer to this question, the strategy chosen requires that Y must provide a significant benefit or be of minimal cost to alter the cost-benefit equation.

The SSL strategy includes the cost of the chosen strategy. Examples of cost may include such factors as:

- Patient considerations for additional tests, procedures, inconvenience, risk, pain, stress).
- Risk of false negative or false positive results from additional tests.
- Risks of omitting additional testing.
- Monetary costs of proposed intervention.
- Side effects of additional testing or procedure(s).
- Treatment delay from options that require additional testing, consultations, etc.
- Prolongation of hospital stay (Fig. 9.4).

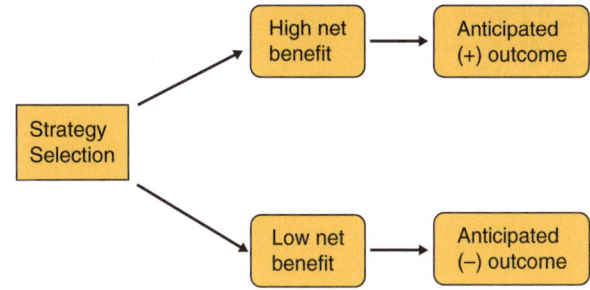

Fig. 9.4 Outcomes of strategy selection

More than any other factor, decision-making and problem-solving strategies are determined by our past experience—the outcomes of decisions we have made in the past. Our decision-making strategies are firstly honed and perfected as we learn from our mistakes and successes and secondarily by our efforts at learning—our formal and informal continuing education. The novice decision-maker must rely on other parameters, however. Those initial preferences may include:

- Prior success or failures with similar situation
- Training/education
- Evidence-based medicine
- Outcomes or actuarial data from published studies
- Institutional or departmental bias
- Institutional capabilities

Based on the outcomes obtained, the clinician is able to evaluate the performance of the strategy chosen in his or her individual experience and, most importantly, is able to learn from that experience or realize that he or she needs further education or that the strategy needs modification. In these ways, physicians are continuously updating the performance of the strategies in their armamentarium and can use those lessons to direct further learning and modify their approach or techniques used. As we shall see later, this type of learning is the essence of evidence-based medicine (Fig. 9.5).

For those in training, the shadow side of selecting strategies in this fashion is that the cognitive aspects of the strategy are unobservable and difficult to teach or replicate. Observers can monitor the actions of the clinician, or infer the rationale behind the strategy chosen, but do not see the strategies discarded or avoided. It is difficult to analyze if the strategy and actual outcome were a good fit or not in terms of the approach used. Focusing on the outcome as an indicator of the validity of the strategy has its limitations as there is not always a linear relationship with the strategy and the outcome. Strategies may produce false positive and false negative outcomes. A successful outcome does not always imply that the strategy was valid, only that the patient (and clinician) may have been lucky. In similar fashion, failure of an operative procedure does not immediately equate to the strategy underlying the decision to perform that operation was a poor choice. Clinicians must, therefore,

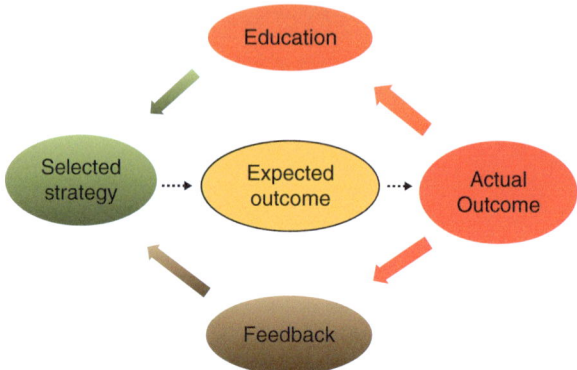

Fig. 9.5 The strategic learning cycle. (Adapted from Rieskamp and Otto 2006)

be aware of the fit between their choice of strategy and the outcome and remain vigilant to the possibility that the strategy was a poor fit for a problem despite a good outcome and vice versa. This is a difficult lesson to impart to trainees who may not appreciate the incongruity between the actions they have observed and the resultant outcome.

In summary, however, the SSL approach has many short- and long-term benefits. It is, in many ways, instinctive and the outcome of how clinical medicine is taught from the student's early days in medical school until the end of his or her training. The benefits of the SSL model include:

- Aids in calibrating our probability assessment—our perception of what variables are optimal and the limits of those variables.
- Provides an objective assessment of our actual results—how accurate our predictions and expectations are and our actual error and complication rates.
- Offsets natural tendency towards overconfidence—we tend to overestimate how much we know or what we think we know.
- Reduces our biases to include overconfidence and expectations of outcomes.
- Reduces tendency to overweigh importance of variables that tend to confirm our hypotheses.
- Reduces our tendency to not collect or to ignore information that does not support our biases.
- Teaches us to use the most appropriate decision-making strategies, thereby reducing the stress on our memory capacity and cognitive processing abilities.
- Identifies variables that contribute to poor judgment or poor decision-making strategies.

9.5 The Hierarchy of Information

There is a difference between quality and quantity of information. We are bombarded with information, yet much of it is not based on sound reasoning or fact. Sorting the difference out is an endless task. Decision-making depends on being able to evaluate data in terms of the relevance and truthfulness of data. We collect massive amount of information in the process of even the most mundane of clinical encounters. Much of this information is qualitative and subject to interpretation. As noted earlier, the savvy observer picks up many cues from the patient and his or her family, and most of these observations revolve around social, demographic, emotional, or psychological factors that have no bearing on the disease process itself but will have a profound influence on how we approach interacting with a patient and his or her family, how we educate that patient, and what course of treatment we recommend. Once we have gathered the relevant information about a patient, we must then review our knowledge about the problem we are faced with and the options we must consider. This is not an easy task.

Much of medical practice is based on unproven principles, personal experience that may not be supported by current research or evidence-based recommendations, faulty memory, or an erroneous understanding of what we think we know. Diagnosis and treatment are often based on the mythology of medicine—concepts or approaches that have been handed down from generation to generation yet cannot stand up to critical or scientific scrutiny. Not all data or observations published in peer-reviewed sources or pronounced by so-called experts is valid. Information or recommendations may have been generated by those who have proprietary interest in a particular drug or treatment center, as evidenced by the explosion of advertising aimed at public consumption. Much of medical therapy is provided to mollify the patient rather than being based on the science of medicine. Why do some physicians prescribe vitamin injections or hormone supplements as a tonic without the presence of a documented deficiency, or why are antibiotics prescribed for known viral infections? The rationale for many therapeutic recommendations is often faulty or scant.

Physicians are ethically bound to evaluate and re-evaluate their practice to include the validity and currency of their knowledge base. In doing so, we must be ever mindful that not all information is the same, depending on source, study design, or experience with that particular entity. Not all problems lend themselves to long-term study, and many conditions are too uncommon to generate statistically significant observations about the presentation or treatment of those entities. There is, therefore a hierarchy of validity for the various sources we rely on for information. This hierarchy can be summarized as follows:

1. Meta-analysis of Randomized Controlled Research (RCR) studies. This approach is commonly used for recommendations from specialty societies and broad-based, independent, multicenter study groups.

2. Evidence from single RCR studies.
3. Evidence from traditional clinical research studies (marginal study and control cohorts, small study groups, single institution studies, limited number of variables analyzed, limited long-term follow-up).
4. Textbooks and general Internet search (often not current and subject to author or editor bias but often a good place to start).
5. Non-randomized, non-controlled studies (case reports, editorials, retrospective or comparative studies).
6. Evidence from subject matter experts, privately funded commercial sources, and individual clinical practice or experience. (Adapted from Burns, Rohrich and Chung 2011).

We are all aware of this hierarchy, but the majority of clinicians rely on items 4, 5, and 6 of the hierarchy as their source of information. It is difficult to convince a physician or surgeon to change time-proven practices, even if it can be demonstrated that those practices are obsolete or based on a faulty understanding of pathophysiology. It is time-consuming work to locate, read, and process the information in items 1, 2, and 3 and also potentially disruptive to hospital and clinic routines. To quote Niccolo Machiavelli's advice in The Prince—*There is nothing more difficult to take in hand, more perilous to conduct, or more uncertain in its success, than to take the lead in the introduction of a new order of things*. Physicians may chafe at Machiavelli's advice—change can be intimidating when well-established routines or prejudices are challenged by new information. Overcoming this natural resistance is a goal of evidence-based approaches and can be eased by using the PICO format which is presented below.

The hierarchy of information model and the PICO format are good ways to teach medical students and residents about the decision-making process. The hierarchy of information model helps them seek out the most reliable sources for information, and the PICO format gives them a focused, sensible approach to gathering and prioritizing information. By simplifying the decision-making process, the resident is now forced to address the question— what data do I really need and what is just nice to have? Approaches to identifying and/or weighing variables will be discussed in the following chapters.

Deciding is easier and more efficient and more accurate if we can limit the options before us. Even though consideration of a larger number of variables seems the more logical and comprehensive and ultimately more accurate way of making a decision, research in the field of cognition and experience with solving complex problems or managing problems has shown that we do not perform at our best when we incorporate a large number of variables into the decision-making process. Having too much information impairs decision-making and leads to poorer decisions.

Understanding which variables are necessary to consider is important in any discipline. Investment consultants, for example, have devised complex and sophisticated strategies to pick stocks and bonds. You would think that, with all the expertise and money poured into this industry that we would all be wealthy just from knowing which investment vehicles will skyrocket in value. Yet, few such consultants seem

9.7 The Decision-Making Continuum 111

to do better than they would if they flipped a coin to determine which company or enterprise will make them rich. Most studies have shown that simple strategies are the most reliable, and many successful investors rely primarily on their intuition. Is medical decision-making any different? It is possible to develop computer programs that include many variables, with each variable being valid or meaningful in terms of its association with a particular disease. These programs are vastly more nuanced and, well, not simple.

Learning what information is vital and what details are not of benefit in the decision-making process is not an easy task. The concept of ignoring information is a recent development in the study of decision-making and for many may seem counterintuitive and uncomfortable, if not distressing. It just goes against the grain. It requires having a good intuitive sense of what is right and what really matters in developing a decision-making matrix. Study of successful CEOs and leaders does show that those who are able to ignore or at least rapidly dismiss superfluous data and focus on what they see as the critical and most essential parameters are not only able to make more efficient and more effective decisions. History is rife with individuals, who had this skill. Steve Jobs, for example, consistently made decisions by focusing only on the key variables, a skill that allowed Apple to maintain dominance in the computer industry even though many of his ideas initially seemed overwhelming, if not impossible.

9.6 The PICO Format

The PICO (Patient or Problem, Intervention, Comparison, Outcome) format is a good approach for the clinician wishing to undertake an evidence-based review of a problem. The PICO format gives a logical, organized and more evidence-based way of evaluating information when constructing a search order or evaluating the validity of data or variables. PICO is the acronym for a four-step approach to reviewing a specific question and stands for:

1. Patient or Problem—What is the relevant problem?
2. Intervention—What are the necessary diagnostic and therapeutic options or available management strategies?
3. Comparison of interventions
4. Outcome—What are the risks, benefits, and outcomes of the disease process, problem, or methods of intervention?

9.7 The Decision-Making Continuum

We have examined the approaches available for making a decision or solving a problem from several angles, but none of these approaches answer the question—exactly how do we go about making a decision? There are several distinct

Fig. 9.6 The decision-making continuum

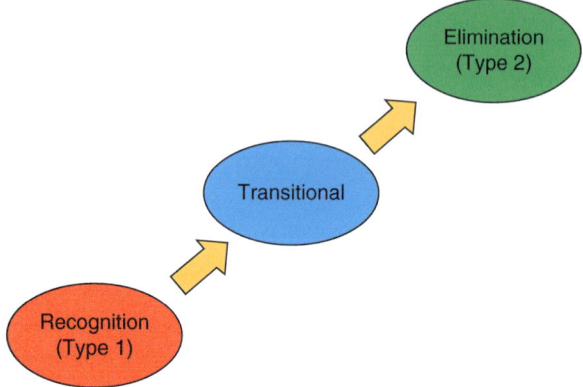

approaches to decision-making, but, if we categorize the different approaches, we find decisions are made by either *recognition* or by *elimination*. Decision-making by recognition and decision-making by elimination involve distinct thought processes or types of reasoning. Some problems require the use of both recognition and elimination. Looking at the various approaches to decision-making that exist within this framework, the processes of decision-making can be considered as a continuum of options. This continuum is not one of increasing difficulty or sophistication but rather an approach that covers the range of reasoning processes that can be called upon to solve a particular problem. These approaches are not mutually exclusive or independent. No approach is ideal for all problems, and no approach is superior or more valid than another. The best approach is usually determined by the clinical situation (Fig. 9.6).

9.7.1 Decision-Making by Recognition

Much of medical practice involves problem-solving by *recognition*. When faced with a problem we have seen before, or one that fits a pattern we are familiar with, or if a problem has few diagnostic or management options, there may be little or no need to pursue alternatives, order extensive testing, or seek additional advice or expertise. We recognize what we are dealing with and can be comfortable with pronouncing a diagnosis and proceeding with management. We can comfortably proceed with a straightforward, expedient approach. Such problems tend to be simple, optimized, and bounded. Such problems generally require procuring only a limited amount of data and have few variables. Decision-making by recognition includes the use of heuristics, maxims, pattern recognition, and intuition. Such approaches are especially useful in critical or time-sensitive situations where there is a need to act quickly and decisively. As

9.7 The Decision-Making Continuum

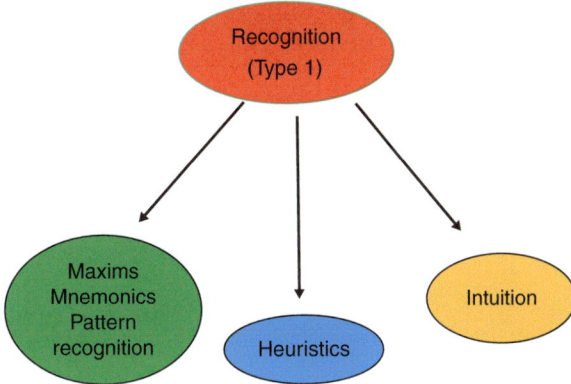

Fig. 9.7 Decision-making by recognition

mentioned previously, these types of decision-making are common in medical practice, but not easy to teach or explain.

Each of the approaches that rely on recognition will be discussed in-depth in the next chapter. Solving a problem by recognition uses the same approach as type 1 or fast thinking, as has been discussed earlier (see Fig. 9.7).

9.7.2 Decision-Making by Elimination

Solving problems by *elimination* is most useful for problems that have multiple options, are ill-defined or ambiguous, or require further research or extensive data. Such problems tend to be complex or complicated or unbounded. The approaches that use elimination will be discussed in Chap. 11 (see Fig. 9.8). Problems that are best approached by elimination require generating options or possibilities and then considering each option in terms of which solution is the best or most reasonable. As stated earlier in this text, solving a problem by elimination uses type 2 or slow thinking.

The approaches that use decision-making by elimination comprise the core of how problem-solving and decision-making are taught in medical school and postgraduate training environments. Unlike decision-making by recognition, they can be formally taught, and the steps of the processes used in a specific or hypothetical situation can be dissected apart, analyzed, and discussed.

Many decisions require a considered, more contemplative, or measured approach and require additional data, study, or thought. These problems usually involve considering multiple options or approaches and are resolved over a period of time. Often such decisions require involving resources such as the patient or their family or primary physician, consultants, or other caregivers. These approaches include use of the differential diagnosis, evidence-based medicine, algorithms, and regression analysis.

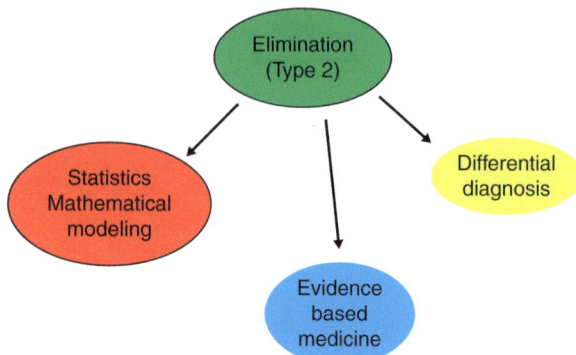

Fig. 9.8 Decision-making by elimination

9.7.3 Transitional Approaches

Not all approaches to decision-making can be neatly classified as either decision by elimination or decision by recognition but use elements of both. Decisions using SOPs or algorithms use recognition and elimination. SOPs and algorithms, which are most commonly designed to be used in specific situations, and guide operator to follow a prescribed pathway. Such decisions depend more on experience and judgment than following a defined process.

Standard operating procedures (SOPs) and algorithms are *transitional models* (Fig. 9.9), as they require the user to make decisions either by elimination or by recognition as he or she progresses through the steps of the process. SOPs provide focused, orderly responses in situations that may be chaotic, confused, or uncontrolled. Most simple problems fall into this spectrum, although a simple problem may still be considered complex if multiple options are available. Reliance on SOPs is a sensible approach, especially for situations that are chaotic, or when it is important not to overlook a critical step. Standard operating procedures can be successfully implemented with minimal training or expertise, but other forms of decision-making by recognition require experience and judgment.

SOPs and algorithms are predetermined pathways for approaching a problem. They can be written by the individual user or created by an organization or team such as intensive care units, cardiopulmonary resuscitation teams, and surgical units. SOPs are designed to aid providers in chaotic or emergency situations or in situations where meticulous attention to detail in a highly technical procedure such as cardiopulmonary bypass is necessary. Often, SOPs are designed for situations where there is a high turnover of personnel or where responders in emergency situations such as cardiac resuscitation find themselves having to administer highly orchestrated care in a situation where they are unfamiliar with the recommended procedures.

Fig. 9.9 Transitional models of decision-making

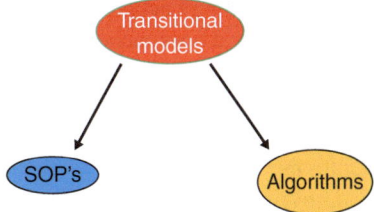

9.8 Selecting a Strategy

> You are never dedicated to something you have complete confidence in. No one is fanatically shouting that the sun is going to rise tomorrow. They know it's going to rise tomorrow. When people are fanatically dedicated to political or religious faiths or any other kinds of dogmas or goals, it's always because these dogmas or goals are in doubt. (Pirsig 1979, p. 152)

How does one decide which decision-making strategy to use? So many approaches have been presented. Having such a wide range of options available may seem intimidating, but the variety of options underscores the fact that it is the rare problem that must be solved by just one approach. Decision-making researchers have argued for decades in favor of their preferred methods and may appear to be in opposing camps—those who argue we ought to use our head and take a formulaic, or actuarial approach, and those who champion a cognitive or a heuristically based approach. Some take the middle ground and claim that a more integrated approach is possible.

9.8.1 Formulaic Versus Cognitive Approaches

Statistical approaches to analyze data have been widely used in medicine, especially in medical research. Actuarial or mechanical approaches to include linear and nonlinear regression, Bayesian analysis and computer-based models have been shown to be more accurate and reproducible than traditional cognitive methods of arriving at a diagnosis, and many argue that medical decision-making should make greater use of actuarial models (Kleinmuntz 1990). An early proponent of statistical analysis was Paul E. Meehl. To quote Paul E. Meehl, who was, arguably, a clinical psychologist and not a physician—*if people have a formula, then they should use their heads only very,* **very** *seldom* (Meehl 1986).

Meehl, a very prolific and influential researcher and writer in the world of clinical psychology, studied the clinical inference in clinical psychology from theoretical (clinical) and probabilistic standpoints (Meehl 1954) and demonstrated that the literature strongly supported statistical prediction. He restudied the problem in 1986 and again in 1996 and made no changes in or retractions of his conclusions. In comparing clinical and actuarial approaches to analysis, Meehl argued that the clinical and mechanical approaches are not interchangeable. They are not capable of being blended or transformed into a hybridized approach. They are separate and distinct. This position may not be valid, especially with the options available today, and blended approaches may provide the clinician with the most flexible and up-to-date solutions.

Grove et al. (2000) duplicated Meehl's finding showing that 47% of studies he considered favored actuarial prediction over clinical judgment alone, and in only 6% did clinical prediction prevail. Many of the sources Grove studied were from the psychology literature and therefore not directly applicable to clinical medical situations (Grove 2005). The massive amounts of data that psychologists accumulate from the instruments they use to evaluate patients cannot be analyzed in a meaningful fashion without the use of computers. A standard psychological evaluation such as the Minnesota Multiphasic Personality Inventory-1 (MMPI-1) considers 567 true/false questions. The MMPI-2RF, a newer measure, has 338 true/false questions. This number of variables cannot be analyzed in an efficient manner without sophisticated computer support. Medical problems do not contain this large number of variables, and the variables used in making most medical decisions are generally more interrelated than the broad scope of questions that the standard psychological tools cover.

Although subject to bias and irrational thinking, clinical practice is primarily based on cognitive approaches. Why? *First, physicians do not want to deal with statistical calculations any more than statisticians want to be around sick people*. Clinicians are not intensively trained in statistics and, even if they are so inclined, are rarely able to perform complex mathematical calculations in the course of a busy clinical practice. Even if clinical problems can be solved more accurately with the use of statistical or actuarial models, physicians gravitate towards heuristics or algorithms to make decisions rather than actuarial or formulaic approaches. Statisticians accept that a baseline degree of error exists in any analysis, whereas clinicians have an almost inbred avoidance towards the probability of errors. Physicians search for familiar cues or patterns and are less comfortable with the more abstract concept of probabilities. Physicians are limited in terms of the time and the resources available to make decisions and are under stress and scrutiny from many vantage points to make high-stakes decisions accurately. In such a practice environment, heuristics are more comfortable (Martignon et al. 2008; Dohami and Harries 2001).

Clinicians can rarely interrupt a patient encounter for any length of time to review additional data, research available literature, or process information using any mechanical or electronic methods. An electronic or mechanical instrument such as an electronic medical record disrupts the patient/physician encounter and diverts the clinician's attention away from the patient and to a computer screen. Patients rightfully expect their physician to be fully engaged, not distracted.

The clinician may gather a large amount of data about an individual patient, but, it is rare that more than a handful of variables have a major impact on establishing a diagnosis or formulating a plan of management. The clinician most often considers a limited number of critical variables, but those variables are often unbounded or qualitative, requiring judgment to weight and prioritize the variables under consideration. Such considerations are not easily captured either qualitatively or quantitatively in a meaningful fashion by a statistically driven survey or questionnaire.

The clinician must first make a diagnosis before he or she can make any comments about a prognosis. There is a profound difference between making a prognosis and establishing a diagnosis, a difference all clinicians are intimately aware of but a difference that underscores the limits of statistical analyses and formulaic approaches. A prognosis is based on data that, when taken collectively, can describe the likely course or a disease in a population with similar situation.

A diagnosis is the correlation of the data gathered about a patient with the clinician's knowledge drawn from his or her experience and accumulated knowledge. Establishing a diagnosis is an iterative process that is refined over time as we have seen in the decision-making cycle in Chap. 4. This process requires knowledge as well as judgment. It requires experience to negotiate unanticipated detours, delays, or conditions that the patient cannot tolerate or is unwilling to accept. Once a diagnosis has been established, the determination of a prognosis can be made within the parameters of the discussion above, but, because of unbounded and individual factors, probabilities gleaned from established data may not match those expected for the individual patient. Outcomes may be predicted but will depend on the response of the individual patient and not necessarily amenable to analysis by any type of a rigid or mechanical model. The validity and utility of statistical approaches for making a prognosis or a diagnosis determine of prognosis and prediction are therefore not congruent. These two tasks are different and require different processes to perform them and ultimately to assess outcomes (Meehl 1954). Traditionally, statistics has been used to describe or determine associations between variables and events. Established statistical methods are available to assure good study design, and statisticians are wary to have their calculations interpreted as providing insight into any causality or ascribe any relationship between the actions and events between the variables studied.

Physicians seek causality, not just relationships between variables. A relationship demonstrated to be statistically significant does not necessarily prove efficacy, nor does it show whether outcomes are the result of false positives or false negatives. A favorable outcome could be the unrecognized spontaneous resolution of the disease process and not the result of the therapy under study. Even though it may seem reasonable to infer causality from the results of a statistical analysis, a statistical analysis cannot provide explanations for why or how a given phenomenon exists or how an intervention can alter the course of a disease.

Clinicians often interpret or infer causality from data, but concluding that data, even if statistically meaningful proves causality is not always logical or valid. *Causal statistics* are a relatively new approach in the field of statistical analysis designed to overcome these limitations.

Causal statistics are a variety of formal methods that can be used to address associations and relationships between variables. The statistics of causality promise to expand the role of statistician beyond their traditional focus on associations of variables and help understand the how and whys of the issues under study and provide a more insightful picture of the nature of the issues under study and the relationships and causes of the outcomes produced by these interactions (Dawid 2007; Dawid et al. 2013; Monleon-Getino and Canela-Soler 2017; Pearl et al. 2016).

9.8.2 Cognitive and Heuristic Approaches

Studies have shown that fast and frugal heuristics often outperform linear or weighted models. *WADD*—weighted additive strategy—heuristics performs as well as and sometimes better than weighted strategies (Gigerenzer and Goldstein 1996; Newell et al. 1996).

Cognitive and heuristic approaches are accurate with a small but situationally acceptable degree of error. That error is offset by the efficiency and cost-benefits of these decision-making approaches. Much of medicine entails dealing with problems that do not lend themselves to evaluation by a formulaic or standardized, algorithmic, or evidence-based approach. In these settings, experience, empathy, and a well-developed sense of intuition are required.

The debate over the validity of mechanical, formulaic, heuristic and cognitive approaches is not an either-or argument. All methods have limitations and advantages, so if different approaches produce comparable outcomes, is debating the process used moot?

Meehl's position that the two approaches are not interchangeable should be questioned. More recent authors (Katsikopoulos et al. 2008; Kleinmuntz 1990) have suggested that the two approaches are complementary and that people should use their heads together with formulas (Einhorn and Hogarth 1978). Researchers in fields considered to be highly analytical and computational have also concluded that problems are also frequently decided by recognition strategies rather than analytical processes (Klein and Calderwood 1991).

Choosing a strategic approach that is either mechanical, cognitive, or heuristic does not apply to a vast amount of medical practice, as many problems are straightforward or routine. Much medicine can be practiced using a cookbook approach. Such problems do not warrant any computer-based or sophisticated support. Good judgment and clinical knowledge are sufficient.

More sophisticated decisions may require mechanical approaches, but before accepting any outcomes data, it is necessary to understand the concepts behind the tools and terminology cited in any publication or communication. Statistical significance does not automatically imply clinical significance, especially in the situation of outcomes derived from small study groups (Tversky and Kahneman 1971). The clinician must be able to recognize unreliable or inaccurate outcomes or conclusions derived from studies that are flawed by suboptimal design, poor execution of the methodology used, or illogical interpretation of the results.

Statistical predictions cannot account for low base-rate phenomena, the incidence of which may dramatically change predicted outcomes or invalidate the utility of the actuarial predictions which, therefore, can legitimately be overridden by clinical judgment. Outcomes of actuarial studies refer to one possible outcome when, in reality, multiple acceptable outcomes may be valid but not supported by the original data (Grove 2005).

Simple algorithms or decision trees derived from outcome studies of large patient cohorts have become widely available. Such recommendations are usually from specialty societies, multicenter trials, or large institutions and have simplified the decision-making for patients with many malignancies or chronic conditions such as hyperlipidemia or diabetes, but it is unreasonable to expect the practicing clinician to be able to personally perform the necessary calculations required to establish such recommendations into their practice.

In spite of the virtues of mechanical approaches, promoting their use is an uphill battle. Baring a major change in medical and postgraduate education, coupled with almost seismic reorientation of how physicians approach their craft, medical decision-making will be accomplished by using one's head rather than formulaic methods. The goal of educating physicians as decision-makers should not be to have them become statisticians but to provide them with the skills and processes required for them to critically and, if necessary, ruthlessly evaluate their decision-making skills.

We cannot create a model to solve many aspects of decision-making such as ethics, compassion, and a concern for the sanctity of the patient, aspects that make the practice of medicine a sacred undertaking. In the end, medicine cannot be reduced to a math problem.

Chapter 10
Decision-Making by Recognition

Summary
Most medical decision-making does not involve intense cerebral effort, extensive review of the medical literature, or use of complex modeling or formulas. We make decisions by recognizing how the problem before us resembles cases we have seen or remembering how we have solved similar situations in the past. Much of this type of decision-making is simple pattern recognition. Decision-making by recognition includes the use of simple rules of thumb, mnemonics or heuristics. Much of decision-making in these situations involves being "in the zone" to use a sports analogy—recognizing the dynamics of a situation and reacting in ways that are intuitive or ingrained by prior experience. We rarely make conscious decisions when performing everyday tasks such as driving an automobile. Routine medical practice, more often than not, falls into this pattern of performing an oft-repeated task. We can dramatically improve our ability to perform such tasks as we develop expertise in a field, a process that has been extensively researched and termed deliberate practice.

10.1 Maxims and Rules of Thumb

Before iPads, cell phones, and instantaneous access to a world of information available in the ether, we carried what we called our peripheral brain, a small notebook that would fit into a pocket of our lab coat. The peripheral brain would contain the pearls of wisdom faculty and would give nomograms, drug-dosing guides, mnemonics, biochemical pathways, flow charts, or any other bits of hard to remember information we might need. A good peripheral brain took years to develop and was a source of great pride. Loss of one's peripheral brain was a disaster. The hope was that with repeated use, we would absorb the information contained in our peripheral brain by osmosis. With the advent of handheld computers, the peripheral brain has gone the way of the black bag given to us by a pharmaceutical company when we started our clinical rotations.

Much of the information we carried in paper form is now available in readily accessible electronic formats to include applications on our cell phones. We cannot rely solely on electronic devices to practice medicine, however. Learning medicine involves training our minds to organize and retain information. Physicians still need ways to jog their memory when writing orders, or remembering which uncommon diseases need what unusual laboratory tests. An efficient physician must develop ways of organizing and remembering the vast stores of knowledge he or she stored in one's long-term memory. These methods include catchy phrases, or more structured and complex mnemonic devices.

Having a large store of knowledge is not sufficient; one must have a filing system. For the master chess player, this filing system is in the subconscious mind. Like any filing system that uses key words or key phrases to identify relevant documents, the master is able to use one fact, one piece of the puzzle, one observation to lead to another point or step in the decision-making process.

In his observations about mastering large quantities of information, Philip E. Ross (2006) noted that chess masters have an enormous store of previous experiences and situations that they can draw upon to compare to a new problem or situation and then, almost intuitively, apply the solutions they have learned from their past experience to the problem they are currently faced with. This store of knowledge is maintained in what Ross described as "a well-organized system of connections". We will look at Ross's work in greater depth shortly.

Aphorisms, maxims, and rules of thumb are examples of mnemonic devices drawn from traditional wisdom and serve as a starting point for remembering a principle or defending an argument. Maxims can express a fundamental principle or truth or rule of conduct. Maxims are short and even folksy or humorous. We all use phrases such as "it is hard to make the asymptomatic patient better" or "the enemy of good is better" or "when you hear hoofbeats, don't think of zebras." Such simple sayings can convey a powerful message about the importance of common sense and reason, and their observance can help us avoid complications or misadventures. These pithy sayings were offered as devices to be relied upon until more advanced or sophisticated lines of reasoning could be developed or overthinking a problem.

I am not a Latin scholar, but one of my favorite aphorisms was the Latin phrase I gave to residents—*nihil novum nocte*—nothing new at night. I would advise against pulling a urinary drainage catheter or nasogastric tube on evening rounds because it would create a crisis if the patient developed a problem after everyone on the team has gone home. Some actions are best left until the next morning.

Aphorisms, maxims, and old saws may not express the latest scientific developments or therapeutic advances, but these guides have kept many a surgeon out of trouble in the middle of the night when alone and required to decide what course is most prudent or safest. Aphorisms and maxims are a part of our decision-making arsenal, as well as the culture of medicine. Physicians ignore them at their peril.

Aphorisms and maxims may be contradictory and disregarded—a practice that was frustrating and confusing for junior decision-makers. These rules are a way of expressing fundamental truths in medicine and provide at least a point of departure for making decisions. Many of the dilemmas the physician faces revolve around uncertainty and ambiguity and require sophisticated reasoning skills well beyond the wisdom provided by a simple aphorism. Diseases do not always present in textbook fashion; patients are not always forthright in their answers or the information they provide. It is not always possible or appropriate to order every conceivable test or study; opinions from specialists can vary widely, leading to further confusion. The social, ethical, and personal framework that surrounds each patient can amplify or conflict with what would seem the ideal approach to the patient. We also use aphorisms or sayings to remind ourselves and teach others fundamental principles. Examples are you can't make the asymptomatic patient better and, a saying always applicable for surgeons, the enemy of good is better.

10.2 Mnemonics

We all learned methods to recall information well before we entered medical school. Those skills were honed as we struggled to learn the cranial nerves or the bones of the wrist. Most of us continued to use mnemonics to make sure we have not overlooked a step. I would often review the five Ps of postoperative care (pain, pulse, position, protein, and piss) when writing postoperative instructions on a particularly complex patient, or in the middle of the night when I was tired, just to make sure I hadn't overlooked anything critical. Not sophisticated or elegant, but a useful way to manage information.

10.3 Chunking

To better understand how we use devices like maxims and mnemonics, let us look at the phenomenon of chunking. Chunking is a process by which we can recall the large amounts of information needed to analyze a problem or remember the steps necessary to manage a problem (Ross 2006). Assume we have two medical students: one from China and one from the United States. Both are fluent in English but had childhood experiences consistent with the cultures in which they were raised. Let us now give these two students a test in the form of five random words written at the top of a piece of paper. The challenge is to place the words in a meaningful order and write any subsequent related thoughts that the words inspire. The words are *a, little, Mary, lamb,* and *had.* Readers raised in an English-speaking culture would immediately identify these words as the first line of a child's nursery rhyme—Mary had a little lamb. Our student from China would probably not have heard this rhyme and, with a bit of thought, might be able to put the words into a recognizable order. His thinking would go no further, as the phrase has no meaning or invokes no memories. Our student raised in

America would not stop there but then go on to write the rest of the verse we all know by heart and could retrieve from our memory bank even though we may not have heard or recited this little rhyme for decades.

Chunking is a memory expander. It is what helps us remember addresses, phone numbers, or words to songs. It is what allows chess masters to recognize a strategy by seeing the position of a few chess pieces on the chessboard. Chunking is an example of the seven plus or minus two concept introduced earlier, allowing us to recall a short list of seemingly unrelated numbers or objects. Such a nonrandom grouping can key our memory beyond the initial chunk as demonstrated with the example of the nursery rhyme (Ross 2006).

Appreciating the limit of our brains to deal with seven plus or minus two items helps us understand how we learn. Our minds are not computers, able to store large chunks of unrelated or random data. This is probably a holdover from our evolution. One does not need to remember a long string of random numbers to extricate oneself from a life and death situation. A decision must be made immediately with limited information. Decisions are sometimes difficult due to the stress of the situation, not having faced this situation before, or not having included this possibility in our planning. The solution is always more obvious after the fact, or with minimal prompting from others. It is not a lack of experience or competence. These events are also a reminder of how our brains evolved. We react quickly to situations we have experienced previously, but not always to new situations.

Chunking is apparent in the game of chess. A chess novice will look at a chessboard with 20 pieces and see it as 20 separate pieces of information. A master will see the position of the pieces and recognize the placement as a pattern. They consider the position of the pieces as five or six chunks—a number within the limit of the mind's working memory. A grandmaster might have access to 50,000–100,000 chunks and can retrieve the information about that position simply by looking at the position of the pieces. Chess masters are very good at recognizing recognized patterns but are not better than amateur players if they are asked to recall the location of chess pieces placed randomly. For example, let highly skilled chess players and non-players be briefly shown a chess board setup with 20–25 pieces as if it was an actual game in progress, and then ask the 2 groups to recall the position of the pieces. Non-players could recall only 4–5 pieces and experienced players perhaps 6–7 pieces. Highly skilled players can recall the location of every piece (Ross). The expert probably does not remember the position of the pieces by their location individually but as packets or small groups.

One can, through effort and training, learn to recall strings of numbers greater than Miller's magical number of seven, but this extra data will not be retained in our long-term memory as we would, for example, a phone number. To remember a significantly larger sequence of information, we link those bits to an already established matrix or format from our long-term memory. That is how we recall the area code for a telephone number—numbers that exceed the seven plus or minus two rules. The area code and the local number are recalled as two separate chunks of information.

Physicians store and retrieve information in chunks also, and experience allows us to remember a greater number of significant details. Reviews show that information about frequency of occurrence is stored in memory by an autonomic encoding process for a wide variety of events (Hasher and Zacks 1984). Such details are probably remembered by categories such as history, past medical history, laboratory results, and so on, not as random bits of data.

Expert chess players rely not so much on a more their ability to analyze problems as they do on having an organized store of experience that allows them to recall situations similar to the game they see before them. Some new problem triggers memories from prior cases that help to rapidly determine what problems and possibilities are present and what strategy to use. Expert chess players access their long-term memory much more frequently than novice players.

A similar process is evident when a student or resident novice surgeon and an experienced surgeon encounter a complex situation such as a large tumor during surgery. The novice can perhaps recall the major features of the patient's tumor, but the master surgeon can also describe the relationships of the tumor to normal anatomic features, anomalies or distortions of normal anatomy, characteristics of the tissues, and any details that are relevant to the decision of how to approach the patient's problem.

Physicians organize the information and experiences they have accumulated in a way that they can recall the data pertinent to the situation, usually by associating the event with an emotional or unique aspect of that encounter. We are more likely to remember that Sally was wearing a red dress than what her initial complaint was. Once we recall the image of the red dress, we are able to recite a voluminous amount about Sally, even years removed from the event.

This limitation is also why the standard lecture format we use for conferences or didactic activities is not the optimal way of presenting information. We are visual and sensory beings and respond best to situations that stimulate our visual cortex and engage as many of our senses as possible.

We are also hands-on or experiential learners. Our memory is even more vividly stimulated if we are a participant rather than being a passive observer. Information that engages our senses or motor cortex provides a stronger hook to help us remember, in context, what may otherwise be recorded as random or isolated bits of data like the example of the Mary had a little lamb nursery rhyme.

10.4 Pattern Recognition

The beginner or inexperienced decision-maker who is not sure what data is relevant to making a good decision can be overwhelmed by a volume of data too large to be easily or meaningfully processed. Here, the novice decision-maker gathers data in an almost straight-line fashion until a pattern emerges out of a forest of data. The inexperienced decision-maker not only collects unnecessary data but is uncertain how the data should be assembled to produce a recognizable picture, an approach that is time-consuming but also expensive and more likely to produce a wrong answer.

The expert does not need to see all the pieces of the puzzle to recognize the picture before him. An experienced decision-maker can rapidly fill in the missing pieces either by relying on past experience or by requesting additional focused data. Such were the analytical powers of individuals like Sherlock Holmes. We all have seen senior clinicians who, when unable to finalize their decision, ask for one or two questions in a laser-like fashion and, after obtaining that data, are able to make the diagnosis or solve the problem. This type of filling in the gaps is a process or minds use all the time. The experienced decision-maker is looking for features in the picture before her that allow creation of an image or figure. This approach is configuration—obtaining just enough data to recognize an image and then fill in the missing pieces using pointed information gathering. For example, if an image resembles a face, but only the eyes and nose are identifiable, we will subconsciously look for other data such as a mouth and ears to fill in the portrait.

Chess masters overcome this dilemma not by intense study, by analysis of strategies, or by analyzing the games of past masters but by playing thousands of games of chess. To get that experience, they play fast chess—they do not labor over deciding which move to make, nor do they spend a great deal of time analyzing the disposition of the chess pieces. Rather, they play thousands of games until they developed an intuition about the situation they are faced with. Their intuition allows them to view the problem in a manageable way by ultimately considering only a few significant variables and not being overwhelmed by all of the data before them. This knowledge cannot be taught, the individual must play game after game until they develop the intuition and board sense that comes with acquiring the patterns they have seen in their long-term memory.

Paintings, for example, do not have all of the details of an object. Instead, flicks of paint from well-crafted brushstrokes are used to suggest details. Our minds complete the painting by filling in the gaps and allow us to visually complete the painting. For the expert, the tipping point in the decision-making process requires only the key features for the pattern to be recognizable. This is an intuitive, not a conscious process. The decision-maker does not immediately jump to a conclusion, however. He or she rapidly and almost subconsciously considers multiple options, multiple ways of putting the pieces together, discarding options that are not feasible or weak until the ideal solution emerges.

This is a highly nuanced process, not readily apparent to the novice or casual observer who is unaware of the options considered and dismissed. The actions of the expert may seem purely reflexive or even impulsive. The expert may not even be aware of the process unless prodded to explain their thinking after the event. *There is no way to teach this process in a didactic forum. It requires repetition of real-world, real-time situations, just like a good chess player who masters the game by playing it over and over until the mental processes of pattern recognition and the analysis of potential moves become more reflexive than conscious.*

Physicians also diagnose problems using pattern recognition. There is a fundamental difference between the game of chess and medical practice, however. Chess is a game with fixed rules and a massive, but limited, number of potential moves. Simple pattern recognition does not account for how we manage ambiguities in an individual clinical situation or how we can compensate for insufficient, spurious or confusing data. Much attention has been given to the application of artificial intelligence in the form of computer programs designed to play chess. Since chess does have defined rules and a finite number of moves, it is theoretically possible to design a program that can outwit even the most gifted and experienced chess player. This approach is of limited value in medicine, as there are an infinite number of variables in resolving clinical problems, as the human organism and disease processes do not follow set rules.

The Achilles heel of this process is misidentification of the image by being too cavalier or superficial in our analysis or misinterpreting the picture due to an inadequate understanding of the subject. The more we know about a disease or a procedure, the more sharply focused and accurate the image will be. It takes experience to know when we have the knowledge, understanding, and data necessary to make a good decision and not merely deceiving ourselves. Looking at the problem in another way, the expert has a detailed and well-organized mind-map that has level upon level of nuance and observations. The novice has a rudimentary and very incomplete map.

Both the chess master and the physician may also use a more deliberate approach that relies on their long-term memory, choosing the best option only after a deliberate analyzing the solutions available from his experience. *The deliberate approach is more structured rather than intuitive or reflexive, and, unlike chunking or pattern recognition, the logic behind the deliberate approach can be explained or taught.*

10.5 Heuristics

Heuristics were introduced earlier in Chap. 2. The term is of Greek origin, meaning serving to find out or discover. Heuristics are now accepted as an indispensable cognitive process to solve problems that cannot be handled by logic or probability theory. Heuristics are practical and effective approaches to making decisions or solving problems. Heuristics use shortcuts in our reasoning processes to efficiently and quickly solve problems. Similar reasoning methods include using a rule of thumb, an educated guess, an intuitive judgment, stereotyping, or common sense. Heuristics are experience-based techniques that speed up the process of finding a satisfactory solution by ignoring or bypassing the desire for gathering more and more information or options, in exchange for making decisions faster and more frugally.

Much of the mythology and wisdom of medicine and surgery are conveyed through heuristics. Medical decision-making relies on heuristics by choosing relevant principles, deciding which laboratory or imaging studies are most likely to aid in diagnosis, or narrowing the range of considerations used in a decision-making matrix. The goal of these actions is to expedite and make the process less wearing and stressful. Decision-making rarely entails a comprehensive consideration of possibilities or alternatives for the problem before us; instead, we consciously or subconsciously pick several variables as being consistent with a certain diagnosis and, then, settle on that diagnosis with comfort if those variables are met.

Heuristics are intended to provide expedient, practical, and efficient solutions— not necessarily the solution that is the best or the most accurate. Heuristics are perhaps the most commonly used approach to problem-solving in medical practice. Decision-making using heuristics relies heavily on judgment or experience, usually by ignoring part of the information available and focusing on the most crucial or salient data. Heuristic thinking is especially useful in urgent, time-sensitive, or unstable situations where gathering more information may not be practical or traumatic to the patient. Heuristics are also useful in situations where information is limited, or the situation being managed involves unusual or anomalous presentations, or problems where there is a low probability of assessing outcomes. Heuristics provide highly accurate and prudent conclusions even though they bypass analyzing all available information or using analytical or formulaic approaches (Gigerenzer and Gaissmaier 2011; Bodemer et al. 2015). Heuristics are therefore more efficient and often more accurate than formal, linear regression types of decision-making approaches (Payne et al. 1988).

Heuristics are useful only if we have a good grasp of the principles inherent in the practice of medicine and understand that decisions based on heuristics require that we remain circumspect and aware that the decision is not always based on highly quantified and analytical levels of knowledge but on more abstract and tenuous assessments such as intuition and assumption. Their usefulness is dependent on the environment or context they are used in. For example, we may tell others to look for horses, not zebras, if they hear hoofbeats. If that person has no knowledge of medicine or disease processes that the analogy refers to, the heuristic will not help them make a sound medical decision. Much of the value of heuristics is reliance on what has worked in the past and what we are comfortable that will generally be efficacious. Most of heuristic thinking emphasizes efficiency and utility over in-depth reasoning. Medical decisions are not unbounded in terms of being able to consider all information and in a uniform fashion; rather they are optimization under constraints.

Heuristics are not good or bad, less valuable, or less valid than other decision-making strategies.

10.5.1 How Do Heuristics Work?

When selecting an appropriate heuristic, we search our memory to find past cases that resemble the problem facing us. That is why so many clinicians rely on cases they have treated in the past, a process denigrated by those who wish to take what they would argue is a scientific or rational approach to diagnosis. We seem to be hardwired for using heuristics. Man has always been faced with having to make critical decisions immediately with incomplete information. Heuristics,

10.5 Heuristics

therefore, serve us as a survival mechanism. We make better and more accurate decisions by ignoring some of the information and by not laboriously considering all options.

All decision-making and problem-solving strategies can be broken down into steps that are usually followed sequentially (Goldstein and Gigerenzer 2002):

- *Search*—Determine the necessary variables in the order of their importance.
- *Stop*—Stop your search as soon as one predictor variable allows it.
- *Decide*—Make a decision according to the most pressing predictor variable.

For medical decisions, I would add an additional step—*exclude. We are obligated to look for and exclude serious, ominous, or life-threatening conditions that are possible if only remote.*

A urologist, for example, would be remiss to not consider or exclude the presence of a testicular tumor when evaluating a patient who presents with an ill-defined scrotal mass that is probably epididymitis. An internist is obligated to exclude the possibility of an underlying carcinoma of the lung in a patient with an infiltrate that initially looks like a simple pneumonia.

As we have learned in our discussions about satisficing and optimizing, not all clinical decisions require the investment of time and effort to find the best course of action. If a patient presents with the classic history and physical and laboratory findings for a minor illness, it is generally not necessary to obtain laboratory or imaging studies or, worse, wait for those results before initiating treatment. Billions of dollars are spent annually for urine cultures, blood counts, serum electrolytes, or imaging studies even when the practitioner has a high confidence level in their diagnosis and minimal need for additional data for other than confirmatory or medicolegal concerns. The underlying fear is that they might miss something, a fear that often has no rational basis. The practitioner must be able to narrow the decision and management options to the minimum amount of data or number of variables necessary to make an appropriate decision. Here, heuristics allow the caregiver to rely on a minimum of data without sacrificing diagnostic accuracy or increasing risk. Few studies have been conducted looking at the benefits of heuristics in streamlining medical decision-making, but studies of the benefits of heuristics in many other fields have shown that monitoring just one critical variable can allow for good decision-making in business and management, without sacrificing accuracy or risk (Gigerenzer and Gaissmaier 2011). To demonstrate how heuristics are used in the clinical setting, let us look at a commonly used heuristic—*one good reason.*

One good reason helps us rapidly and effectively approach many problems, especially problems seen in emergency or time-sensitive situations. This heuristic is based on reaching a decision based on the presence of one critical variable. We look for one significant, pivotal clue rather than analyze a variety of data points. In the world of peacock biology, I am told, peahens looking for a mate assess a small number of peacocks and choose the one with the largest number of eyespots on his tail feathers. Here, the sample size considered by the peahen is small, but the weight of that one cue—the number of eyespots—appears to determine, at least for peahens, the decision.

Years ago, I performed a complicated reconstruction of the urinary tract on a young boy born with spina bifida. He was suffering from the usual complications of that condition to include recurrent episodes of pyelonephritis and lack of bladder and bowel control. The surgery was uneventful, and the child did well for several months. I took a vacation to go fly fishing in a remote area of Rockies, as was my custom every year, and returned to learn that the child had died during my absence.

The boy developed a urinary tract infection and was given antibiotics at a rural medical facility. He did not improve, and he was taken to the university medical center I was affiliated with, where he was evaluated by an emergency department physician and given a different antibiotic. My backup was not notified, and the patient sent home, where he expired. I suspect those in the emergency department did not understand or were intimidated by the complexity of this child's medical condition. Despite the unusual and complex nature of this child's underlying medical problems, reliance on a simple heuristic, borne of common sense, could have avoided this disaster. The heuristic applicable to this situation, an obviously septic young child with a dramatic elevation in white blood cell count, should have been *one reason only*. The only reason needed to decide whether or not this child required admission and immediate evaluation was the presence of a major infection in a high-risk child that had not responded to the initial therapy.

Another example of this heuristic occurred when I was on a neurosurgery service as a senior medical student. One morning, as the team was passing through the emergency department on our way to breakfast, an emergency medicine resident asked us to take a quick look at a patient that had just arrived. The patient was a middle-aged, healthy man who was a supervisor at the state prison. He had fallen down a flight of concrete steps that morning and was brought for routine evaluation. The gentleman was well-spoken, calm, and apologetic at having interrupted our morning. His neurological examination was totally normal, and he had no major signs of trauma. We asked the emergency department physicians to obtain imaging studies. In those days, initial studies were limited to plain films of the skull and neck. We advised the gentleman we would be back soon and then continued to the cafeteria.

We had no sooner set our breakfast trays down when we were notified by an emergency room nurse that our patient was now confused and combative. We left our breakfast and ran back to the emergency room. The patient now had signs suggestive of an intracranial bleed and was taken to surgery to evacuate an epidural hematoma caused by a skull fracture. Our patient recovered without incident. Again, the principle used to change the management of this patient was—*one reason only*—a sudden change in mental status.

Take the best is another commonly used heuristic. When a decision about management must be made rapidly, we consider the constellation of findings before us to provide a quick sketch of the patient's situation but often rely on one critical variable to determine the initial course of action. A variation of the one good reason heuristic that demonstrates this point is *take the best*. Here the problem is approached by prioritizing the variables and selecting the one that is most appropriate to the situation, using the following steps: (1) search through cues in predetermined order, (2) stop the search as soon as a cue—the best— justifies a course of action, and (3) initiate the appropriate response.

Take the best can also be called the variable plus 1 ($v + 1$) approach. For example, any patient with a cardiac history or acute cardiac symptoms requires immediate attention. The dilemma is not determining whether the patient needs further observation or management or not but, rather, deciding the environment that could best provide that care. Not everyone needs to be admitted to the cardiac intensive care unit (CICU), and there are only so many beds in any CICU, so admissions there must be selected carefully. One study looked at a wide range of variables to include electrocardiogram abnormalities, ST segment changes, resting chest pain, the patient's response to nitroglycerine, or a history of a prior myocardial infarction or CICU admission, to determine which, if any variable, was the most the most reliable indicator of an infarction, or incipient infarction (Green and Mehr 1997). Their study showed that even though the other findings were all good indicators of an acute cardiac event, the most reliable was ST segment depression on the electrocardiogram obtained in the emergency suite. For this study, ST segment depression was the $v + 1$ variable.

Heuristics like one good reason, take the best, and $v+1$ are like binary nodes in an algorithm or decision tree where the matrix demands proceeding on one of two distinct pathways. It is a fork in the road, and one must take the left or the right fork. This form of reasoning is based on Bayes' theorem, which is used to calculate the probability of events having a binomial distribution such as our fork in the road. Bayes' theorem helps us look at binary cues or variables. Each piece of information or bit of data can be considered a variable or v. The need for a greater or lesser number of variables is dependent on the situation, the decision-maker's experience, and needs of the individual patient. As v increases, the computations necessary to solve the problem become more difficult, and, as the options available increase, the decision-making matrix becomes more complex, requiring an increase in time, effort, and resources. Surprisingly, such an increase in variables may also increase the risk of errors in the decision-making process. This is why computer support is necessary for multivariate problems and also why physicians opt for a more efficient way of making decisions in highly complex or time-sensitive situations.

The increase in variables may also require additional diagnostic testing and add significantly to the cost of medical care. Additional tests also delay institution of appropriate therapy and often expose the patient to additional risk and discomfort. Heuristics help to minimize or even avoid these factors. This method has been shown to be as accurate as sometimes better than regression analysis, especially when the number of variables is large. As we have seen, this number of variables is still way beyond the individual's ability to manage without some form of mechanical support.

Another example of the use of the value of heuristics in situations where multiple variables may be present was demonstrated in a study of the utility and role of MRI scanning vs. clinical evaluation for patients presenting with dizziness. In one study (Kattah et al. 2009), the authors compared simple bedside techniques to MRI scanning to diagnose dizziness due to a brain stem or cerebellar stroke. This is a difficult diagnosis to establish with error rates in an emergency department environment up to

35 per cent of cases. Katta's bedside examination required only three steps to establish a stroke as the cause of a patient's dizziness. This bedside technique had a higher accuracy rate than MRI, took one minute, and correctly identified 100 percent of patients with a stroke as contrasted with an 88 percent detection rate on magnetic resonance image imaging (MRI), with a false positive rate of only 4 per cent.

10.6 Approaches to Using Heuristics

10.6.1 How We Make Choices

Heuristics help us make choices. For many choices in life, to include purchases at the grocery store, a new automobile, home, or a radio or television program, we stop search as soon as we find an option that satisfies our search criteria. This heuristic applies to medical decisions as well. We rarely consider an exhaustive list of possibilities in our initial differential diagnosis. Instead, we are more likely to settle on a diagnosis that seems most probable or likely. When faced with a patient who is ultimately found to have an unusual or atypical disease, that option is rarely considered from the beginning. We perform many complex activities without considering all the variables present.

It is the difference between an expert driver who controls his automobile in a smooth, effortless fashion and the new driver who has difficulty coordinating the break, gear-shift and accelerator. We learn when to slow down when approaching an intersection or speed up enough to safely enter a stream of moving traffic. This level of intuition was what our primitive ancestors had to master when trying to hit a moving deer with an arrow or spear. Just as a golf professional improves his or her game by using a coach, learning to shoot an arrow accurately can be aided by good mentoring and by instruction. In the same way, surgical residents benefit from having a mentor that can point out ways to hold an instrument better, or place stitches more accurately and efficiently. None of this learning can be acquired in a lecture or by reading a book. There is no language to pass on these skills. The nuances of surgery are not acquired by intelligence or knowledge. They can only be acquired by practice, introspection, observation, and coaching. The student must have a sense of how their innate mental and physical capacities are compatible with and suited for the specialty they choose to pursue. Knowing a heuristic is not sufficient for the inexperienced or beginner; the learner must have a sense of their own innate mental and physical capacities as well as the domain in which they are learning. Having the knowledge about how an appendectomy is performed is not adequate; the student must understand and apply their capabilities within the context of the task. In this fashion, the student learns to apply their intuition about the nature of surgery to best advantage (Gigerenzer 2007). Over time, this intuition is honed to a point that much of what is done in the setting of making a diagnosis, managing a patient, or performing a procedure becomes a subconscious and natural process, and one that we can modify or adapt to meet the challenge of the moment, even if we have never been faced with the exact configuration of the problem we have before us.

Deciding is easier and more efficient and more accurate if we can limit the options before us. Even though consideration of a larger number of variables seems the more logical and comprehensive and ultimately more accurate way of making a decision, research in the field of cognition and experience with solving complex problems or managing problems has shown that we do not perform at our best when we incorporate a large number of variables into the decision-making process.

Investment consultants have devised complex and sophisticated strategies to pick stocks and bonds. You would think that, with all the expertise and money poured into this industry, we would all be wealthy just from knowing which investment vehicles will skyrocket in value. Yet, few such consultants seem to do better than they would if they flipped a coin to determine which company or enterprise will make them rich. Most studies have shown that simple strategies are the most reliable and many successful investors rely primarily on their intuition. Is medical decision-making any different? It is possible to develop computer programs that include many variables, with each variable being valid or meaningful in terms of its association with a particular disease. These programs are vastly more nuanced and, well, not simple.

10.6.2 Fast and Frugal

Heuristics involve fast and frugal thinking, a concept that has already been introduced in Chap. 1. Fast and frugal thinking reduces the effort required for practical yet good and highly accurate decision-making. Fast and frugal approaches are easy to teach and easy to memorize. Fast and frugal guidelines are, therefore, an immense aid to the busy clinician. All heuristics rely on effort reduction and, upon first consideration, appear similar. These differences are subtle, yet fundamental, especially when introducing the concepts to students, or discussing how a decision was arrived at (Ericsson 1996).

Fast and frugal has a precise meaning. For example, in the case of decision trees, the frugality of a decision means that the tree uses the fewest number of questions or nodes. Fast refers to reducing the number of steps or operations necessary to reach a decision. First, fast and frugal trees must, under conditions of limited time, information, and with minimal computation, produce a definitive answer. Second, fast and frugal trees can make only qualitative predictions—a finding or value must be absolute and not subject to interpretation. Third, the cues are not combined but considered one at a time. Fast and frugal trees use a one reason only form of decision-making option—they do not use probabilities or options (Martignon et al. 2003). Fast and frugal trees must be designed to yield a definitive answer with limited time, information and computation.

10.6.3 Examining Fewer Cases

Rather than performing an exhaustive review of literature or available experience, the decision-maker can limit his or her search to examples that meet the variables under consideration. This is not a substitute for in-depth reading about a particular disease, syndrome, or approach to therapy, but it does help the decision-maker to focus their initial efforts on the information at hand rather than being overwhelmed by new data which can be distracting when a decision is required in a timely manner.

10.6.4 Limiting Consideration or Retrieval of Variables

Decisions can be streamlined without sacrificing validity by limiting consideration or retrieval of cue values or variables. Each request for a laboratory test, imaging study, or consultation should be viewed as a binary event, the outcome of which forces the decision matrix in one direction or another, not just to gather additional information. Limiting values or variables must be done in a deliberate and considered manner, not arbitrarily.

10.6.5 Simplifying the Weighting of Variables or Cues

Experienced decision-makers prioritize or rank information from a set of variables both in terms of the variables considered, and also in the significance they assign to each variable, so that the presence, absence, or value of one finding may be adequate to tip the decision-making scales. This approach may seem obvious, but mastering this skill requires judgment and experience.

10.6.6 Examining Fewer Alternatives

When developing a management plan using the concept of fast and frugal, the decision-maker should consider only the most efficacious, expedient, or least invasive approaches to therapy rather than developing an encyclopedic list of all therapies that might be tried. A thorough review of the available alternatives may serve as an excellent teaching device, and may be required in complex or puzzling cases, but creating an exhaustive differential diagnosis is rarely practical in a busy clinical environment.

10.6.7 Less Is More

With heuristics theory, there is an inverse relation between accuracy and the amount of information, computation, or time available. More information is usually harmful not better, and an excess of information can either delay a decision or stymie the decision-maker into inaction.

10.6.8 Ignoring Part of the Information

This is another advantage experience provides. Experience allows the decision-maker to be able to discriminate between data points that are critical and those that are of little importance, or even misleading. This type of thinking leads to more accurate judgments and weighting and adding all information: this is especially true in instances involving diseases or situations where the data available has been derived from small samples, or unproven or novel techniques, or outcomes have not been sufficiently studied to make reasonable predictions.

10.6.9 Recognition Memory

In the course of analyzing a problem, two approaches for the solution are identified: one approach is familiar or recognized and the other approach is unfamiliar or foreign; the decision-maker is prone to assign a greater degree of validity or comfort to the familiar approach. If both alternatives are recognized and seem equivalent, the decision will favor and then infer that this alternative has the higher probability or better fit with respect to the criteria. We have encountered this default mechanism in the prior discussion of pattern recognition.

10.6.10 Take-the-First

The take-the-first approach is similar to take the best. Even the most sophisticated and experienced decision-maker is biased towards the first alternative that comes to mind. It takes time and effort to discard a solution that appears reasonable or workable. There appears to be a neurological basis for this pattern of thinking. Studies using MRI imaging to test the two processes of recognition and evaluation have shown that the recognition heuristic may be default mechanism for making expedient or decisions or rapidly settle on an initial management plan, especially in a crisis situation. Some forms of heuristics may be default mechanism or reaction to an event that has been incorporated into our thinking from evolution like the scenario of the Paleolithic who responds to danger instinctually rather than analytically.

10.6.11 Heuristics Can Be Taught

Heuristics are selected and learned by teaching and modeling informally through social or communal interactions such as discussions about patients on ward rounds. Heuristics are a valid approach to problem-solving and understanding the value of and appropriate application of heuristics needs to be included in the medical school and postgraduate educational experience. If students and residents can identify the particular heuristic they are applying to a problem, their decision-making skills will be sharpened, and their thinking can be objectively critiqued. By employing commonly used and understood definitions of various types of heuristics, the communication between mentors and students can be improved, and the speed at which trainees understand and employ the fundamental cognitive skills of medical practice can be accelerated.

10.7 Intuition

If you visit Taos, New Mexico, where I live, you will want to see the Rio Grande Gorge. The gorge is a rift valley formed 29 million years ago by the shifting of the Earth's crust. Beginning near the Colorado border to the north, the gorge is over 50 miles long, and, where it passes by Taos, it is 800 feet deep. The Rio Grande River runs through the bottom of the gorge, providing world-class rafting, fly fishing, and breathtaking scenery. It is a wild place filled with critters.

While hiking along the rim of the gorge one early spring, I had an encounter with one of the local residents—*Crotalus viridis*—the prairie rattlesnake, an event that provided me with much grist for my thinking about dealing with unexpected events in medical practice. As the name would suggest, the prairie rattlesnake is usually green—actually a pale, sage green precisely the color of the desert sagebrush that grows here. When I encountered this snake, the foliage of the sagebrush had not bloomed depriving the snake of his normally excellent camouflage. Even though he was at least a yard long and lying in plain view as he enjoyed an early warm spring day on the edge of a well-travelled trail, many passed him by; I stopped and watched him for a while and thought—there is a lesson here. What did cause me to notice that something was not quite right, that something on the side of the trail was out of character with its surroundings, that, perhaps, this unusual bit of color was an indication of a threat and that I should immediately focus on that something and be cautious and ready to react. I could no longer continue along the path intent on my goal of reaching a particular overlook just down the trail. That "something" was out of place and allerted my intuition. Intuition is defined as the ability to perceive, know, or understand a situation immediately without the need for reasoning. Intuition has also been called gut feeling or gut reaction.

We rely heavily on intuition when making decisions and judgments. Intuition or "gut reactions," "second nature," or "hunches" seem unscientific, if not primitive. I have already mentioned Herbert Simon the Nobel Prize laureate. Simon wrote: "Intuition is nothing more and nothing less than recognition." Intuition is, like emotions, heavily influenced by our subcortical centers. Intuition is only of benefit in situations where, like chess masters, we are able to relate past experiences with the current situation. Our Paleolithic ancestor was aided in his escape from a lion by relying on his intuition, rather than his higher cortical centers. Without experience to fall back on, his response to a threat would be autonomic rather than intuitive.

10.7 Intuition

Our intuition is also integrated with our muscle memory. There is a major difference between a rifle shooter trying to hit a fixed target and a shotgunner trying to break a clay pigeon. In a competition, where accuracy is paramount, the rifle shooter deliberates and studies her shot, while the shotgunner engages his/her target using the muscle memory and hand-eye coordination that is the result of hours of practice. Another example is the driver who controls his automobile in a smooth, effortless fashion, engaging the analytical portions of his/her cortex only when an unanticipated situation presents. We unconsciously slow down when approaching an intersection or speed up enough to safely enter a stream of moving traffic and engage our conscious mind only when faced with having to decide if one needs to turn right or left at an unfamiliar intersection. Success is possible only with practice, however.

Intuition is a major factor in helping us to make a decision using much less information and time as we learned when looking at decision-making curve. The clinician with a well developed sense of intuition may recognize the best option before analyzing the available information in a conscious or deliberate manner. That clinician may be able to explain the evidence-based or technical rationale for a given decision but may not be able to articulate the role his intuition played in coming to that decision. Intuition does require practice and repetition—the neural pathways need to be established and the cortical responses primed by experience and practice.

Our neurotransmitters help us develop and access our intuition. Our neurons are exquisitely responsive to a surge in dopamine, and perhaps other, yet to be identified, neurotransmitters. Dopamine provides an intense feeling of pleasure. More importantly, perhaps, our neurons anticipate and expect this dopamine surge whenever we are in situations where we expect to perform well or be rewarded. The monkey in a research lab can be trained to perform a task and then rewarded for successfully completing that task. That reward will be followed by a surge in dopamine. If the monkey fails in the task, and the anticipated dopamine surge doesn't happen he will exhibit stress. The monkey becomes acutely aware of the failure or mistake, and he is startled into being more aware of the failure. His body tenses and his brain is hyper-focused. Just like the monkey, we learn from our experiences and *really* learn from our mistakes. The inexperienced resident does not relate these signals to either danger or reward and is less likely to benefit from a given experience than an experienced physician. Surgeons also experience this phenomenon when watching a resident dissect a blood vessel incautiously, not sensing that one more snip may precipitate disaster. The resident does not have the knowledge or intuition the senior surgeon has. Unlike the monkey, the human brain has much greater connections between the emotional and logical brain allowing even more extensive and faster transmission of neural signals, a fact for which our patients should be very thankful.

The feeling of pleasure generated by this dopamine burst has more impact on our learning than even the best lecturer. It is the teachable moment, an opportunity for learning that should never be allowed to pass without re-enforcement—ideally positive re-enforcement—which further stimulates dopamine secretion and the cementing of knowledge. Browbeating or intimidating the resident only activates their fear centers and suppresses the resident's receptivity to teaching. The resident's neural networks have already been activated and are busy rewiring themselves to react more effectively in the next similar situation. With this rewiring, not only are your neural network cells prepared, they have learned to anticipate what will happen next. This sense of anticipation may be the beginning of what we collectively call intuition.

An experienced surgeon knows the milestones for the normal clinical or postsurgical course and can sense when something is not quite right before the problem is obvious. If a patient's course doesn't fit the expected pattern, the diligent surgeon will sense that an untoward event may be imminent and start looking for additional information to support or allay that premonition. They see the snake others walk by.

Much of medical decision-making is based on qualitative, subtle observations that cannot be considered in an algorithm or regimented or standardized approach. This intuition takes years to develop and perhaps even longer to appreciate or listen to.

Our brains change when we undertake a new skill or practice. The areas of the cortex being stimulated show increased myelin around nerve sheaths and nerve fibers. Dendrites will proliferate and form new connections. The capability of the brain to change in response to practice or rigorous mental activity continues throughout one's life. The buildup of myelin is slow, in parallel with the time and effort required over time to achieve true mastery in a field (Zull 2002).

The neural changes seen with this type of focused effort and the communication required to impart and receive knowledge may be due to cells called *mirror neurons* (Rizzolatti and Craighero 2004; Kilner and Lemon 2013). Mirror neurons, first identified in primates, and later in humans, are motor neurons that fire when a specific action is performed and also will fire when they observe another primate performs the same action. Engagement of mirror neurons is what allows the student to absorb information and physical skills from a mentor. It takes time and effort from both the mentor and student to link these motor neurons in a way that information and principles are efficiently transmitted. The depth of this interchange ultimately eclipses the level of simple conversation, and the student and teacher begin to communicate on a synergistic and unspoken level and share wisdom and insight normally shared with acquaintances or colleagues comparable to the relation between spouses or the information and ancient knowledge a tribal shaman would share with his or her protégé.

Intuition is pattern recognition. Put another way, intuition is the sense that the pattern before the observer is, in some way, incomplete or faulty. These patterns are analogous to the mind-maps we develop for a disease or a problem. These behavior patterns will, with time, become more extensive and nuanced, and the data contained within the pattern more interrelated. We use these maps as templates to interpret what is in front of us and rapidly, almost without thinking. Using our experience, we are rapidly able to recognize the pattern of diseases and medical problems we are presented with. Intuition is not a science, and there is much we do not understand about this aspect of our behavior. Several general statements can be made about the nature of intuitive thinking, however:

10.8 Flow
139

- Intuition or how a decision using intuition was arrived at cannot be explained using our current understanding of neurophysiology.
- Intuition is not analytical or linear.
- Intuition is, to a large degree, applied pattern recognition.
- Intuition requires the ability to sort and prioritize rapidly.

Making a decision by intuition may seem a random or loose approach to solving a problem, but intuition is developed only after deliberate and critical analysis of the processes inherent and outcomes of prior experiences and decisions. It is applied experience and judgment. Intuition is not a substitute for developing the fundamental clinical skills such as observation, focused history taking, and judicious use of ancillary data. Rather, intuition is knowing what elements of the patient's history and examination are most critical combined with the ability to apply those observations in a focused and decisive manner. Intuition cannot be taught directly or formally. Much of postgraduate training is directed at developing an individual's intuitive skills in informal settings such as ward rounds and discussion of individual patients or with case studies and conferences where the rationale behind a given decision is discussed using a Socratic rather than a didactic approach. This method allows the student to reflect upon and analyze the lessons in the events discussed and gradually integrate that teaching into their unique and personalized approach to decision-making.

10.7.1 The Shadow Side of Intuition

There is a shadow side to our intuition. We search for and impose patterns on events that are, in fact, totally random, events such as a sportscaster's comments about a basketball player having a scoring streak or the so-called "hot hands" phenomenon. Our desire to ascribe patterns to other random events has been shown in studies of other phenomena to include other sports and horse racing, as well as in the stock market (Gigerenzer 2007; Johnson-Laird 2011). We also have selective and inaccurate memories about prior events and replay those errors in our memory as if they were factual. This is why several witnesses to a crime or automobile accident can have a totally different explanation of the events they observed. Also, good intuition in medicine is acquired by having extensive experience in the domain of medicine—it does not confer having good intuition in a domain you have no expertise in.

10.8 Flow

Driving an automobile is a skill that can be performed by an experienced driver almost automatically. Just as it is inconceivable that a top tier race car driver would speed around the track in a race without being fully engaged as to how his or her vehicle is performing, and what the other drivers are doing, there is no way a surgeon can conduct an operation without being fully engaged with everything that is going on in the operating room: the status of the anesthesia, the concerns and activities of the operating room personnel, and also the events unfolding in the surgical field. The good surgeon will rapidly note when there is a change in the patient's pulse rate, or the level of activity in the room.

Mihaly Csikszentmihalyi (born 1934), professor of psychology and education at the University of Chicago, performed extensive research studies to determine what constitutes optimal experiences for human beings in order to improve skills and capabilities. To explain his findings, he coined the term *flow*. The concept of flow and flow experiences is recognized in many areas, especially sports. According to Csikszentmihalyi, "Flow is that optimal condition of human experience in which we are fully engaged in the activity we are participating in to produce a state of complete immersion in and satisfaction with that activity and that moment in time" (Csikszentmihalyi 1990). We have all experienced this phenomenon while participating in sports, games, or hobbies, or in our professional activities, notably surgery. Flow, therefore, is the intersection between one's level of skill and a situation that challenges one's skill. Flow, and achieving a state of flow, has many facets as listed in the sidebar.

We learn best and perform best when we are in a state of flow. All athletes know this, and we are familiar with the sports commentators' observation that "he is really in the groove," meaning the athlete is experiencing a state of flow. To get into a state of flow is actually easy according to Csikszentmihalyi—we need to set tasks and situations that stretch our skills by just a small increment. We do not want to repeat what we have already mastered: it is boring and we rapidly lose interest. The task before us should not be significantly beyond our skills or knowledge: we will find the task frustrating. *The optimal learning experience must stretch our capabilities just enough to keep us engaged, productive, and in control*. This also means we need to attend to the environment we are working in so that we can concentrate and not be unduly distracted, and we should engage in activity when are fresh, not tired. We are able to concentrate on a given task for only a brief period of time, perhaps no more than 90 minutes, preferably an hour or less. The optimal practice environment has been extensively studied by others and termed *deliberate practice*, a concept we will take up next. To this end, we must be cognizant of the environments that produce flow and thereby optimal learning experiences, as well as those activities that interfere with optimal learning. These parameters may seem impossible in the medical training environment, but it is important to know what they are and give thought to how we can best alter schedules and clinical experiences to optimize learning.

We cannot disassociate our thinking from our emotional brain. The learning cycle may seem regimented and structured, but in fact, we cannot disregard that our brains have evolved and that our education and experiences are heavily influenced and reinforced by our emotional brains: our limbic system. Remember our Paleolithic ancestor: our learning is heavily influenced by the emotional milieu in which we experience and learn and make decisions. Our thinking and decision-making does not happen in the sterile and isolated environment in which our computers operate. Our emotional centers are activated by and supply input to any experience, decision, or action we undertake, milliseconds before our cortex is activated before we are conscious of what is happening. We are not as logical, scientific, or analytical as we would like to think. Optimal learning requires a balance between emotions such as fear, a feeling of not being entirely in control, and the emotions of joy, enjoyment of the process, and a sense of accomplishment.

Individuals who are in a state of flow are able to perform at a high level seemingly without effort. Those pursuing mastery of a given domain cannot rely on this level of performance if they wish to improve but must consciously engage in what they are doing. They cannot be satisfied with an uncritical approach to their performance. Just as it is inconceivable that a top tier race car driver would speed around the track without being fully engaged as to how his vehicle is performing, and what the other drivers are doing, there is no way a surgeon can conduct an operation without being fully engaged with everything that is going on in the operating room.

Sidebar: Flow
- Flow requires intense, laser-like thinking and concentration and utilization of our talents and skills.
- Flow tends to occur in activities that have a clear set of goals that require appropriate responses such as sports, games, and surgery or highly technical procedures.
- Flow activities provide immediate feedback (skiing, creative arts, surgery).
- Flow occurs when a person's skills are fully involved in overcoming a challenge that is just about manageable. Flow does not happen if you are performing mundane, repetitive tasks, neither does flow occur when involved in a situation where you are out of control or beyond your level of expertise.
- During flow experiences, challenges and skills are in balance. The participant is fully absorbed in the activity. Performing activities that stretch your capabilities and skills provide real growth in technical and cognitive expertise. Stretching does not require undertaking a major challenge, just a challenge that is a few degrees more difficult than what you are comfortable with. For example, to improve, musicians do not practice what they have already mastered, but what is just beyond their level of competence.

10.9 Deliberate Practice

Practice does not make perfect, perfect practice makes perfect.
—Vince Lombardi

The best surgeon I ever worked with was my mentor during my fellowship. He was not the fastest surgeon I ever saw but was the most efficient and most deliberate and delicate when handling tissues. During operations, he gave a running commentary on his philosophy of surgery, lessons learned about the problems he was dealing with, his experience with different techniques and why he preferred a particular approach, dissertations on his understanding the normal and abnormal function of the urinary tract, and on and on. It was truly a mesmerizing experience. As someone with a worldwide reputation, he was very intimidating to the residents around him. Most were too afraid to ask him questions during procedures for fear of offending him or interrupting. These budding surgeons were missing an incredible opportunity. My mentor was actually very approachable and was happy to stop what he was doing and elaborate on a fine point of technique. He did not reach the pinnacle of surgical expertise by innate talent or gifts, although he was certainly in possession of an abundance of talent. What he had done was approach each problem he saw from a very analytical and basic start and then break the approach to a given problem into its component steps.

For a surgical procedure, for example, he thought about the optimal positioning of the patient, how he should stand or sit, and how his instruments should be organized and laid out. If he had to, he would work with an instrument manufacturer to design instruments to make a particular step or maneuver easier and more facile. This approach began when he first met the patient in consultation and continued through the patient's convalescence. He did not know it, but he engaged in *deliberate practice* and how deliberate practice could be incorporated into a surgical career. He was also meticulous in his thinking about pathology and the workings of the urinary tract. He was a past master of deliberate practice not only in his surgical skills but also in terms of his thinking.

The secret to attaining expertise in any field is not just practice, although practice is a key component, it is the process of practicing in an expert, or thoughtful, and meticulous or deliberate way. Becoming an expert is not a function of innate talent, although talent does help. Becoming an expert is, more importantly, practicing with the goal of achieving excellence. The quote attributed to Vince Lombardi at the beginning of this segment says it best—one needs to practice like an expert. (This quote has also been attributed to the baseball great, Cal Ripken.)

The term deliberate practice is attributed to K. Anders Ericsson, a Swedish psychologist whose work focused on the psychology of expertise and human performance. Ericsson began his research on mastery of a discipline studying violin students at the Music Academy of West Berlin (Ericsson et al. 1993).

For this study, students whose potential varied from average (prospective music teachers in the music education department) to good (potential professional violinists) to best (potential premier or solo violinists) were chosen by their professors according to their ability, divided into age and experience matched groups, and their practice habits and lifestyles monitored and compared. Ericsson and his co-workers analyzed the length of time these students practiced, how they practiced, what they practiced, as well as their extra-curricular activities to include their sleep habits.

Ericsson found that students in the top group practiced significantly more than those in the other two groups. Not only did they practice longer and harder, they practiced smarter. They practiced in short bursts of sustained and highly focused activity. They did not focus on passages or pieces they already had mastered. Instead, the top performers worked diligently on rehearsing the fundamentals and also passages or techniques they found challenging or difficult. The practice was deliberate, hence the term deliberate practice. Ericsson and his co-workers were also able to list several behaviors that the researchers felt aided the students in achieving mastery. Those in the best group tended to practice in the mornings when they were fresh. They also slept longer at night and took afternoon naps.

It is not easy for residents or the busy clinician to incorporate deliberate practice into one's daily activities, but residents can adopt many of the habits that Ericsson's premier violin students demonstrated. Several eminent physicians of the past have done so. Hospitals and groups seem to deliberately discourage or at least put roadblocks in the way of a physician interested in deliberate practice.

Harvey Cushing, father of neurosurgery, was also a consummate follower of deliberate practice. He was talented as an illustrator and drew pictures of the pathology he encountered and surgical approaches he used. He laboriously developed his techniques for approaches to problems such as acoustic neuromas and pituitary tumors. These were tumors that had not been dealt with effectively, and as a pioneer in the field, he spent a great deal of time and energy working with cadavers and postmortem specimens to improve existing approaches or develop a new management technique. He consistently reviewed his complications and failures in an attempt to minimize the morbidity inherent in neurosurgery before the age of antibiotics and modern general anesthesia. His concern for fastidious and sterile technique resulted in infection rates and surgical mortality rates that were impressive even by today's standards. He seemed to have no limits when it came to doing what it took to solve a problem with his work. On one occasion, he even posed bent over nude so that Max Broedel, the famous medical illustrator at Johns Hopkins, could draw his backside to demonstrate the course of the sacral nerve roots. Cushing was acutely aware of the technical limitations of the time and took advantage of the opportunities he had to define the problems he faced and then develop methods to overcome those obstacles.

When engaging in deliberate practice, goals must be very specific, focused on a limited and manageable aspect of one's performance. It is not adequate to have as a goal something like "I want to have better outcomes with a particular surgical procedure" or "I want to improve the accuracy of my diagnoses." Goals and outcomes are easier to define for the more technical, quantitative, or administrative aspects of care such as complication rates for a surgical procedure, or length of hospital stay, but any aspect of medical care to include patient flow, appointment scheduling, clinic wait times, or appointment reminders, prescription costs, to name but a few aspects of one's practice that can be chosen for improvement. These more mundane aspects of a medical practice are an important but often neglected aspect of providing the highest quality, masterful care. A renowned specialist is not providing the best quality of care if his or her clinic wait times are excessive and if his office does not strive to make patients comfortable. Goals to improve outcomes may be as specific as developing ways to minimize blood loss or postoperative pain and improve one's fluidity of motion and use of ergonomics in the operating or examination room. Goals for improvement of the more qualitative aspects of care such as patient satisfaction with the functional or cosmetic results or a surgical procedure or the adequacy of pre- or postoperative education are more difficult to evaluate but are still of concern for the practitioner who wants to master their specialty (Ericsson et al. 1993; Ericsson 2004, 2008, 2009).

Chapter 11
Transitional Models

Summary
Not all medical situations can be addressed by recognition. To address more unusual or complex issues, we may need to rely on transitional methods, methods that fall between the more intuitive and reflexive approaches described in the proceeding chapter and the more analytical or cognitive approaches that will be described in the next chapter. Transitional models insure the consideration of necessary or uncommon variables in complex, emergency or highly technical situations. Standard operating procedures or protocols (SOPs), algorithms, decision support systems, decision trees, or decision support systems, can be standardized for use throughout a system or institution such as in the operating rooms or emergency or intensive care departments, modify the protocols for specific areas or situations such as adult or pediatric situations, and create computerized templates for rapid access and data input and retrieval. The ability to use computer templates for these protocols allows the information to be reviewed for quality assurance and shared for logistical purposes. For example, templates used as checklists for the operating room could be shared with the hospital medical equipment and supply department to aid in maintaining appropriate inventories.

11.1 Checklists

Physicians and surgeons are often reticent to use checklists. Checklists do allow the more mundane aspects of performing a surgical operation or preparing for a highly technical undertaking such as making sure all of the required equipment and supplies are present and functional, to be made with minimal drama, and free the team captain to concentrate on the job at hand. Checklists also reduce diagnostic errors (Ely et al. 2011; Gawande 2009). Using checklists can, therefore, improve our decision-making by allowing one to focus on the critical elements of the problem at hand. Checklists should, therefore, not be viewed as a crutch, but as having another set of eyes and ears available to keep one out of trouble and insure that we have not failed to consider the appropriate options or variables. Checklists, time-outs and pre-frontal pauses, are accepted as a standard part of medical practice. We should also be aware of the other, less obvious advantages to using these tools, either as a part of a standard operating protocol or an individualized approach to working through a task such as developing a differential diagnosis, writing patient care orders, or developing a management strategy. These maneuvers should become habits. Advantages of such adjuncts include decreasing reliance on memory alone, stepping back from immediate problem to consider options and reasoning processes, developing strategies to avoid bias, and countering fatigue or distraction.

11.2 Standard Operating Procedures

Standard operating procedures (SOPs) are widely used in trauma units, operating rooms, and by cardiac arrest teams, situations where decisions and interventions need to be started immediately, often in the face of considerable chaos. Triage personnel and screeners are often provided with algorithms. These ancillary health-care providers can use an algorithm to answer telephone requests and decide when a patient calling their office needs immediately or not. With the shortage of physicians we are facing today, algorithms used by ancillary care providers may be the way to allow physicians to spend their time dealing with more complex problems.

SOPs require that decisions be made by both elimination and recognition as one progresses through the decision-making process. Both algorithms and SOPs operate by having decision nodes at critical points in the process. As one progresses through an algorithm, the decision-maker will be forced to either eliminate or decide upon which branch of a node to take next. The decision-maker cannot, follow the pathway blindly—a choice must be made, and if the best choice is not obvious, appeal to a colleague, consultant, or, in the case of a non-physician screener, a supervisor is necessary.

11.3 Algorithms

Algorithms are a variation of the SOP. Algorithms rely on a structured, binary approach to assessing a problem based on presence or absence of predetermined findings or factors. Algorithms force the user to evaluate critical factors at nodes or forks along the decision-making pathway in a sequential fashion. These nodes serve as markers that prevent the user from overlooking key steps. For that reason, algorithms can also be used by inexperienced decision-makers allowing them to progress through the decision-making process with minimal supervision or experience. *Algorithms are, therefore, an excellent teaching tool.* They provide a structured and logical approach to the diagnosis and management of a specific problem and can highlight key decision-making junctures and pitfalls. They can also be used as the format for a case-based discussion on the wards or in more formal conference settings.

We rely heavily on algorithms—established, step-by-step guidelines or rules that guide us in the evaluation and management of patients with specified conditions. There is a large volume of research showing that algorithms are a more reliable tool for solving problems than expert judgment (Lewis 2017; Margolis 1983). Algorithms take the guesswork out of managing crisis situations, or problems that entail multiple sequential steps, allowing one to devote their cognitive skills to assessing and managing the chaos and multiple aspects of emergencies or other stressful situations. Algorithms, like mnemonics, are very useful tools even if they appear simple or like following a recipe in a cookbook. Algorithms are useful for even the most skilled clinician, especially when faced with an unusual problem or treating a condition that might require multiple unusual laboratory studies or management steps such as major electrolyte or fluid disturbances. Such guides are especially helpful when harried or sleep deprived (Hoffman 1960; Hoffman et al. 1968).

Algorithms can also be used to assist non-physicians to screen and even diagnose medical problems. Algorithms have been used in the military to allow enlisted personnel trained as medics to screen and manage patients with acute minor illnesses. Several studies demonstrate this point well (Lewis 2017; Goldberg 1970, 1978). A study performed by the Oregon Research Institute showed radiologists failed to identify the presence of stomach cancer in a high percent of cases when shown with upper gastrointestinal radiographs of patients with suspected gastric malignancy in a double-blinded fashion. The research group lead by Goldberg then asked the radiologists to develop an algorithm containing the generally accepted radiographic findings of patients with stomach cancer. The result was a seven-point scale ranging from findings showing a definite malignancy to a study being definitely benign. The algorithm using the variables determined by the radiologists proved to be more accurate than the trained radiologists.

The researchers then performed a similar experiment, using clinical psychologists and psychiatrists, to devise an algorithm that could be used to determine at what point it was safe to discharge psychiatric patients from hospital. Graduate students using the algorithm proved to be as accurate as trained psychologist in determining which patients should be discharged (Lewis 2017).

A study by Martignon et al. demonstrates that a well-developed algorithm does not have to be complicated to provide a high degree of diagnostic accuracy and also that the processes that physicians use to justify their diagnoses may not always be as nuanced and esoteric as they would have us believe (Martignon et al. 2008). It also shows that, to be of value, algorithms must be followed.

11.3.1 Computer Enhancement of Algorithms

The marriage of the immense volume of data collected in electronic health records (EHR) and computer-enhanced analytics has produced opportunities to develop even more sophisticated algorithms (Obermeyer and Lee 2017). For example, one group analyzed electrocardiograms looking for miniscule changes that might be associated with sudden cardiac death. These changes cannot be evaluated by even the most astute cardiologist on a standard electrocardiogram, but with computer enhancement, this study show that computationally generated cardiac biomarkers could be used to assess risk profiles of patients who had experienced an acute coronary syndrome (Syed et al. 2011). The ability to sift through data captured in electronic health records also provided the statistical power necessary to identify subtle correlations. Computationally based algorithms are therefore able to provide answers to management questions about management recommendations and patient risk patterns that even the most broad-based multicenter studies of the past have been able to provide. Such algorithms have the additional advantage of being able to be continuously refined as new data is collected.

11.3.2 The Shadow Side of Algorithms

Algorithms do have their downsides. They need to be carefully crafted and based on adequate data and valid treatment protocols. Even a well-constructed and proven algorithm may not account for individual differences between patients. Also, treatment guidelines in an algorithm may not meet patient expectations or preferences. Algorithms are, therefore, not a substitute for good clinical judgment and consideration of the needs of the individual patient. The best algorithm is of limited value if it is not followed.

11.4 Decision Trees

Decision trees are a more complex form of an algorithm. Decision trees, as a device to show relationships, go back to the third century AD where they were used to record the genealogy of royal dynasties and to depict the hierarchy within organizations. Unlike the algorithm, the nodes or decision points in a decision tree can be binary or multiple—several options or different paths can be present in the node of a decision tree, unlike the simple binary arrangement of an algorithm.

To be valid and of clinical use, a decision tree must be carefully constructed to be both logical and visually unambiguous. A decision tree is a graphic or visual representation of a rule or sets of rules, the nodes depicting the objects to be classified, and each branch representing a different answer to the question. The rules of decision inherent in the tree should be simple and listed at the earliest possible times. The order of relationships between the variables in the tree should be context-specific and avoid uncommon cue combinations. The branches should be causally organized by cause or major to indicate presence or absence of a factor. Decision trees, therefore, require greater thought and analysis in their construction than simple algorithms. Decision trees, by nature of the fact that they may require consideration of more than two options, also require greater judgment and consideration from the user than an algorithm.

Decision trees can be full, indicating all possible options, or truncated or pruned, showing only the major branches or decision paths. A truncated decision tree may be drawn to present a more simplified or optimal decision-making processes. Pruned trees can therefore be thought of as a method of depicting the decision process in a fast and frugal format (Martignon et al. 2003).

11.5 Decision Support Systems

Decision support systems (DSS) are computer-based systems designed to analyze the data available about a particular problem or condition to help clinicians make decisions about the diagnosis or management of those conditions. They are like algorithms and decision trees, but more extensive and computationally complex, requiring a large database that makes them cumbersome or overwhelming for users and may disrupt workflow. Decision support systems have been used in large organizations, especially in situations where executive decisions are required for complex, unstructured situations such as gate assignment systems for an airline or warehousing needs for a large, multiple facility, scheduling for railway use by multiple companies.

Clinical decision support systems (CDDS) are feasible today because of the advances made over the past few decades in the fields of artificial intelligence and electronic medical record systems. CDDS are the computer age answer to algorithms or decision trees. Support systems like those mentioned in the preceding paragraph have a long way to go before they are widely adopted in medicine or available to the clinician. CDDS have been shown to be useful in making antimicrobial treatment decisions, as they can screen for current local drug resistance patterns, drug allergies, contraindications, drug interactions, cost containment, and adequate dosing.

Optimal support systems are dependent on up-to-date databases and therefore must evolve over time. The factors cannot be maintained manually—they are too extensive and complex and thus rely on well-constructed software. Such systems must be well-structured, unambiguous, and rule based so that all users can understand and work with the system efficiently and accurately. They must not be so cumbersome as to intrude unnecessarily on the clinician's already overloaded schedule. A CDSS must be flexible and adaptable to the conditions unique to the patient in question and also the institution in which care is provided. A CDSS must also be highly contextually oriented so that the clinician can rapidly access the pertinent information without having to dig through a large amount of data not applicable to the problem at hand.

Building a CDDS requires extensive statistical assessment of the pertinent literature within the domain of interest, input from experts within that domain to include consideration of regional differences and institutional capabilities. Formulating such a system may require developing unique mathematical approaches and domain-specific rules of application. A valid CDDS must also be based on an adequate volume of patient experience. CDSS are most valid for cardiovascular diseases, certain infectious diseases, malignancies, public health, or environmental health problems where large, multicenter trials have been conducted or outcomes data are available.

Any CDDS, no matter how complete, will rapidly become obsolete and will require constant updating and assessment. This work will require teams of experts to develop a good system and will be costly and time-consuming. An obvious problem with all three of the instruments discussed here is the question of who will provide the funds, expertise, and computer support required to develop and maintain them.

Chapter 12
Decision-Making by Elimination

Summary
Some decisions require analysis or maintenance of extensive amounts of data. Some decisions require in-depth review of the medical literature or outcomes of clinical research studies. Some decisions require consideration of multiple options or modification of treatment regimens due to the presence of conflicting factors such as multiple disease processes. For these situations, decisions by recognition or use of transitional models may not be appropriate. Decisions requiring the situations just listed can be categorized as decision-making by elimination. These approaches include the use of statistical and mathematical models or review of outcomes-based research, reliance on evidence-based medicine, or developing a formal differential diagnosis. These approaches are more time-consuming and more useful for complex, complicated, or very uncommon disease processes or conditions where data from large, prospective clinical trials or studies are available.

12.1 Statistics and Mathematical Models

As has been noted earlier, it is mandatory that the physician be educated in the theories behind statistical analyses and how to incorporate statistically verified outcomes from research studies into their medical practice. This is all part of the practice of good medicine and the decision-making process. The role of statistics in everyday clinical practice does need to be put into perspective, however. The clinician cannot expect to be a statistician.

As powerful as statistical and mathematical have become for enhancing our understanding of health and disease, they still remain somewhat of a mystery for clinicians. The reasons are obvious. First, even with the advent of pocket calculators and the ubiquitous presence of computers, the busy clinician does not have the training or time to be navigate statistical packages at the bedside. The time may come when this capability is mature enough for widespread usage, but that era has not been realized. Second, and of more importance, clinicians are not statisticians. Yes, we have all had some rudimentary training in this field, and most understand the basic concepts, and have a limited vocabulary of statistical terminology, but individuals with a sophisticated and working knowledge of statistics remain rare in medical institutions, even academic centers.

Textbooks have been written about the use of statistics and mathematical models in medicine, and discussion about statistical methodology is beyond the scope of this book, for several reasons. First, to apply statistics and mathematical models requires a level of knowledge and expertise beyond the vast majority of clinicians. Second, mathematical models are complex and cumbersome for use in routine clinical practice. Third, texts on mathematical models or statistics for medical applications do not address the fundamental question that this book endeavors to answer—how does the practicing clinician or surgeon go about making decisions? Fourth, as has been discussed previously, much of medical decision-making involves unbounded considerations, and such considerations do not lend themselves to reduction to a mathematical formula, except in situations where large numbers of patients or events can be collated and analyzed. Data from such analyses or studies does give the clinician useful and powerful information about the behavior of a disease process, but the physician still must exercise his or her knowledge and judgment when using this information to aid an individual patient. The physician must still make the necessary decisions. We can anticipate that computers will become more accessible in the clinical environment and that clinician-friendly programs and packages will be developed to provide the support necessary to use the data available from relevant resources in an efficient manner.

Should our colleagues in the worlds of statistics, computer science and artificial intelligence continue to search for ways to improve the ways we can analyze data and better understand what research studies can tell us? Absolutely. Progress will almost certainly be slow and incremental, and the surgeon faced with a patient with an acute abdomen in the middle of the night, or the oncologist faced with deciding the optimal approach for an individual with advanced carcinoma, will still have to rely on their judgment and experience for the foreseeable future. Statistics will never replace but only support good clinical judgment.

Data, to be meaningful, generally requires looking at large populations, yet we deal with one patient at a time. Causation is just the beginning of solving a medical problem and may be unrelated to the solution for the problem. We know that a smoker should stop that habit, but the fact that he is a smoker has little or no direct bearing on the fact that he now has lung cancer. Even if we know that smoking causes lung cancer, there is no certainty that smoking was the cause of an individual patient's cancer. We do not deal in a world of absolutes. Even if we have a well-supported diagnosis, the decision-making process must still consider many other variables, uncertainties, and unknowns resulting in the fact that, as Aristotle noted, the real wisdom involved in making the decision is judgment and practical reasoning (Gold 1985).

As we have seen in the last chapter, an increasing interest in applying mathematical models and developing equations algorithms allows medical decision-making to be more quantifiable, rational, and reproducible. Some of this interest has been driven by insurance and regulatory bodies in an attempt to develop standards of best practice or determine best outcomes. The computational power of computers combined with large collections of data we can access today can provide answers to vexing clinical problems if we can identify the important clinical variables or analyze the vast body of published data. Such an approach may help in public health, communicable diseases, or oncology where studies of a large cohort of patients are available. Such studies, no matter how large the data base or profound the outcomes, are still only a guide when dealing with an individual patient. Indeed, most medical research involves small numbers of patients, making the conclusions one can draw from most clinical studies of limited value. We cannot divorce our decisions from the reality that patients do not behave in a predictable or consistent way and are subject to the uniqueness of their genetic constitution, personality, and lifestyle. The potential value of mathematical approaches to problem-solving is exciting and these tools may become more prevalent in the day-to-day clinical practice in the future, but such such approaches are currently of little value to the practicing clinician faced with a time-sensitive problem at the bedside of an individual patient. Absorbing and understanding a body of knowledge proven to be statistically or computationally of merit are achieved, not at the bedside but during the course of the physician's efforts at mastering the information in the quiet hours given to study or contemplation.

12.2 Statistics and Mathematical Models: The Shadow Side

12.2.1 Statistics and the Individual Patient

Medical decision-making, especially in the academic environment, is heavily influenced by statistics and the use of statistical significance from research. The reliance on statistics has the authority of mathematical or objective significance but can be improperly applied if based on small samples, poorly defined study group characteristics or inappropriate parameters. Recommendations or inferences based on data from one institution may not be appropriate for another institution due to many factors to include variation in technical abilities or expertise (equipment or operator), variations in terminology or inclusion or exclusion criteria for a particular study, appropriateness of statistical methodology used, resources available, methods of data collection, and interpretation.

How often after a presentation on some aspect of clinical or basic science research has anyone seen a member of the audience contest the statistical methodology used to analyze the data in the paper? I am not a statistician and certainly have a minimal appreciation of the best tools to use for analyzing a set of data in a given project. I am a clinician. I know very few community-based even academic physicians who can discuss knowledgably which statistical approaches are best for a given study. Yet, we are quick to accept the statistical methodology used for a given project without question. I am not arguing that we should become experts or even conversant in statistics, just that we retain a degree of skepticism about the validity or methodology of analysis used to support or defend an argument (Willenheimer 2001).

12.2.2 Computational Intractability

> A problem is called "intractable" if the only known way of finding the perfect solution requires checking a number of steps that increase exponentially with the size of the problem. (Gigerenzer 2007)

Most medical decisions are made by considering a limited amount of data or number of variables. The human mind can only consider a handful of variables at any one time, and attempts to consider more than the fingers on one hand carry the risk of arriving at a poor decision.

There are also practical limits to programming a calculator to predict outcomes from a set of data with multiple variables. The number of potential outcomes can rapidly exceed the capability of a computer to identify outcomes in a timely or meaningful fashion. Since the number of outcomes increases exponentially with the addition of each new variable, medical problems do not often lend themselves to computer modeling. Simple algorithms can be rapid and accurate if the variables are limited in number and discrete, but many medical problems cannot be distilled down to a limited number of variables or established conditions without human intervention on an almost case by case basis. The game of chess, for example, has more possible moves or responses to a move that the average personal computer can process in a timely fashion. To date, it has not been possible to design a computer program that will consistently outperform a chess master. Games such as chess also have set rules, and, as such, outcomes are not contestable. The conditions for declaring a winner in a game of chess are also well defined. This is not the case in medicine where any rules are ill-defined and outcomes not fixed or certain. There is often no best or defined outcome. Certainly, having a lot of data about prior patient histories can be used to compute probability of outcomes obtained through hindsight, but predictability of an outcome in a new patient is not the same as probability of outcomes documented in prior cases (Gigerenzer 2007).

Another problem with computer models of medical problems is that the computer has no compassion for or connection with the patient at hand. The computer is therefore incapable of reading the subtle, verbal and nonverbal messages a patient provides to an empathic physician, thereby allowing that physician to pick up on the soft, unquantifiable data the patient projects.

12.2.3 Ethical Considerations

Can physicians use statistical predictions to make decisions, or are they bound to exercise critical judgment as well? The probabilities or prognoses generated in long-term, large surveys may provide data that is the most up-to-date or accurate, but such data may not be the most reasonable or appropriate for an individual patient or an isolated set of circumstances. The same arguments can be made for recommendations generated by evidence-based approaches. What are the moral and ethical responsibilities of the physician in these situations? Obviously, a comprehensive discussion of these issues is not within the scope of this volume, but it is appropriate to, at a minimum, make the reader aware that these adjuncts to decision-making do carry an ethical and possibly a legal component (Dawes 2002). When does failure to apply statistical predictions or probabilities or ethics-based recommendations constitute failure to provide the best standard of care? Are such recommendations to inform and educate the clinician or make the physician aware of current standards or levels of practice? Should such recommendations be accepted as the benchmark for practice standards or superior to clinical judgment, thereby absolving the clinician of adding his or her judgment or experience to the diagnosis or management matrix?

12.3 Evidence-Based Approaches

> The dogmas of the quiet past are inadequate to the stormy present. The occasion is piled high with difficulty, and we must rise with the occasion. As our case is new, so we must think anew and act anew.
> —Abraham Lincoln

Evidence-based medicine (EBM) has become a powerful asset in our decision-making. EBM does not require that we become statisticians and allows us to remain clinicians working at the bedside where we belong. Using EBM is nothing more than applying a more formalized approach to evaluating and understanding the empiric principles of medical therapy and disease we were all taught in medical school and during our training, an approach to practicing reasonable and judicious medicine or surgery.

EBM is the conscientious, disciplined, and informed use of the best or most objective data or information available in evidenced by controlled and well-performed clinical research and is arguably the best, most rational, and most scientifically grounded approach to solving clinical problems, especially problems without an obvious intuitive answer or problems involving high risk or uncertain outcomes.

Medical practice is rife with myths, prejudices, tradition, and reliance on what is now obsolete information. EBM forces us to critically examine the available data and our practice patterns in an attempt to discard inaccurate or less than valid practices for those that are at the vanguard of our understanding of disease and medicine.

Evidence-based medicine, or the practice of making medical decisions based on considered and statistically driven analysis of published experience, outcomes, and other data, has helped to place medical decisions on a more logical or scientifically grounded basis. There is no question that data and clinical findings that have been subjected to the rigors of analysis that define EBM allow us to practice better medicine and make more rational decisions. EBM is not a decision-making tool in the same way as an algorithm, or heuristic, however. EBM is a deductive or type 2 way of thinking. EBM may require extensive reading or the digestion of evidence-based reviews provided by journals or specialty societies. These tasks form the basis of the practical and knowledge basic skills necessary for good medical practice and are what defines empiric medical practice. Evidence-based medicine should therefore be the most current and best and hopefully the most efficient and cost-effective approach to management of a particular disease or process.

The EBM approach is also a more effective way to advance one's knowledge. We all have trouble keeping current. Medical journals publish articles at a rate no one can keep up with, and most of the articles, even in a specialty journal, are of little immediate or practical benefit. The topics covered are just too wide ranging, and it is not enough to merely read articles; one must integrate, contemplate, and, ideally, discuss pertinent articles. An article relevant to one's practice should also stimulate further reading rather than moving on to the next article in the latest issue of a journal like one would read a popular magazine.

12.3.1 What EBM Is Not

EBM is not a cookbook approach to medical practice. Neither does EBM involve abandoning traditional practice patterns and conventions—just those that do not stand up to the scrutiny of good evidence.

EBM is not a substitute for clinical judgment, nor is it a mandate for pursuing a particular therapy or for initiating an established and reasonable approach to therapy. It is conceptual rather than prescriptive.

EBM does not detract from the individual practitioner's ability to decide what course might be best for an individual patient in an individual clinical or geographic situation, but EBM does trump personal bias or individual experience in favor of the outcomes of large, combined, and rigorous, well-designed studies.

Evidence-based medicine does not alter the fundamental skills necessary or essence of medical practice. It does help in teaching and clarifying our thinking to put decisions on a more rational and qualitative basis.

Basing decisions on an unfiltered or pure application of evidence-based principles does not always guarantee an optimal outcome, nor it is always the best course for a given patient or practitioner. Blind application of an evidence-based approach does not alter the fact that judgment and clinical experience are necessary for good decision-making. There is too much variability between patients and the presentation of disease entities and the response of interventions in biological systems too variable.

12.3.2 The Shadow Side of EBM

Given all the benefits EBM provides, it is just one tool we have, and it does not resolve all of the issues the practitioner is faced with. Given the increased interest in alternative or homeopathic medicine and the increasing tendency for patients and families to question or be wary of what the doctor recommends, the line between standard medical dogma and patient preferences has become increasingly blurred. No longer is the physician always considered right or the definitive spokesperson for an individual's attitudes towards health care, nor is medical advice taken at face value.

EBM cannot provide solutions to all the problems of clinical practice. Not all problems are readily subject to the scrutiny of meta-analysis or analysis of variance. This applies especially to those who are engaged in surgical and interventional specialties. Surgeons are, as a rule, slower to incorporate recommendations that demand a major change in their practice from any source to include EBM. This is not due to a lack of understanding of the concept behind EBM or an intrinsic distrust of attempts to standardize medical thinking. There are many reasons for their reluctance.

Sidebar: Evidence-Based Medicine and Surgery
1. Many surgical problems do not lend well to long-term, randomized, controlled, and prospective studies.
2. There is often an editorial and regional bias inherent in studies from single institutions. A standard practice in Chicago may not be accepted in Phoenix, and a protocol in a large city may not be appropriate for a small rural community.
3. The findings of a large prospective study may not be directly or totally applicable to an individual patient, surgeon's experience or skills, or institutional capacity, nor do they always account for the patient's cultural or personal beliefs, geography, or individual needs.
4. Most clinical studies in surgery are based on a relatively small number of patients, and those patients may not be well stratified or rigidly selected. They represent the collated experience of the institution, not a broad-based population.
5. Most surgeons do not like being the first or the last to adopt a new technique. They want to see that novel recommendations or new techniques first stand the test of time. Journals are filled with articles that show new research findings and breakthroughs in our knowledge and encourage new techniques that have minimal follow-up. Much of the information published does not weather the test of

time. How can a surgeon apply this information confidently in his or her practice, knowing that he, and not the authors of a journal article, is responsible for the outcome of their procedures for an individual patient?
6. Surgeons trust what works in their hands and tend to be slow to change habits. The outcome of a surgical procedure is not just the result of one factor but the combination of multiple events and factors.

There is a risk that hospitals, insurers, or government agencies mandate strict adherence to the conclusions of evidence-based reviews issued by specialty societies or other official bodies, using the argument that deviation is prima facie evidence of substandard or inappropriate practice. This also gives attorneys a potent argument to criticize an individual practitioner's decisions or actions. Medical practice would be easy if there were generic, cookbook guidelines for each problem, and no other considerations were necessary. As humanists and guardians of the welfare of our patients, physicians have responsibilities beyond the impartial application of recommendations based merely on EBM. Physicians must also consider the *implied tasks* of medical practice which include:

- Delivery of health care in a humane, caring, and compassionate manner
- Practice within the ethical boundaries of the profession
- Adherence to the standards and expectations of society (Pellegrino and Thomasma 1981)

The implied tasks cannot be reduced to a formula or easily followed guidelines. We must temper our management recommendations to fit the individual patient's situation. An evidence-based review can consider the ethical and humanistic factors of medical care in only a broad and generic way, if at all. These facets of medical decision-making are arguably the most difficult to master and apply. The decision to operate, begin chemotherapy, or institute any type of intervention is not always easy, even when armed with an extensive, evidence-based support for the optimal approach.

Two equally qualified and experienced radiologists can read imaging studies differently. Laboratory tests have an inherent error rate, many physical findings are subject to interpretation, and the patient's history may be misleading and is certainly subject to listener bias. The results of research studies and published observations of clinical cases are also liable to different interpretations. Our best attempts to place medicine on sound scientific footing do not eliminate uncertainty or ambiguity or legitimate difference of opinion. EBM will never resolve the uncertainties inherent in this process. Advances in knowledge will always help, but medical decisions will always be shadowed by some degree of uncertainty and chaos. Decisions will always, to some degree, be unbounded. EBM will never replace good clinical judgment, and the decision regarding the best course for a particular patient will always remain a challenge.

EBM does not take into account local capabilities, resources, levels of expertise and experience, geography, or a patient's financial resources for travel or other family needs.

Our brains are not programmed to handle data in a purely logical or analytical way. Decisions are rarely based on pure mathematical or statistics driven analysis. We have, with experience, a self-calibrated bias towards events or situations we encounter. Our calibration may be very inaccurate, skewed by experiences with untoward outcomes of previous patients, inflated or exaggerated ideas of just how good our treatment results are for a given problem. We may be using the wrong data. We may think that the probability of a certain event or outcome is 10 per cent when in reality it is 25 per cent. We may think that the complication rate for a given procedure is 5 per cent in our hands, but we may have not performed enough of that procedure to accurately state the complication rate in one's personal experience. Just because the complication rate in a published report is 13 per cent does not mean that an individual surgeon will have an identical result. A junior or newly minted surgeon will not have had sufficient experience with any procedure to be able to truthfully tell a patient that "in my hands, the incidence of this particular complication rate is x per cent." It may be years before a surgeon can truthfully make that statement.

Management of the anomalies and outliers cannot be reduced to an algorithm or best practice guidelines. The unique case may not have the statistical power necessary to justify an evidence-based approach. The clinician must rely on his or her clinical skill, experience, and judgment.

Opting for a treatment that is not in synch with EBM guidelines because of any of these factors does not constitute bad medicine as long as the physician and the patient fully understand those implications. Opting for radiation or chemotherapy because that modality is available locally is an acceptable alternative to surgery, even if surgery is the ideal choice if the patient does not want to travel to an institution that does the surgery or has other objections to surgery. Those that would wish to mandate therapeutic decisions exclusively on EBM guidelines do not appreciate that medical decision-making is a holistic endeavor and should not be bound to impersonal or, worse, financially driven mandates.

12.4 The Differential Diagnosis

We are all taught how to develop a differential diagnosis by the time we begin our clinical rotations. Learning to create a differential diagnosis is a fixture in medical education and a logical and useful exercise for the student, resident, or mature physician faced with a difficult case. Formulating and working through a differential diagnosis may be the best decision-making tool available for those in training. It is especially valuable for vague or ill-defined problems that may have a number of causes such as hypotension, tachycardia, or shortness of breath. It allows the formulation of a thoughtful explanation for the patient's narrative and the first step in designing a plan for evaluation and, ultimately, treatment and can help the clinician avoid overlooking uncommon causes for common symptoms. Medical decision-making should always favor the principle of Occam's razor—the search for the simplest and most straightforward explanation for the patient's symptoms. A well-thought-out list of potential diagnoses helps to keep our thinking fresh and broadly based, not falling into the trap of biased or narrow thinking.

Using the differential diagnosis method to manage patients does have limitations and pitfalls. That diagnosis is a label for a work in progress, subject to change as new information is obtained and as the patient's condition or response to therapy evolves. It is not a final decree. In this regard, the differential diagnosis should be thought of as an information management or thinking tool. Once a list of potential diagnoses has been created, the clinician must still be engaged in further evaluation and decision-making, always thinking beyond the diagnoses that have been considered. To consider a list of differential diagnoses as rigid or complete blunts our lateral thinking or considering possibilities that were not immediately apparent. Unlike a horse race, where, once a bet is placed, it cannot be changed, the differential diagnosis is always a work in progress.

We may be guilty of labelling a patient with a diagnosis too casually or prematurely. For example, if a patient is admitted to hospital with the diagnosis of a myocardial infarction, that diagnosis is likely to shadow the patient throughout his hospital course. Would it not be better to use an admitting symptom such as chest pain and force the receiving and consulting services to consider the etiology of the symptom rather than accept a diagnosis that might have been formulated in haste or based on incomplete information in the emergency department?

The challenge of a complicated diagnostic problem is, for many, the joy and excitement of medicine, what keeps one's passion for the profession alive. Problems that have well-defined solutions are rarely debated. It is the anomaly, outlier, or exception to the routine that we seek. The patient with a perplexing problem may be the beginning of the trail that, if followed, would provide a significant advance in our understanding of a disease process. Unfortunately, the busy clinician rarely has the time to pursue rare or elusive problems; he is more interested in what is immediately useful and practical. For some, such a case is the siren song that lures them into academics or research. In this sense, medical situations are more like dealing with a problem in particle physics chaos theory than staying in the cause and effect world of Newtonian physics.

Some presenting complaints, such as a lacerated finger, may be obvious with the differential diagnosis consisting primarily of issues that need to be excluded such as injury to adjacent structures such as nerves or tendons. The clinician must consider whether the laceration may be safely sutured in the emergency department or if a specialist needs to take the patient to surgery for more extensive exploration or repair. That scenario is very different from the patient who presents with a fever of unknown origin or shortness of breath. The student will see more complex problems over and over in their practice, so it is of great benefit for the novice to reinforce their thinking about such problems over and over again using the tool of the differential diagnosis.

12.4 The Differential Diagnosis

The creation of a differential diagnosis is therefore an excellent training exercise for students and junior residents. It teaches them pattern recognition for complaints that patients commonly present with. It also aids in the shift from centrifugal to centripetal thinking. The process is inefficient and costly if the novice is allowed to pursue each diagnosis with the testing required to search each rabbit trail separately. They do not have the ability to discriminate between diagnostic possibilities and have not developed the breadth of experience the practiced clinician possesses.

12.4.1 The Differential Diagnosis and the Beginner

The medical student beginning his or her clinical rotations will have difficulty developing a sound differential diagnosis. Their education has been predominately centrifugal, and now they are challenged to reverse their thought processes and think centripetally. In addition, they do not have a frame of reference for which diagnoses are possible or more probable. For them diagnosis #1 has the same relevance as diagnosis #2. They have a limited frame of reference with which to differentiate one diagnosis from another and cannot order diagnoses in terms of either relevance, practicality, or urgency. This is not a criticism of the novice, but a reflection of the limitations they are working with when learning this process. Their ability to appreciate nuances or subtle distinctions between possible diagnoses and their feel for the relative probabilities of one disease over another are limited. They may know that pneumonia is worse than the common cold, but for the purpose of establishing a correct diagnosis, their ability is very limited. For the novice, all diagnoses are equivalent or equally likely, as represented in the diagram by the circles of equal size. Without being able to discriminate, the learner must give equal attention to each possibility—an inefficient way to solve the problem. Developing a differential diagnosis is a way of practicing one's mind-mapping skills (Fig. 12.1).

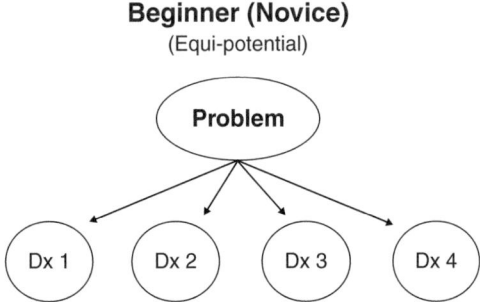

Fig. 12.1 The beginner's differential diagnosis

12.4.2 The Intermediate Learner

With a growing knowledge base and more clinical experience, the trainee can approach the differential diagnosis from a more sophisticated perspective. No longer is it adequate to just create a list. One can be more selective as to probability of a particular diagnosis being more likely and which diagnoses are more ominous and require more diligent consideration. The intermediate learner is learning to prioritize diagnoses based on probability, pattern recognition, and their ability to accumulate the appropriate data. Diagnosis #1 may be likely, but not nearly as attractive as diagnosis #2, and diagnosis #3 assumes the position of a distant possibility. No longer are the circles the same diameter, but the process is still less than optimally efficient. The diagram has bi-directional arrows indicating that the intermediate learner must evaluate and exclude each possibility before arriving at the optimal diagnosis (Fig. 12.2).

12.4.3 The Master

The experienced clinician cannot only develop an adequate list of possible diagnoses; she has the knowledge, experience, and judgment to rapidly triage the possibilities and focus on the most likely solution. She can create an appropriate list of potential diagnoses but, with her experience, is able to rapidly focus on the most probable diagnosis and place a low priority on a diagnosis that is only remotely possible. The lines between the problem and diagnoses are of different width indicating that she can prioritize the potential diagnoses. She is also able to consider that while diagnosis #2 is most probable, other diagnoses must not be dismissed out of hand, especially if those diagnoses carry a significant risk to the patient if overlooked. The arrows also go both ways: The judicious clinician cannot, without overwhelming

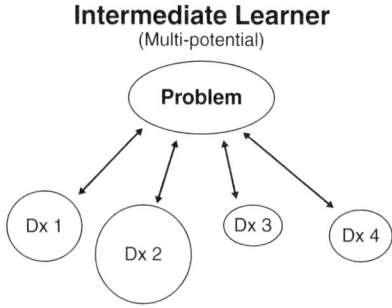

Fig. 12.2 The intermediate learner

12.4 The Differential Diagnosis

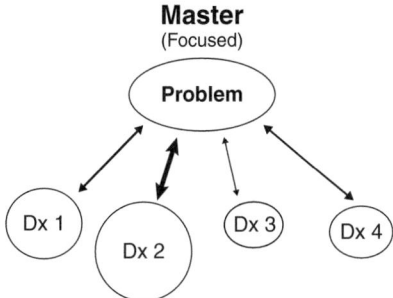

Fig. 12.3 The master decision-maker

evidence or the urgency of the clinical situation, forget about the possibility of the remaining diagnoses, even if they initially appear remote. The differential diagnosis one initially constructs is not to be regarded as a one-way process but always subject to review and, if necessary, expansion (Fig. 12.3).

Chapter 13
Managing Errors

> *We are also unduly attached to opinions or beliefs that we like to think are true but, in fact, are not well supported (Author unknown).*

Summary

We all commit errors—both errors of commission and errors of omission. It is an inevitable part of medical practice. Some errors are due to bad or poorly thought-out decisions. Errors may be due to technical failures or inexperience with a particular procedure or concept, inadequate preparation, poor judgment, and inadequate or erroneous information. We must also distinguish errors due to poor decision-making from errors due to technical, equipment, or organizational failures.

13.1 Errors: An Overview

No one sets out to make an error. Physicians have a well-developed capacity for self-criticism and probably learn more from their mistakes than they do from the multitude of decisions and actions that go well. Unfortunately, the litigious world we live has given birth to a legion of observers and critics that are anxious to point out any shortcomings in our actions. Practicing defensive medicine is an accepted but somehow less than satisfying strategy. Not only do we need to be critical of our own decisions, but we are frequently placed in the position of having to judge our peers or those we supervise or teach. We can be blind to shortcomings in our judgment and thinking, and well-intentioned attempts to improve our decision-making or technical skills can be immediately met with hostility and permanent damage to relationships. Criticism is easy, but helping ourselves and those we work with to improve their performance and thinking is an art form. Learning to recognize biases and faulty thinking in ourselves and in others is a part of maturing as a physician. What is more difficult, and ultimately more valuable, is learning how to help ourselves and others in a constructive and encouraging way. As with all aspects of decision-making in medicine, there is value in looking at the common errors and flaws in our thinking. Hopefully, those who have ruminated about these errors will be better prepared to either recognize them in themselves or provide meaningful and not damaging input to their peers, team members, and students when called upon to address the actions of others.

We all make errors. An unpleasant yet mandatory part of medical training is to realize this truth and to learn to recognize and manage errors appropriately and learn from one's mistakes. Recognition of errors and learning is compounded by the fact that there is rarely immediate feedback. A repair that looked good in the operating room may not heal properly, and the surgeon may not make the correlation between his technique or decision-making and a poor outcome when he sees the patient several weeks after the patient has been discharged from hospital. This problem is compounded by the medicolegal system that penalizes those who dictate procedural summaries. Dictated summaries provide an excellent vehicle to discuss difficulties encountered in the course of a procedure, considerations for alternate approaches one might have had during the procedure, notations of how the course of the procedure could have been improved or portions where techniques or materials could have been altered. Unfortunately, such an introspective approach provides grist for the medico-legal mill instead of helping the surgeon to improve his or her skills and surgical procedure notes and written consultations are not as valuable as they could be.

A major task for medical educators and clinical faculty is to provide a direct and frank model of how physicians are monitored, controlled, and indoctrinated into the guild of medicine to include development of appropriate attitudes towards errors. To this end, decision-making, and the teaching of that skill, becomes an integral part of the acculturation of medical students and physicians in training. Much of this process is informal and unspoken as students and junior physicians learn the norms of the profession, what behaviors are expected, and what aspects of their interactions are privileged and sacrosanct (Bosk 2003).

Medicine is an inexact discipline, and outcomes are subject to a myriad of unknowable or unpredictable variables. Still, we all must work to minimize errors, a process that requires absolute dedication, attention to detail, and personal honesty. Mistakes and errors are a part of every type of medical practice but are particularly visible and common in highly technical and invasive specialties and in the training environment. Errors always raise the question of whether a poor decision was responsible. Errors take three basic form—*technical errors, normative errors, and judgment errors* (Bosk 2003).

13.2 Technical Errors

Technical errors are just errors in technique or procedure. Technical errors can be due to ignorance of or unfamiliarity with a particular protocol, or lack of training. In underlings, technical errors are more indicative of a systems failure such as lack of proper instruction or supervision. When performed by individuals lacking proper credentialing or experience, these errors should be considered a problem of judgment and regarded seriously, especially if there is a pattern of such behavior. Technical errors committed can be due to systems problems such as equipment or supply problems. Complications with a technique do not always imply that an error was committed. Poor or unexpected outcomes are inevitable, and often beyond the control of the responsible person, and do not automatically warrant an accusation of negligence. Technical errors in the hands of experienced persons may warrant review to determine preventable causes such as a genuine need for a better technique, a situation that is again more of a systems problem than a failing of the individual. More ominous causes can be present in the form of issues such as sleep deprivation, psychological or emotional distress, or substance abuse. Errors in that situation should be regarded as judgment errors and signal the need for intervention by appropriate forums.

Of the three types of errors, technical errors are usually the easiest to identify and often have the most glaring consequences. That said, management of technical errors is perhaps the easiest to manage. We focus on the technical aspects of medical practice because they are easy to identify, examine, correct, and quantify. Most of the efforts in programs for quality improvement, peer assessment, 360^0 evaluations, or other incentives directed towards evaluating outcomes or systems and operational management revolve on these more concrete factors. Technical errors are usually the easiest for mentors or instructors to deal with in the training environment-.

13.3 Normative Errors

Normative errors are due to a failure to discharge role obligations conscientiously. Normative errors include errors of omission and of commission. Normative errors are seen at all levels but more common with younger residents who are still learning their responsibilities and limits (Bosk 2003).

Quasi-normative errors are breaches of the standards of performance and are seen at all levels. This form of error does not include physician-specific quirks or eccentricities that are excusable in senior physicians who have earned their spurs in terms of experience and judgment. An example of this situation would be a disagreement among experienced surgeons over which suture would be best in a particular situation or whether or not temporary drainage or diversion is the optimal choice. The decision for watchful waiting over immediate intervention in a specific instance can also be considered a quasi-normative error but, again, is more of an issue of judgment rather than technique. Such errors are not easily dismissed when committed by junior physicians who do not have the experience-based background to defend their decision. Normative and quasi-normative errors, when committed by junior physicians who do not have the clinical experience to defend their decision, should not be tolerated but handled gracefully unless the resident has exhibited a pattern of inappropriate behavior over time.

13.4 Bias and Cognitive Errors

Our decisions are affected by emotional and proprietary biases. Some of this bias is subconscious, but one must also guard against bias generated by our particular prejudices for or against a particular approach such as a surgeon's natural bias for recommending surgery over radiation therapy. In these situations, we may be biased by virtue of our specialty, institutional, or group affiliations. There are also economic biases. For example, if a medical group has a financial interest in a laboratory or radiation therapy center, they are more likely to recommend that patients use those facilities even if the laboratory does not have the expertise needed by a particular patient or if radiation therapy is not the ideal option for a specific problem. The same concerns exist for selective referral within a group or specialty.

Our approach towards patient care is profoundly affected by the errors we make and those we observe. Errors and shortcomings are perhaps the best teacher, but our actions are also affected by biases we unconsciously adopt. Biases are not borne of errors as much as they are prejudices or strongly held opinions. Biases are not intrinsically unreasonable but may have no basis in truth or fact, nor are they necessarily logical or rational. We all have biases. I know of one department chairman who was strongly biased against using a running suture to close abdominal incisions and was convinced that using interrupted sutures was the only appropriate method. He further believed that it was important to use a permanent suture and in situations where the closure was the least bit tenuous to use wire. His bias was forcefully shared whenever a wound closure using other methods failed. The debate over optimal methods for closure of abdominal wounds raged for years in the department even though the chairman's stance was not supported by the literature published on the subject. We all harbor biases and prejudices. Some of those opinions may help us to sleep better at night, but we must realize that a bias is a bias and not necessarily fact or truth. We rely on biases in decision-making at our peril.

13.5 Judgment Errors

Judgment errors occur when an incorrect strategy of treatment is chosen. Judgment errors are rarely seen in underlings or subordinates; they are more commonly encountered with more senior residents as treatment plans and major decisions are generally relegated to those with more training.

These errors occur most commonly when an incorrect strategy of treatment is chosen or when there is a lapse in integrity, focus, or priorities. Judgment errors become more prominent as one gains experience and responsibility and are therefore more common in physicians in the latter phases of their training.

Unfortunately, the current medicolegal climate interferes with decision-making and understanding how decisions are made. Much time is spent in medical conferences discussing decisions, how a particular decision was arrived at, and why other options were discarded or not deemed to be the best. This is rarely an issue with verbal discussions or in the context of a conference where information is protected from legal discovery. This is not the case for information recorded in a patient record or in correspondence. As mentioned earlier, the unfortunate and unintended effect of this dichotomy is that the consultant who is trying to think on paper or expound on his or her analysis of the problem cannot do so without fear of medicolegal reprisal. The physician faced with the dilemma of deciding what is going on with a particular patient and how best to approach management of a particular patient feels exposed if he commits his uncertainty or deliberations to paper. This is also true in the context of a post-operation note where the details of what suture was used and how each step was accomplished are rarely as insightful and instructive as a good description of the findings at surgery and expository comments or discussion about the challenges presented and the deliberative process used to make a decision about the best option apparent at the time. Rather than having these documents be a vehicle for learning and insight, they have become a weapon for attorneys to use against the thoughtful physician potentially creating a self-inflicted wound.

13.6 Errors in Preparation

We do not always perform at our best in a crisis. Preparation in anticipation of a crisis helps to overcome this natural reaction to stress. We will perform better if we have thought about a potential problem and have read or studied how others have approached a similar situation. This type of preparation has been heavily studied in the field of research management (Reynolds and Blickensderfer 2009). It is how airline pilots prepare for handling a disaster, and it is how military leaders have prepared themselves for dealing with combat situations they may encounter. Most of the successful military leaders have been diligent readers and lifelong students of military history. Training programs should spend a great deal of time discussing crisis management with their residents, presenting scenarios that will make them think about what they would do if they encountered an emergency such as potentially lethal crisis on the ward, clinic, or operating room.

13.7 Dealing with Errors

Highlighting categories of errors begs the question—what can be done to prevent or manage errors? Discussing, analyzing, preventing, and learning how to deal with errors and poor outcomes are significant parts of educational and training environments. Critical and in-depth consideration of errors is less apparent, but no less important once one is away from the teaching environment. Examination of errors in technique, judgment, or decisions can be informal and private or conducted in a variety of educational or conference settings. Grievous errors can also be dealt with in a rigorous, controlled, institutionally mandated forums with ominous and permanent consequences. With the exception of this last approach, management of errors should be conducted in a more informal, collegial, and instructive environment. Traditionally, many of the traditional venues for these interactions have become abusive, demeaning, and critical rather than constructive and educational. These attitudes have become part of the rite of passage in some training programs and a vehicle for toughening trainees up, rather than mentoring. Historically, residents have been struck, physically and verbally berated, and publicly mocked for their shortcomings. The medical training environment has become more humane and respectful, but examples of these former behaviors are not hard to find today. The disruptive or abusive physician is no longer tolerated.

13.7.1 Are Conferences an Effective Way of Looking at Errors?

The training environment relies heavily on formal conferences to discuss untoward outcomes, but conferences, and the way they have been traditionally been conducted, may not be the most effective way of identifying mistakes. The manner in which these are conducted is important if such conferences are to be effective ways of identifying mistakes and help the involved clinicians or trainees to further their education and improve their personal performance. Published analyses of these types of conferences suggest that they might not be as effective as we believe. One study shows that just less than half of regular attendees, to include trainees, found the traditional M&M conference of significant educational value or an aid to reducing surgical errors (Kohn et al. 2000). Another lengthy polemic (Meehl 1973) provided multiple well-constructed examples of the deficiencies of traditional case review conferences, examples all of us who have suffered through similar experiences can identify with. Discussions in conferences are subject to interpretation, personal opinions, and bias, degrading the educational value of these forums. We can improve the manner in which such conferences are conducted.

After-action reviews performed in a formal and deliberate manner in the airline industry, nuclear power plants, and the armed forces are examples of the efficacy of a more formal and deliberate approach and should be considered within medical organizations and residency training environments. After-action briefings such as those conducted by commercial aviation, nuclear power facilities, and the military are more structured and do not rely on the authoritarian pronouncements, commentaries, or recollection of past patient experiences that are a common part of medical conferences. A systems approach as outlined in the section the decision-making cycle or formal mind-mapping techniques may improve the utility of these conferences.

Chapter 14
Decision-Making Styles and Specialty Choice

Summary
Not everyone makes decisions in the same way. The decision-making strategy that one is most comfortable with or suited for is individualized. The person who enjoys the decisions made in a hectic emergency room may not prefer the more contemplative decisions required in a field such as internal medicine. Some prefer making decisions by elimination, some by using transitional models, and some by recognition. The decision-making strategies an individual prefers should, therefore, be a major factor in deciding upon the specialty they might be best suited for and what type of environment they would feel most comfortable working in. As a student progresses in their education and training, he or she will become aware of their unique decision-making style, and that insight should be discussed with mentors and advisors to help the individual choose a specialty or career path that will make optimum use of their unique strengths and preferences.

14.1 The Quadrants of Care

What specialty are you interested in? What do you plan to do when you finish medical school? These were standard questions for students that rotated through my service. The answers students gave to these questions were, for them and for me, critical to the experiences they would be given when on my service and also provided insight as to the personality and interests of each student. I am certain that every physician they encountered asked the same questions. Unfortunately, students do not always get the best advice for what they should do to best prepare for their life in medicine. Faculty advisors are frequently not clinicians but basic scientists or are in an administrative position that has removed them from direct patient care. Poor guidance, even if well intended, can lead to students pursuing a specialty they are not suited for, resulting in a loss of time, money, and unnecessary emotional and mental stress.

I asked these questions of a student that had a post-graduate degree in neurophysiology. He replied that because of his post-graduate training, he assumed or, rather, he was resigned to pursuing neurology. I asked if he had any exposure to neurology or understood what neurology was all about. He had no exposure to that field and was, upon further questioning, more interested in a primary care specialty such as family practice. He was worried that if he didn't pursue neurology, his previous education would have been a waste. He did not want to pursue an academic career, a direction where his post-graduate education may have been put to use pursuing research or teaching.

This student's background was somewhat atypical, but many students feel compelled to pursue a field that may not be suitable for their skills and interests. Just because your father or mother was a surgeon is a poor reason to pursue a career in surgery. Likewise, just because you like children, it does not follow that you should like or even want to pursue pediatrics. Being enamored of cardiac physiology is, by itself, also a poor reason to pursue cardiology. What then can teachers and advisors use as a tool to help students sort through this complicated and perplexing decision? A major part of deciding on a specialty is understanding the environment where you will spend the majority of your time. Do you prefer a quiet, thoughtful, and personal encounter with your patients such as a psychiatrist or internist might have, or do you prefer the excitement of a high stress and more impersonal patient contact one has in the emergency department? The answer to this question is determined by one's interpersonal skills, level of emotional intelligence, and, very importantly, one's decision-making and problem-solving preferences. Physicians or surgeons within the same specialty are not uniform in their approaches to decision-making but generalizations can be made. Trauma surgeons are not generally contemplative by nature. They make decisions best when under time constraints. Plastic surgeons, on the other hand, may spend hours considering the best approach to a difficult problem with reconstruction. Both the trauma surgeon and the plastic surgeon are happiest when in their optimal environment. The same is true for an internist who specializes in intensive care medicine. She is happiest when barraged by multiple, often conflicting problems that need to be rapidly assessed, prioritized, and deftly handled. The oncologist, on the other hand, is more comfortable when thoroughly considering the options for treatment before him and taking care to consider all of the family and personal concerns his patient is having to deal with.

The default or comfort zone that these practitioners functioned best in was a critical, even if unconscious, consideration as they considered the career options before them. Failure to answer these questions candidly might lead to a specialist who is unhappy, disgruntled, or likely to resort to drug or alcohol abuse, suicide, and depression, or have dysfunctional interpersonal and family relationships. We have all had to cope with the disruptive physician. Most of these individuals are deeply unhappy and angry about the practice environment they live in. Rarely do superficial remedies such as increasing salaries, change of practice type or location resolve

14.1 The Quadrants of Care

their discontent. Many have just chosen a specialty for which they are congenitally not well suited.

John P. Zubialde, MD, a family practitioner and associate dean at the University of Oklahoma Health Sciences Center, looked at health-care systems from the standpoint of what he termed *Quadrants of Care* (Zubialde et al. 2005). This model was developed for health-care systems and institutions, and not necessarily the world of the individual provider. Zubialde's model divided care into four quadrants based on whether the problems are acute or chronic and management is simple or complex. The medical and systems requirements in each quadrant vary by specialty, practice environment, resources available, and many other variables. The quadrants of health-care model was originally developed to look at health care from a systems or institutional level, but the model can be applied to illustrate how the work and environment of an individual physician will be affected by choice of specialty.

This model gives a lot of information about where the optimal style of work falls different specialties and practice environments. Physicians have a comfort zone within this spectrum: a zone in which they have the best outcomes and feel most at home. It also highlights the skills and traits beneficial for the physician working in each different environment. Most importantly, for the purposes of this book, it gives an insight into the decision-making skills each quadrant will require (Fig. 14.1).

Physicians usually prefer practice in one quadrant over another, not only because they enjoy the challenges each quadrant offers and because the fundamental skill set and temperament are different in each quadrant but because the decisions one is required to make in each quadrant are different. Study of this model provides the student with insight about the skills, problems, and type of work he would encounter working in each quadrant. Preference for working within a given quadrant affects several aspects of one's practice to include choice of specialty, practice environment, caseload, patient demographics, and the need for ancillary or more extensive resources. A study that looked at the distribution, by quadrants, of patient problems seen in a university-based family practice program showed the following distribution: straightforward problems quadrant I (straightforward) 20–30%, quadrant II (acute/complex) 5–10%, quadrant III (chronic/straightforward) 25–30%, and quadrant IV (chronic/complicated) 35–40% (Evans 2007).

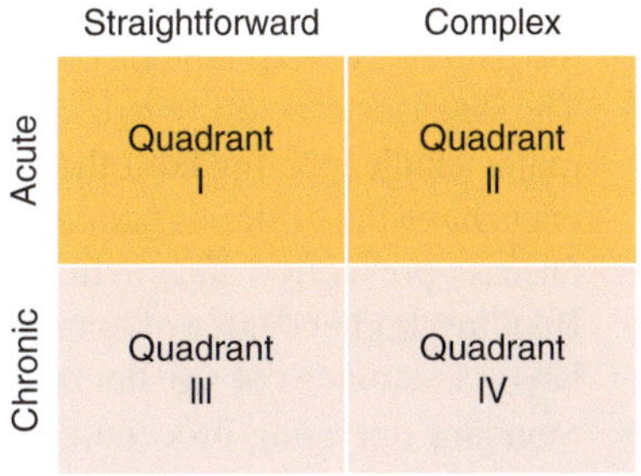

Fig. 14.1 The quadrants of care matrix. (Modified from Zubialde et al. 2005)

	Straightforward	Complex
Acute	Quadrant I	Quadrant II
Chronic	Quadrant III	Quadrant IV

In general, as one progresses from quadrant I to quadrant IV:

- Technical skills and requirement for more advanced or sophisticated technological support increase.
- The level of institutional and organizational complexity required for management of problems in each quadrant increase. Problems in quadrant I are more commonly seen in acute care or general clinic settings, while quadrant II and III problems frequently require inpatient or specialized units. Quadrant IV problems are more common in hospice or long-term care facilities.
- The incidence of uncommon diseases and presentations increases.
- The human factor becomes more prominent as one moves from quadrant I to quadrant IV. There is less direct, long-term contact required for patients with a self-limited problem such as a laceration or appendicitis (quadrants I or II), than for chronic problems such as hypertension or diabetes (quadrants III and IV).

14.1.1 Specific Characteristics of Problems by Quadrant

Quadrant I
- The cause and effect of problems are generally easy to define and manage.
- Problems lend themselves to protocol-based approaches, enabling the use of physician extenders.
- The long-term impact of problems in this quadrant is generally minimal and patient/physician relationships are less important.
- Continuity of care is minimal.

Quadrant II
- Problems straddle the continuum between simple and complex.
- Problems may require a high degree of technical expertise but are limited in terms of time and opportunity for significant continuity.
- Requires more multitasking and organizational cooperation but less than situations where multiple consultants, specialties, or treatment modalities are involved.
- Requires more resources and access to other providers.

Quadrant III
- The longitudinal nature of problems in this quadrant creates a greater impact on the patient's life and the physician—patient relationship.
- The diseases due to lifestyle decisions such as smoking and obesity may create major challenges for both the patient and physician—issues that not all physicians have the desire or patience for.
- Disease prevention and environmental issues begin to emerge.
- Requires higher degree of longitudinal support, monitoring, and greater resources beyond resources of smaller or community hospitals.
- Standard operating procedures and protocols become less useful, except in the face of emergency situations.
- Requires deeper relationships with the patient.
- Relational, spirituality, beliefs, and value systems become more important.

Quadrant IV
- Outcomes hard to define or predict and determined on a case-by-case basis.
- Increasing diagnostic and therapeutic uncertainty.
- Role of specialist may become limited, episodic or supportive.
- End of life, spiritual needs more prominent and perhaps dominant.
- Organizational and payer resources and reimbursement policies may impair delivery of optimal care.

This list is not exhaustive and consideration of other potential characteristics of a practice within each quadrant should be a part of a student's career decision-making calculus. Geographic factors such as one's desire to practicing in a rural or metropolitan locations will influence the distribution of problems within each quadrant. The quadrants of care model has other applications to include the short- or long-term assessment of organizational, personnel, and resource needs.

14.2 The Quadrants of Care and Choice of Specialty

Just as there are many approaches and styles of decision-making, not everyone is comfortable with all the environments in a hospital. Some are not most comfortable being in a hospital and feel more comfortable in a clinic environment. Knowing the environment you are most comfortable in and knowing if you like the types of decisions that environment requires are key factors in choosing a specialty. We do not present that framework to medical students as they rotate through each area of the hospital. By taking some liberty with the quadrants of care model, it is possible to place a problem within a quadrant based on whether the problem is acute or chronic or straightforward or complex.

Why a person winds up in a particular specialty is a mysterious and often serendipitous process. The process is not foolproof, as evidenced by the high number of residents who change from one field to another. For some specialties, the attrition rate is as high as 23 per cent (Andriole et al. 2008; Longo et al. 2009). This represents a loss of precious time and manpower and resources within a system that is stretched thin. Training programs cannot afford to lose residents because of a change in career interest.

The challenge for medical students is to find a specialty you will feel at home in. Just because you have an advanced degree in neurophysiology does not mean you should limit yourself to considering neurology or neurosurgery. You may not be suited for either of those specialties and find yourself thrown in with residents and faculty you don't identify with.

When meeting a medical student and once you have established where they went to college and what their undergraduate major was, physicians, being to the point and direct, will spring the question: "What specialty are you going into?" It is the medical equivalent of the common question addressed to children: "What are you going to do when you grow up?" For many students, the answer is easy. "I love kids have always wanted to be a pediatrician" they may say. "I like the idea of being in a rural environment and taking care of people's basic medical needs so I think I will go into family practice" is a common answer. "My grandfather died from lung cancer so I want to become a cancer specialist," or "My brother was born with a heart defect so I want to become a cardiologist." Or, "I don't know, and am keeping my options open." That response is not popular with surgeons as they wonder why anyone would want to do something other than surgery. I would argue that most of these reasons are based on considering the wrong variables as evidenced by the response listed above. I would also argue that students do not take an approach that considers looking at a specialty from the standpoint of how they best make decisions. Most students receive poor guidance as to selection of specialty or preparation for a specific specialty. Their guidance may come from well-meaning but uninformed relatives or a faculty advisor who is not aware of the nuances of the areas of interest to the student or who is not a clinician. There may be an inherent bias in the medical school if that school has the mandate to provide primary care physicians rather than specialists. The aspiring surgeon, for example, may experience a department that is dysfunctional, malignant, or focused on research and not medical students.

By plotting one's interests, preferences, and strengths into the appropriate quadrant, the student will have a better sense of the specialty in which he or she may feel most comfortable. The same model can be used to plot other factors inherent in choice of a specialty, practice location, or ideal environment:

- Working within a quadrant includes several aspects of the individual physician's practice
- Practice environment
- Case load
- Patient demographics (socioeconomic profile)
- Resources

When presented with this model, a student can easily visualize which quadrant he or she would feel most comfortable and most professionally satisfied. The student can also understand the relationship or degree of continuity required to care for patients in each quadrant. Do you enjoy brief encounters with patients whose medical needs are minimal and have a high probability of resolution with minimal residual, or do you want to manage intricate, technically challenging problems in a patient who will recover and may never need your services again? Do you want to manage patients with challenging but chronic problems that you will develop a relationship with that may last years, or do you want the challenge of patients who are severely compromised with complex, more acute problems?

14.3 Does the Expert Make Better Decisions?

An array of approaches to decision-making have been covered in the preceding chapters to include an argument that the expert or master decision-maker uses a different approach from the novice or intermediately experienced decision-maker. This proposal does beg the question—do experts make better decisions than their less experienced colleagues?

The definition of expertise, and what it takes to become an expert, is beyond the scope of this book, but it can be safely stated that expertise in any domain takes years to achieve and requires more than just having been on the job for a prescribed length of time. A good definition is certainly worthy of further pursuit. Few physicians or surgeons are recognized as being true experts. Becoming or being recognized as an expert decision-maker is a goal all physicians wish to achieve, so, in the context of considering the subject of decision-making and problem-solving in medicine, the issue of expertise in this skill is worth, at least, of brief consideration.

Several investigators have demonstrated that expertise is a skill acquired in stages (Dreyfus et al. 1986; Shanteau 1992). Only recently have physicians and surgeons had their outcomes made public and compared to their peers. Methods for accumulating and deciphering such data is, arguably, still in its infancy and highly contentious, but there is no doubt that hospital privileges and other recognitions are linked to one's ability to demonstrate such standards. Experience, knowledge, and skill are not easy to measure and do not always correlate with outcomes, and the same can be said for decision-making skills. We all have a duty to improve our outcomes throughout our careers, and many physicians do not take this process beyond the minimum requirements in terms of CMEs required for maintenance of their license. We all would like to be on the extreme right of the bell curve in whatever system we are evaluated in, but it is a steep hill to climb.

Malcolm Gladwell, English-born journalist and author, is generally credited with popularizing the 10,000-hour rule, a rule that proposes that mastery requires 10,000 hours of dedicated practice (Gladwell 2008). The validity of the 10,000-hour rule has been challenged, but there is no argument that expertise in any discipline take years of develop.

As we have seen earlier in the discussion on how physicians with various skill levels approach the standard differential diagnosis, novices think in a backward or retrograde fashion, moving from unknowns to givens in a more linear or sequential, or deductive fashion. Experts are more efficient, using chunking techniques and pattern recognition to reduce the list of potential diagnoses to the most likely possibilities first and then pursuing a very focused approach to verify their choices.

Residents are, by definition, novice decision-makers. They may have an excellent fund of knowledge and skill acquired from years of study but lack the judgment needed to make decisions, in great part because they do not have the experience to make the associations the expert can. They cannot reliably and confidently put the pieces of the diagnostic puzzle together efficiently.

Experts are comfortable with a variety of decision-making strategies to include technical and operational expertise, teamwork, flexibility, and ability to perform in dynamic, chaotic, unfamiliar, or ambiguous environments. Clinical medicine is predominately a left brain activity. We spend most of our time managing repetitive, often mundane tasks. The expert, however, must be proficient with using both cerebral hemispheres and be able to learn. Experts must have a willingness to recognize, take on, and grapple with right brain tasks. They must work at the extremes of left brain (analytical) and the right brain (creative) yet maintain balance and proportion and be aware of what problems are solved by right or left brain—when to be analytical and when to be creative or intuitive. The expert should seek difficult cases and perform at the limits of their discipline.

While the expert may have achieved this level of efficiency and confidence in their decision-making skills, it is important to point out that the expert needs to act like an expert, demonstrating self-confidence, communication skills, adaptability, responsibility, and humility, combined with control of their ego and a sense of being comfortable with themselves. Rigidity and a lack of humility about one's decisions are characteristics of novices.

The expert must have laser-like attention skills, a sense of what is relevant, and the ability to identify exceptions to rules and standard approaches (Shanteau 1992).

It is difficult to provide an objective definition of expertise in clinical medicine is difficult to arrive at. Becoming an expert requires having the right psychological and mental attributes as well as working hard to reach the status of becoming an expert. Being an expert does not make one immune to making errors in their decision-making, avoiding biases, difficulty judging probabilities, making predictions, or dealing with uncertainty as evidenced by the work of Kahneman (2011) and Tetlock (2005).

14.4 Beyond Clinical Practice

The emphasis of this treatise has been on decision-making in the clinical environment, but none are able to escape the fate of having responsibilities, often by choice but sometimes by decree, to assume committee, administrative, or leadership roles. Such jobs present other arenas in which decision-making skills are needed. It is unfortunate that medicine does not offer more opportunities for leadership development and honing our management skills, as these positions make us more well-rounded, thoughtful, and effective practitioners. Medicine needs more good leaders. Opportunities to develop these skills should not be avoided but actively pursued. Our current system does not address the needs of younger physicians have for acquiring such skills. It is not even on the radar screen of most academic institutions. Most medical organizations or large clinics do not have programs to develop potential leaders. Once training has been completed, there is little informal and no formal effort given to career development beyond continuing medical education. The default approach is for an individual to attend a graduate business or management degree in their off hours, and it is debatable how much leadership or decision-making skills are provided at such programs. Decision-making and leadership are a lifelong pursuit, not acquired by adding initials to one's signature block. Some management and decision-making skills may be acquired through our formal education, but the vast majority of those skills are learned on-the-job, hopefully during well-chosen assignments, thoughtful career decisions, and also from strong mentoring and coaching, opportunities rarely offered in the average, hectic medical environment.

The decision-making skills required of an administrator, department head, or committee chair are no different than those we all use on a daily basis to manage our patients and run a practice. Organizational decisions tend to be more unbounded and complicated or complex with multiple, competing, and unrelated variables. They are type 2 or elimination problems. Such decisions are different than the day-to-day problems of patient management or diagnosis but still can be resolved with many of the approaches presented in this book.

Medical organizations tend to be very hierarchical, relying on control and centralization, an arrangement that may not be the most functional or productive for health-care organizations today. Physicians are more than capable and more than willing to work to improve their environment. Physicians want to make decisions and have the ability to make decisions and take responsibility. It is what they do every day in their practice. It is a part of their nature. Organizations with a well-developed approach to developing leadership in their staff may give potential leaders assignments that stretch their management and leadership skills. It is a long-term investment, and few medical organizations think of growing leaders over time and keeping them there long enough to benefit from the lessons to be learned in a position that challenged and developed their skills.

A more inclusive and visionary approach is to view management and administrative positions as an integral part of physician development and the organizational culture of an organization, not just an additional assignment or duty. Perhaps not all physicians would want to participate; perhaps some would rather just attend their clinics and patients. This approach may be tolerated just because there are never enough providers to care for the clinical load, but a robust and forward-thinking organization should be looking to develop future leaders.

Medical organizations must encourage and take advantage of the creative potential and the desire to improve that all physicians possess. You can't beat creativity out of someone; neither can you demand passion or commitment. This boils down to the fundamental attitudes of an organization's senior management and the value that senior management places on development of it's employees. Most physicians are race horses and they should be allowed to run not plough a field. These should be the goals of any medical organization. Steve Jobs was an excellent example of a leader of highly motivated and educated employees. Even though Jobs was a hard taskmaster, his employees consistently produced products that met his vision and standards, overcoming obstacles that were though by many to be insurmountable. Jobs knew his workforce was magnificently talented, and he let them do their job, generously rewarding them for their contributions: an admirable model for any medical organization. In spite of the wealth Apple created, it is interesting that neither Jobs nor his partners were driven by economic reward: their passion was in the creation. In fact, Jobs worked as the CEO of Apple for years while taking an annual salary of one dollar a year (Issacson 2013).

Chapter 15
Conclusions

15.1 Sitting by the Fire

> We will always need to be making adjustments so that the place we are is the place we belong (Leider and Shapiro *Claiming Your Place at the Fire*, 2014, p. 60).

For generations, our ancestors sat by the fire at night discussing the events of the day or recalling stories and legends. To sit by the fire was an honor reserved for the tribal elders, the wise men, the chiefs, and shamans. The younger members of the tribe sat or stood behind their elders and listened and learned. Their guidance was rarely sought (Leider and Shapiro 2014).

So, it is with medicine, especially academic medicine with its hierarchical and rigid social structure. The younger members of the tribe are not only learning about the particulars of patient care and the management of problems, they are learning how to be incorporated into the tribe. Young physicians and medical students must wait to be fully accepted into the culture of medicine and the subculture of the specialties they have chosen. There is nothing wrong with this. Senior faculty have earned their pride of place. It is the job of the residents and students to watch, listen, and learn.

There is a problem with sitting by the fire if all that is discussed are the stories that explain our traditions, superstitions, and beliefs. It is not just about passing on stories, or even knowledge. Those learning their way also need to the know the processes used in the practice of medicine, and for the purposes of this book, how to make decisions. This skill has traditionally been acquired by trial and error, observation, and mentoring, but today, learning by observation or doing is just too costly and inefficient. Our students must become capable of rapidly and confidently managing the problems they encounter in their education and throughout their careers. Critical thinking as it applies to decision-making needs to be taught, contemplated, discussed, and honed.

We can spend hours discussing the surgical approaches for a carcinoma of the kidney, or the nuances of managing septic shock, but a discussion about a clinical problem can become an uncomfortable event if someone asks what steps the mentor took to make the decisions necessary to address those problems. Such a question appears almost intrusive. Mentors must be ready to explain the rationale behind their decisions. We assume that the knowledge necessary to solve a clinical problem is obvious, or will be revealed with time and experience. When discussing this issue with a mentor, I asked: "how to you teach decision-making?" He replied: "they just learn over time". That approach perpetuates the mystique of medicine many would like to maintain but does not help the student. Decision-making is a skill that is objective, reproducible, easily understood, and teachable.

Decision-making is analogous to the proverbial elephant in the room, likely to be ignored because the other guests find the subject uncomfortable or awkward. We all know the elephant is there and that he takes up a lot of space and energy, but he is rarely talked about.

This elephant must be engaged. He has wise and insightful observations to share and is very approachable. This elephant is nonpartisan and a rational, reasonable creature. He is easily tamed and housebroken.

Decision-making is a process, not an endpoint. Discussing this process allows the participants to break the decision-making process into its component parts, identify cognitive errors, missed opportunities, wrong turns, and faulty reasoning. Such an exercise improves our decision-making skills. It is easier to teach how decisions are made than have students stumble down unproductive paths. Students and residents who have a map to reach a goal will know better what is expected of them and will be faster, more efficient learners. Having a formal method to look at the decision-making provides a quantitative approach to the subject rather than giving vague, confusing comments about the skills students and residents are desparate to learn. A good decision, one that is rational, well formulated and capable of being effectively implemented. Good decisions create good will between the physician, patients, consultants and colleagues. Making a good decision is what we are being asked to provide in every encounter. The best decision-maker is one who can deliver that decision with conviction and also with grace and humility. Good decisions lead to safer, more efficient and cost-effective care.

15.2 Decision-Making in the Future

This book has focused on the fundamental processes of thinking, problem-solving, and decision-making, but this discussion would be incomplete if it did not address how new technology and capabilities are changing our approaches to gathering information and solving problems. New and improved technology will not alter the responsibilities of the physician who is caring for patients. Medicine will remain a contact sport. The fundamental concepts and approaches of decision-making will not be changed by new technology, only enhanced and made easier to master and apply.

15.2 Decision-Making in the Future

Understanding and being able to implement these developments will require changes in how physicians are trained. These changes should include updating the requirements for admission to medical school to insure that students have been exposed to the concepts new technology has been derived from. Likewise, the content of the medical school curriculum and postgraduate training programs need to incorporate an expanded exposure to statistics, computer modeling and artificial intellegence as they pertain to clinical practice (Obermeyer and Lee 2017).

I hope this book provided an incentive for all practitioners to become better decision-makers. If I accomplish this goal to any degree, the efforts required to bring this project to completion will have been worth the time. This book has also presented ideas and observations that many might find controversial. The jabs at the convention are intentional and with a purpose in mind—to stimulate thinking and discussion about the nature of medical decision-making. It is my wish that we enter a constructive dialogue about what can be done to improve our thinking and decision-making skills and how we can become better teachers and mentors as we work to incorporate students and residents into our profession, and, as individual clinicians, consider how we can include at least some of these ideas into our practice.

Disclaimer

This book presents many concepts that have been developed by others or are discussed in detail elsewhere and concepts that are my own. The concepts I present as my own may, unbeknownst to me, be available elsewhere. I studied the literature in several disciplines in the course of writing this manuscript, but any review of such a broad topic could never be comprehensive. Totally new ideas are rare, and most of the concepts in the field of decision-making are based on previously published work. I have been careful to give the originators of ideas credit but recognize that some of my ideas may have been developed by others and not encountered in my research. To that end, I apologize and graciously give them their due credit.

I especially want to thank the many researchers and authors whose publications made this book possible. Much of this work is not readily available to the practicing physician, physician in training, or the physician writing about decision-making. One of my biggest challenges has been distilling their work into a format that the busy physician can put to immediate and practical use. My purpose was not to claim ownership of these concepts but to bring this information to an audience that can benefit from the insights of the experts who have created these ideas. For these reasons, I have gone to great lengths to ensure that those authors and researchers have been given credit for their work. Any oversights in my efforts are unintentional.

Bibliography

Andriole DA, Jeffe DB, Hageman HL, Klingensmith ME, McAlister RP, Shelan AJ. Attrition during graduate medical education: Medical school perspective. *Arch Surg* 2008; 143(12): 1172–1177.
Aristotle. (Ross D, translator). *The Nicomachean Ethics*. Oxford, UK: Oxford University Press; 2009.
Athanasiou T. *Mind Over Machine: The Power of Human Intuition and Expertise in the Era of the Computer*. New York, NY: The Free Press (Macmillan); 1986.
Baron J. *Thinking and Deciding*. Fourth Edition. New York, NY: Cambridge University Press; 2008.
Beach LR, Mitchell TR. A contingency model for the selection of decision strategies. *Acad Management Rev* 1978; 3: 439–449.
Bentley JL, McGeoch C. Amortized analyses of self-organizing sequential search heuristics. *Communications of the ACM (Association for Computing Machinery)* 1985; 28(4): 404–411.
Beresford EB. Uncertainty and the shaping of medical decisions. *Hastings Center Report* 1991; 21(4): 6–11.
Bilalic M, McLeod P. Why your first idea can blind you to a better one. *Scientific American*. March 2014. (See also: The Editors, How psychologists study the Einstellung effect in chess, *Scientific American*. 2014.)
Birkmeyer JD, Dimick JB, Birkmeyer NJO. Measuring the quality of surgical care: Structure, process, or outcomes? *Journal of Am Coll Surgeons* 2004; 198 (4): 626–632.
Bodemer N, Hanoch Y, Katiskopoulos KV. Heuristics: Foundations for a novel approach to medical decision making. *Internal and Emergency Medicine* 2015; 10(2): 195–203.
Bosk CL. (2003). *Forgive and Remember: Managing Medical Failure*. Second Edition. Chicago, IL: University of Chicago Press; 2003.
Boudreau JD, Cruess S, Cruess RL. Physicianship: Educating for professionalism in the post-Flexnerian era. *Perspectives in Biology and Medicine* 2011; 54(1): 89–105.
Burns PB, Rohrich RJ, and Chung KC. The levels of evidence and their role in Evidence-based medicine. *Plast Reconstr Surg* 2011; 128(1): 305–310.
Csikszentmihalyi M *Flow*: *The Psychology of Optimal Experience*. First edition. New York, NY: Harper and Row; 1990.
Dawes RM. The ethics of using or not using statistical prediction rules in psychological practice and related consulting activities. *Philosophy of Science* 2002; 69(S3): S178–S184.
Dawid CAP, Musio M, Fienberg SE. From statistical evidence to evidence of causality. *Bayesian Analysis* 2013; 11(3): 725–752.
Dawid CAP. Fundamentals of statistical causality. Research Report No. 279. Department of Statistical Science. September, 2007; University College London, London, England.

de Madariaga S. *Essays With a Purpose.* New York: Richard West Publishers; 1989.
Dieckmann A, Todd PM. Simple ways to construct search orders. *Proceedings of the Annual Meeting of the Cognitive Science Society* 2004; 26(6): 309–314. https://escholarship.org/uc/item/1x06tqn.
Dohami MK, Harries C. Fast and frugal versus regression models of human judgement. *Thinking and Reasoning* 2001; 7(1): 5–27.
Donabedian A Evaluating the quality of medical care. *Milbank Memorial Fund Quarterly* 1996; 44: 166–206.
Ibid. Evaluating physician competence. *Bull World Health Organization.* 2000a; 78(6): 857–860.
Dreyfus HL, Dreyfus SE, Athanasiou T. *Mind Over Machine: The Power of Human Intuition and Expertise in the Era of the Computer.* New York, NY: The Free Press (Macmillan); 1986.
Eddy DM. Practice policies: where do they come from? *JAMA* 1990; 263: 1265–1275.
Ibid Evaluating physician competence. *Bull of the World Health Organization.* 2000b; 78(6): 857–860.
Einhorn HJ, Hogarth RM. Confidence in judgment: Persistence of the illusion of validity. *Psychol Rev* 1978; 85(5): 395–416.
Ely JW, Graber, ML, Croskerry P. Checklists to reduce diagnostic errors. *Acad Med* 2011; 85(3): 307–313.
Ericsson KA. Deliberate practice and the acquisition and maintenance of expert performance in medicine and related domains. *Acad Med.* 2004; 79:(10 Suppl): S70–S81.
Ericsson KA. Deliberate practice and acquisition of expert performance: A general overview. *Acad Emerg Med* 2008; 15: 988–994.
Ericsson KA, editor. *The Road to Excellence: The Acquisition of Expert Performance in the Arts and Sciences, Sports and Games.* New York, NY: Psychology Press; 2009.
Ericsson KA, Prietula MJ and Cokley ET. The making of an expert. *Harvard Bus Rev.* 2007: On-line Version, pp 6–7.
Ericsson KA, Krampe RTh, Roemer, CT. The role of deliberate practice in the acquisition of expert performance. *Psychol Rev* 1993; 100(3): 363–406.
Evans, L, Trotter DRM. Epistemology and uncertainty in primary care: An exploratory study. *Fam Med.* 2009; 41(5): 319–326. (See also: Scherger, J. Letters to the Editor, *Fam Med.* 2009; 41, 690–693).
Evans L. (2007). Using the quadrants of care model for applying the bio-psychological model (Personal communication).
Gawande A. Annals of Medicine: The bell curve: What happens when patients find out how good their doctors really are? *The New Yorker.* 2004. http://www.newyorker.com/archive/2004/12/06.
Ibid. *The Checklist Manifesto: How to Get Things Right.* New York: Picador; 2009.
Gigerenzer G. *Gut Feelings: The Intelligence of the Unconscious.* New York: The Penguin Group; 2007.
Gigerenzer G, Gaissmaier W. Heuristic decision making. *Ann Rev of Psychol* 2011; 62: 451–482.
Gigerenzer G, Goldstein DG. Reasoning the fast and frugal way: Models of bounded rationality. *Psychol Rev* 1996; 103: 650–669.
Gigerenzer G, Todd PM and the ABC Research Group. *Fast and Frugal*: The Adaptive Toolbox. *Simple Heuristics That Make Us Smart.* New York, NY: Oxford University Press; 1999: 3–34.
Gladwell M. *Outliers: The Story of Success.* New York, NY: Little, Brown and Company; 2008.
Gleick J. *Chaos: Making A New Science.* New York, NY: Penguin Books; 1988.
Gold HJ. *Mathematical Modeling of Biological Systems.* New York, NY: John Wiley and Sons; 1985.
Goldberg LR. Man versus model of man: A rationale, plus some evidence for a method of improving on clinical inferences. *Psychol Bull* 1970; 73(6): 422–32.
Goldberg LR. Simple models or simple processes? Some research on clinical judgments. *American Psychologist* 1978; 23(7): 483–96.
Goldstein DG, Gigerenzer G. Models of ecological rationality: The recognition heuristic. *Psychol Rev* 2002; 109(1): 75–90.

Grebogi C, Ott E, Yorke JA. Chaos, strange attractors, and fractal basin boundaries in nonlinear dynamics. *Science* 1987; 238(4827): 632–638.

Green L, Mehr DR. What alters physicians to admit to the coronary care unit? *J Fam Practice* 1997; 45: 219–226.

Greene R. *Mastery*. New York, NY: Penguin Books; 2012.

Griffin D, Tversky A. The weighing of evidence and the determinants of confidence. *Cognitive Psychol* 1992; 23(3): 411–435.

Grimshaw JM, Russell IT. Effect of clinical guidelines on medical practice: a systematic review of rigorous evaluations. *Lancet* 1993; 342: 1317–1322.

Groopman J. *How Doctors Think*. New York, NY: First Mariner Books, Houghton-Miflin Company; 2008.

Grove WM, Zald DH, Lebow B., Snitz BE, Nelson C. Clinical versus mechanical prediction: A meta-analysis. *Psychol Assessment* 2000; 12(1): 19–30.

Grove WM. Clinical versus statistical Prediction: The contribution of Paul E. Meehl. *J Clin Psychol* 2005; 61(10): 1233–1243.

Guyatt G, Cairns J, Churchill D, et al. (The Evidence-Based Medicine Working Group). Evidence-based medicine, A new approach to teaching the practice of medicine. *JAMA* 1992; 268: 2420–2425.

Hampton JR, Harrison MJG, Harrison JRA, and Seymour C. *Relative contributions of history-taking, physical examination, and laboratory investigation to diagnosis and management of medical outpatients*. BMJ. 1975; 2: 486–489. Cited by Montgomery K. *How Doctors Think: Clinical judgment and the practice of medicine*. New York, NY: Oxford University Press; 2006: 223.

Hasher L, Zacks RT. Automatic processing of fundamental information: The case of frequency of occurrence. *American Psychologist* 1984; 39: 1372–1388.

Hoffman PJ. The paramorphic representation of clinical judgment. *Psychological Bull* 1960; 57: 116–131.

Hoffman PJ, Slovic P, Rorer LG. An analysis of variance model for the assessment of configural cue utilization in clinical judgment. *Psychological Bull* 1968; 69: 338–349.

Hubbard DW. *How To Measure Anything: Finding the value of intangibles in business*. Hoboken, NJ: John Wiley and Sons, Inc.; 2007.

Issacson W. *Steve Jobs*. New York, NY: Simon and Schuster Paperbacks; 2013.

Johnson-Laird PN. *How We Reason*. New York, NY: Oxford University Press; 2011.

Kahneman D. *Thinking, Fast and Slow*. New York, NY: Farrar, Straus and Giroux; 2011.

Kahneman, D. *Summary: Thinking, Fast and Slow*. Epic Summary (Book 11). Independently published (Available on Amazon Books, amazon.com) 2019.

Kahneman D, Tversky A. On the psychology of prediction. *Psychol Rev*1973; 80(4): 237–251.

Katsikopoulos KV, Pachur T, Machery E, Wallin A. From Meehl to fast and frugal heuristics (and back): New insights into how to bridge the clinical – actuarial divide. *Theory and Psychology* 2008; 18(4): 443–464.

Kattah JC, Talkad AV, Wang D., Hsieh YH, Newman-Toker DE. HINTS to diagnose stroke in the acute vestibular syndrome: Three-step bedside oculomotor examination more sensitive than early MRI diffusion-weighted imaging. *Stroke* 2009; 40(11): 3504–3510.

Kenworthy B. quoted by Roger Lowenstein in "Intrinsic Value", *The Wall Street Journal*, Page C-1. June 1, 1995.

Kilner JM, Lemon RN. What we know currently about mirror neurons. *Current Biol* 2013; 23(23): R1057–R1062.

Klein GA, Calderwood, R. Decision models: Some lessons from the field. *IEEE Transactions on Systems, Man, and Cybernetics* 1991; 21(5): 1018–1026.

Kleinmuntz B. Why we still use our heads instead of formulas: Toward an integrative approach. *Psychological Bulletin* 1990; 107(3), 296–310.

Kohn LT, Corrigan JM, Donaldson MS, eds. *To Err is Human: Building a safer health system*. Washington, DC: National Academy Press; 2000.

Kolb, DA. *Experiential Learning.* New York, NY: Simon and Schuster; 1983.

Kolb DA. *Experiential Learning: Experience as the source of learning and development.* Second Edition. Englewood Cliffs, NJ: Prentice Hall; 2015.

Konnikova M. *Mastermind: How to think like Sherlock Holmes.* New York, NY: Penguin Books; 2013.

LeDoux JE. *The Emotional Brain: The mysterious underpinnings of emotional life.* New York, NY: Simon and Schuster; 1996.

Leider RJ, Shapiro DA. *Claiming Your Place At The Fire: Living The second half of your life on purpose.* San Francisco, CA: Berrett-Koehler; 2014.

Lerher J. *How We Decide.* New York, NY: Houghton Mifflin Harcourt; 2009.

Lewis M. *The Undoing Project: A friendship that changed our minds.* New York, NY: W. W. Norton and Co.; 2017.

Liebow EM. *Dr. Joe Bell: Model for Sherlock Holmes.* Madison, WI: Popular Press; 2007. (Originally published by Bowling Green University Popular Press, 1982 and reprinted by the University of Wisconsin Press, Madison, Wisconsin, Copyright, 2007, The Board of Regents of the University of Wisconsin System).

Longo WE, Seashore J, Duffy A, Udelsman R. Attrition of categoric general surgery residents: Results of a 20-year audit. *American Journal of Surgery* 2009; 197(6): 774–778.

Lorenz EN. Deterministic nonperiodic flow. *The Journal of Atmospheric Sciences* 1963; 20(2): 130–141.

MacIntyre A. *After Virtue.* Third Edition. Notre Dame, IN: University of Notre Dame Press; 2007.

Marewski JN, Gigerenzer G. Heuristic decision making in medicine. *Dialogues in Clinical Neuroscience* 2012; 14(1): 77–89.

Margolis CZ. Uses of clinical algorithms. *JAMA* 1983; 249(5): 627–632.

Martignon L, Katsikopoulos KV, Woike JK. Categorization with limited resources: A family of simple heuristics. *Journal of Mathematical Psychology* 2008; 52: 352–361.

Martignon L, Vitouch O, Takezawa M, Forster MR. Naïve and Yet Enlightened: From Natural Frequencies to Fast and Frugal Decision Trees. In: Hardman, D. and Macchi, L, eds. *Thinking: Psychological perspectives on reasoning, judgment and decision making.* Hoboken, NJ: John Wiley and Sons; 2003: 189–211.

Masic I, Miokovic M, Muhamedagic B. Evidence based medicine—New approaches and challenges. *Acta Informatica Medica* 2003; 16(4): 219–225.

Meehl PE. Causes and effects of my disturbing little book. *Journal of Personality Assessment* 1986; 50(3): 370–375.

Ibid. *Clinical Versus Statistical Prediction: A Theoretical Analysis and a Review of the Evidence.* Minneapolis, MN: University of Minnesota Press; 1954.

Ibid. Why I Do Not Attend Case Conferences. In: Meehl, PE, ed. *Psychodiagnosis: Selected Papers by Paul E. Meehl.* Minneapolis, MN: University of Minnesota press; 1973: 225–302.

Miller GA. The magical number seven, plus or minus two: Some limits on our capacity for processing information. *Psychological Review* 1956; 63: 81–97.

Monleon-Getino A, Canela-Soler J Causality in medicine and its relationship with the role of statistics. *Biomedical Statistics and Informatics* 2017; 2(2): 61–68.

Montgomery K. *How Doctors Think: Clinical judgment and the practice of medicine.* New York, NY: Oxford University Press; 2006.

Newell BR, Weston NJ, Shanks DR. Empirical tests of a fast-and-frugal heuristic: Not everyone 'takes-the-best'. *Organizational Behavior and Human Decision Processes* 1996; 91: 82–96.

Obermeyer Z, Lee TH. (Perspective) Lost in thought—The limits of the human mind and the future of medicine. *NEJM* 2017; 377: 1209–1211.

Payne JW, Bettman JR, Johnson EJ. Adaptive strategy selection in decision making. *Journal of Experimental Psychology: Learning, Memory, and Cognition* 1988; 14(3): 534–552.

Pellegrino ED, Thomasma DC. *A Philosophical Basis of Medical Practice.* New York, NY: Oxford University Press; 1981.

Pearl J, Glymour M, Jewell NP. *Causal Inference in Statistics: A primer*. Chichester, UK: John Wiley and Sons; 2016.
Pirsig RM. *Zen and the Art of Motorcycle Maintenance: An inquiry into values*. New York, NY: First Morrow Quill paperback edition; 1979.
Potchen EJ, Cooper TG, Sierra AE, et al. Measuring performance in chest radiography. *Radiology* 2000; 217(2): 456–459.
Reeves CA, Bednar DA.. Defining Quality: Alternatives and implications. *The Academy of Management Review*. 1994; (Special issue: Total Quality) 19(3): 419–445.
Reynolds R, Blickensderfer E. Crew resource management and shared mental models: A proposal. *The Journal of Aviation/Aerospace Education and Research* 2009; 19(1): 15–23.
Rieskamp J. The importance of learning when making inferences. *Judgment and Decision Making* 2008; 3: 261–277.
Rieskamp J, Otto PE. SSL: A theory of how people learn to select strategies. *Journal of Experimental Psychology and Genetics* 2006; 135(2): 206–236.
Rizzolatti G, Craighero L The mirror-neuron system. *Annual Review of Neuroscience* 2004; 27(1): 169–192. https://doi.org/10.1146/annurev.neuro.27.070203.144230. Accessed 2 April, 2019.
Ross PE. The expert mind: Studies of the mental processes of chess grandmasters have revealed clues to how people become experts in other fields as well. *Scientific American*. 24 July 2006.
Saposnik G, Redelmeier D, Ruff CC, Tobler PN. Cognitive biases associated with medical decisions: a systemic review. *BMC Med Inform Decis Mak*. 2016; 16: 138. https://doi.org/10.1866/s12911-016-0377-1. Accessed 5 Aug 2019.
Savage LJ. *Foundations of Statistics*. Second Revised Edition. Mineola, NY: Dover Publications; 1972.
Schmidt HG, Norman G, Boshuizen HPA. A cognitive perspective on medical expertise: Theory and implications *Acad Med* 1990; 65(10): 611–621.
Schön DA. *Educating the Reflective Practitioner: Toward a new design for teaching and learning in the professions*. San Francisco, CA: Jossey-Bass; 1987.
Schön DA. *The Reflective Practitioner: How professionals think in action*. New York, NY: Basic Books, The Perseus Group; 1983.
Shanteau J. Competence in experts: The role of task characteristics. *Organizational behavior and Human Decision Processes* 1992; 53: 252–266.
Shelton W. Can virtue be taught? *Acad Med* 1999; 74: 671–674.
Shiralkar U. *Smart Surgeons Sharp Decisions: Cognitive Skills to Avoid Errors and Achieve Results*. The Surgical Psychology Series, TFM Publishing. Shrewsbury, UK; 2011.
Simon HA. A behavioral model of rational choice. *The Quarterly Journal of Economics* 1955; 69(1): 99–118.
Ibid. Rational decision-making in business organizations. Nobel Memorial Lecture, December, 1978: 343–371.
Syed Z, Stultz CM, Scirica BM, Guttag JV. Computationally generated cardiac biomarkers for risk stratification after acute coronary syndrome. *Science Translational Medicine* 2011; 3: 102. DOI: https://doi.org/10.1126/scitranslmed.3002557. Accessed 2 April, 2019.
Taleb NN. *Antifragile: Things That Gain From Disorder*. New York, NY: Random House; 2012.
Ibid. *Fooled by Randomness: The hidden role of chance in life and in the markets*. New York, NY: Random House; 2004.
Ibid. *The Black Swan: The Impact of the highly improbable*. Second edition. New York, NY: Random House trade paperbacks; 2010.
Tetlock E. *Expert Political Judgment: How good is it? How can we know?* Princeton, NJ: Princeton University Press; 2005.
Tversky, A, Kahneman D. Belief in the law of small numbers. *Psychology Bull* 1971; 2: 105–110.
Volz KG, Gigerenzer, G. Cognitive processes in decisions under risk are not the same as in decisions under uncertainty. *Frontiers in Neurosciences* 2012; 6(105): 1–6.
Wheatley MJ. *Leadership and the New Science—Discovering order in a chaotic world*. Second edition. San Francisco, CA: Berrett-Koehler; 1999.

Willenheimer, R. Statistical significance versus clinical relevance in cardiovascular medicine. *Progress in Cardiovascular Diseases* 2001; 44(3): 155–167.

Wilson TD. *Strangers to Ourselves: Discovering the adaptive unconscious.* Cambridge, MA: Belknap Press of Harvard University; 2002.

Wubben M, von Wangenheim F. Instant customer base analysis: managerial heuristics often 'get it right'. *Journal of Marketing.* 2008; 72: 82–93.

Wycoff J. *Mindmapping: Your Personal Guide to Exploring Creativity and Problem-Solving.* New York, NY: Berkley Book; 1991.

Zubialde JP, Shannon K., Devenger N. The quadrants of care model for health services planning, *Families, Systems, and Health* 2005; 23: 172–185.

Zull JE. *The Art of Changing the Brain: Enriching the practice of teaching by exploring the biology of learning.* Sterling, VA: Stylus Publishing; 2002.

Index

A

Abductive reasoning, 20, 21
Abstract hypothesis, 72, 73
Acculturation, 41
Active testing phase, 73
Adaptive unconscious, 10
Ancillary health care providers, 146
Assertive and stalwart approach, 6
Availability bias, 14

B

Bias and cognitive errors, 168
Biases, 8
    cognitive bias, 10–12
Biomedical ethics, 55
Black swans, 35–36
Blended/mature knowledge, 30
Bounded/optimized decisions, 27–29
Butterfly effect, 34, 36

C

Calibration, 11
Causal statistics, 117–118
Centrifugal reasoning, 21
Centrifugal thinking, 68–70
Centripetal reasoning, 21
Centripetal thinking, 68–70
Chaos theory, 32–34
Chunking, 123–125
Clinical decision support systems (CDDS), 149, 150
Clinical presence, 57, 58
Cognitive and heuristic approaches, 118–119
Cognitive bias, 10–12

Communication, 58
Community-based physicians, 8
Complex decision-making matrices, 27–28
Complex problems, 31, 32
Complex reconstructive procedure, 5
Complicated problems, 31, 32
Comprehensive maternal-fetal-neonatal unit, 60
Computational intractability, 154
Computer malfunction, 34
Concept-mapping, *see* Mind-mapping
Concrete experience, 71, 73, 74
Confirmation bias, 13
Cost-benefit analysis, 104

D

Decision point, 99
Decision support systems (DSS), 101, 149
Decision threshold, 100, 101
Decision trees, 148, 149
Decision-making approaches
    by elimination, 16
        computational intractability, 154
        differential diagnosis, 159–161
        ethical considerations, 155
        evidence-based medicine, 155–159
        intermediate learner, 162
        master decision-maker, 162, 163
        statistical and mathematical models, 151–153
        statistics and individual patient, 153, 154
    by recognition, 16
        aphorisms, 122
        chunking, 123–125
        deliberate practice, 140, 142–144

Decision-making approaches (cont.)
    flow, 139–141
    heuristics (see Heuristics)
    intuition, 139
    maxims and rules of thumb, 121–123
    mnemonics, 123
    pattern recognition, 125–127
  conceptual model, 98, 99
  continuum
    algorithms, 114
    by elimination, 113, 114
    flow diagram, 112
    by recognition, 112, 113
    standard operating procedures, 114
    transitional approaches, 114, 115
  decision support system, 101
  decision threshold, 100, 101
  information hierarchy, 109–111
  Kaleidoscope model, 93–95
  knowledge and technical skills, 94
  multitasking, 93
  PICO format, 110, 111
  professionalism and judgment, 94
  risk and uncertainty, 92
  search orders, 101, 102
    simple swap rule, 104
    SSL (see Strategy selection and learning)
    tally swap rule, 104
    tally systems, 103
    validity rule, 104
  search rule, 102
  strategy selection
    cognitive and heuristic approaches, 118–119
    formulaic vs. cognitive approaches, 115–118
Decision-making continuum
  algorithms, 114
  by elimination, 113, 114
  flow diagram, 112
  by recognition, 112, 113
  standard operating procedures, 114
  transitional approaches, 114, 115
Decision-making cycle
  algorithms, 45
  best practice models, 45
  characteristics, 46
  clinical situations, 45
  clinical-pathology conference presentations, 46
  definition, 45
  fiduciary and ethical responsibilities, 46
  GPS-RADAR model, 47–49
  morbidity and mortality conferences, 46
  pre-operative conferences, 46
  principles, 44, 45
  standardized protocols, 45
  succinct and accurate assessment, 46
Decision-making matrix, 8, 29
Deductive reasoning, 21–23
Deep learning, 71
Deliberate practice, 140, 142–144
Descriptive thinking, 24

E

Ego/practice habits, 8
Einstellung effect, 12
Emotional brain, 4, 5, 7
Emotional/subconscious thinking, 5
Emotions, 4
  color decision-making, 9
  color perception, 8
Empiric thinking, 20
Empiricism, 20
Ethical and humanistic dimensions, 55
Ethical decision-making, 55
Ethics, 55
Evidence-based medicine (EBM), 155
  advantages, 156
  blind application, 157
  deductive/type 2 way of thinking, 156
  definition, 155
  implied tasks, 158
  mathematical/statistics driven analysis, 159
  medical practice, 155
  radiation/chemotherapy, 159
  shadow side, 157
  unfiltered or pure application, 156
Experiential learning, 71
Explicit learning, 10

F

Fast thinking, 15, 16
Flight simulators, 52
Flow, 139–141
Formal logic, 17
Formal/algorithmic approaches, 20
Framing bias, 14, 89

G

Game of solitaire, 3
Gather, Process, Store, Retrieve, Analyze, Decide, Act (GPS-RADAR) model, 47–49

H
Heuristic approach, 15
Hindsight bias, 14
Human short-term memory, 3

I
Implicit learning, 10
Inductive reasoning, 21–23
Informal process, 52
Information bias, 11
Information gap, 99
Information hierarchy, 109–111
Initial/intuitively appropriate response, 52
Intellectual virtues, 54
Intermediate learner, 162
Intuition, 88
    clinical or post-surgical course, 138
    definition, 136
    factors, 137
    'hot hands' phenomenon, 139
    mirror neurons, 138
    muscle memory, 137
    myelin, 138
    neurotransmitters, 137
    pattern recognition, 138
    random/loose approach, 139
    resident's neural networks, 138
    shadow side, 139

J
Judgment errors, 169

K
Kaleidoscope model, 93–95

L
Large world (unbounded) decisions, 26
Leadership, 59
Learning-cycle
    abstract hypothesis, 71–73
    active testing phase, 71, 73
    cementing data, 72
    computational/working memory, 72
    concrete experience, 71, 73, 74
    experiential/deep learning, 71
    limitation, 72
    mind-mapping, 72
    reflection, 73
    reflective observation, 71, 72
    traditional methods, 74
    transformation point, 72
Linear/mechanical view, 32
Logic, 17, 18

M
Macroeconomics, 27, 28
Management plan development, 59
Managing errors
    bias and cognitive errors, 168
    dealing with errors, 166, 171
    educational value/reducing surgical errors, 170
    formal and deliberate approach, 171
    judgment errors, 169
    normative errors, 167
    overview, 165, 166
    preparation, 169–170
    technical errors, 166, 167
    training environment, 170–171
Master decision-maker, 162, 163
Mathematical models, 20, 24, 27, 28
Memory, 8
Microeconomics, 27, 28
Micro-medical clinical decision maker, 28
Military operations, 52
Miller's research, 3
Mind-mapping
    basics, 78
    capturing and organizing information, 77
    case conference, 77
    death by PowerPoint, 75
    easy and informal process, 78
    fever and confusion, 84
    in-depth treatment, 78
    initial evaluation and management, 83
    learning techniques, 76
    medical educators, 76
    numerous systems, 77
    orthopedic resident, 76
    plan and team assignments, 83, 84
    repetition or rote memory, 76
    urinary tract infections, 79
        clinical applications, 82
        febrile, 80
        format, 79
        in ICU, 81
        informal/formal learning setting, 79
        pediatric, 82
Minnesota Multiphasic Personality Inventory-1 (MMPI-1), 116
Mirror neurons, 138
Mnemonics, 123
Moral virtues, 54
Multi-factorial decision-matrix, 27

N

Narrative thinking, 63, 64
National or global health care policy, 27
Newtonian mechanics, 32
Normative errors, 167
Normative thinking, 25

O

Optimal support systems, 149
Optimization, 25, 26
Organizational and operational awareness, 60, 61
Outpatient surgical center, 5
Outside-in reasoning, 21

P

Paleolithic ancestor, 2
Pattern recognition, 125–127
Physicians, 65, 66
Physicianship, 54
PICO (Patient or problem, Intervention, Comparison, Outcome) format, 110, 111
Posteriori knowledge, 30
Pre-frontal cortex, 5, 6
Prejudices, 8
Prescriptive thinking, 24
Priori knowledge, 30
Problem solving
  acculturation, 41
  algorithms, 70
  argumentation, 91
  complicated problems, 38
  current practice/outcomes benefit, 91
  daily practice, 91
  vs. decision-making, 38, 39
  education, 40
  framing, 89
  gathering information, 90
  intuition, 88
  logic, 91
  medical or surgical treatment, 89
  open-ended questions, 90
  residency training, 39
  resolving disorders, 37
  prostatic obstruction, 91
  simple or straight-forward problems, 38
  structured approach, 88
  rhetoric, 91
  training, 40, 41

Q

Quadrants of care
  characteristics, 176–177
  choice of specialty, 177, 178
  clinical environment, 180
  decision-making and leadership, 180
  default/comfort zone, 174, 175
  expertise, 179, 180
  faculty advisors, 173
  inclusive and visionary approach, 181
  matrix, 175
  medical organizations, 181
  organizational decisions, 181
  physicians/surgeons, 174
  pursuing research/teaching, 174
  university-based family practice program, 175
  Zubialde's model, 175
Quality, 55–57
Quality of care, 55
Quasi-normative errors, 167

R

Radiation therapy facility, 5
Reasoning
  abductive, 20, 21
  deductive, 21–23
  definition, 20
  induction, 21–23
  retroductive, 20
Recency bias, 13
Red Volkswagen' paradigm, 14
Reflection, 73
Reflective observation, 72
Reinforcement learning, 105
Representation/anchoring bias, 14
Retroductive reasoning, 20
Retrospective process, 64

S

Satisficing, 26
Search orders, 101, 102
  search rule, 102
  simple swap rule, 104
  tally swap rule, 104
  tally systems, 103
  validity rule, 104
Search restrictions, 105–108
Search rule, 102
Sherlock Holmes, 65–67
Short-term memory, 4

Simple problems, 31, 32
Simple swap rule, 104
Simulation centers, 52
Slow thinking, 15, 16
Small world decisions (bounded), 26
Some clinically useful training (SCUT), 51
Standard operating procedures (SOPs), 114, 146
Statistical analysis of data, 28
Steady state/homeostasis, 33
Stop rule, 103
Strange attractor, 34
Strategic learning cycle, 107, 108
Strategy selection and learning (SSL)
    cost-benefit analysis, 104
    cost elements, 106
    initial preferences, 105
    outcomes, 105, 107
    reinforcement learning, 105
    search restrictions, 105–108
    strategic learning cycle, 107, 108
Sunk cost bias, 14

T
Take the best (TTB), 103
Tally swap rule, 104
Tally systems, 103
Teamwork skills, 59
Technical errors, 166, 167
Technical skills, 60
Thinking fast and slow systems, 15, 16
Top-down reasoning, 21
Transformation point, 72
Transitional approaches, 114

Transitional models
    algorithms
        computer enhancement, 148
        excellent teaching tool, 147
        shadow side, 148
        structured and logical approach, 147
        variation, 146
    checklists, 145, 146
    clinical decision support systems, 149, 150
    decision support systems, 149
    decision trees, 148, 149
    optimal support systems, 149
    standard operating procedures, 146

U
Unbounded/unoptimized decisions, 27, 29
University-based family practice program, 175
Unpacking bias, 13
Urinary tract infections (UTIs), 79
    clinical applications, 82
    febrile, 80
    format, 79
    in ICU, 81
    informal/formal learning setting, 79
    pediatric, 82

V
Validity rule, 103, 104
Virtue, 53

Z
Zubialde's model, 175

MIX
Papier aus verantwortungsvollen Quellen
Paper from responsible sources
FSC® C105338

If you have any concerns about our products,
you can contact us on
ProductSafety@springernature.com

In case Publisher is established outside the EU,
the EU authorized representative is:
Springer Nature Customer Service Center GmbH
Europaplatz 3, 69115 Heidelberg, Germany

Printed by Libri Plureos GmbH
in Hamburg, Germany